Positively No Filipinos Allowed

In the series

Asian American History and Culture,
edited by Sucheng Chan, David Palumbo-Liu, Michael Omi,
K. Scott Wong, and Linda Trinh Võ

A list of additional titles in this series appears at the back of this book

Positively No Filipinos Allowed

Building Communities and Discourse

Edited by

Antonio T. Tiongson, Jr.,
Edgardo V. Gutierrez,
and Ricardo V. Gutierrez

Foreword by Lisa Lowe

Temple University Press
Philadelphia

Temple University Press
1601 North Broad Street
Philadelphia PA 19122
www.temple.edu/tempress

⊗ The paper used in this publication meets the requirements of the American
National Standard for Information Sciences—Permanence of Paper for Printed
Library Materials, ANSI Z39.48-1992

Library of Congress Cataloging-in-Publication Data

Positively no Filipinos allowed : building communities and discourse / edited by
   Antonio T. Tiongson, Jr.; Edgardo V. Gutierrez, and Ricardo V. Gutierrez ; foreword by
   Lisa Lowe.
      p.   cm. – (Asian American history and culture)
   Includes bibliographical references and index.
      ISBN 1-59213-121-2 (alk. paper) — ISBN 1-59213-122-0 (pbk. : alk. paper)
      1. Filipino Americans—Ethnic identity.   2. Filipino Americans—History.   3. Filipino
   Americans—Social conditions.   4. Community life—United States.   5. United States—
   Race relations.   6. Racism–United States.   7. United States—Relations—Philippines.
   8. Philippines—Relations—United States.   9. Imperialism—Social aspects—Philippines.
   10. United States—Insular possessions.   I. Tiongson, Antonio T., 1968– .   II. Gutierrez,
   Edgardo V. (Edgardo Valencia), 1969– .   III. Gutierrez, Ricardo V. (Ricardo Valencia),
   1971– .   IV. Series.

E184.F4P68 2006
305.89′921073—dc22

                                                                        2005049888

2 4 6 8 9 7 5 3 1

Contents

7   On the Politics of (Filipino) Youth Culture
     Interview with Theodore S. Gonzalves   111
     ANTONIO T. TIONGSON, JR.

8   Colonial Amnesia
     Rethinking Filipino "American" Settler Empowerment in the
     U.S. Colony of Hawai'i   124
     DEAN ITSUJI SARANILLIO

IV RESIGNIFYING "FILIPINO AMERICAN"

9   "A Million Deaths?"
     Genocide and the "Filipino American" Condition
     of Possibility   145
     DYLAN RODRÍGUEZ

10   Reflections on the Trajectory of Filipino/a American Studies
     Interview with Rick Bonus   162
     ANTONIO T. TIONGSON, JR.

11   Do You Mis(recognize) Me
     Filipina Americans in Popular Music and the Problem
     of Invisibility   172
     ELIZABETH H. PISARES

12   A Different Breed of Filipino Balikbayans
     The Ambiguities of (Re-)turning   199
     S. LILY MENDOZA

     Notes   215

     About the Contributors   245

     Index   247

LISA LOWE

Foreword

Writers, artists, and scholars—from Alfrredo Salanga, Angel Shaw, and Carlos Bulosan to Oscar Campomanes and Reynaldo Ileto—have commented that *forgetting* characterizes the Filipino encounter with the United States, both in the Philippines and in the United States. Nations, collectivities, and individuals have forgotten wars, eras of colonial rule, sojourns, settlements, sufferings, and survivals. With memories left unrecorded, locations destroyed or abandoned, and sequences of events disrupted, the past is lost to narrative history. Yet while a past defined and constituted by such forgetting can never be made available whole and transparent, it may often reappear in fragments. It may perhaps be read in the cultural practices, social spaces, scholarly and political work of immigrant formations. The immigrant presence in the metropolis itself may be the *revisiting* of the empire by its imperial past.

The essays collected here in *Positively No Filipinos Allowed* are written against the injunction to forget. They are eloquent testaments to the dialectical necessity that inscribes the project of remembering, committed, as Walter Benjamin was, to the idea that "nothing that has ever happened should be regarded as lost to history." The work here discusses the legacy of U.S. colonization of the Philippines, the *manong* as a U.S. immigrant labor force in the early part of the twentieth century or that of the female domestic laborer in the latter half, or the many social spaces of political activism and organizing by Filipino immigrants in the United States. In doing so, the essays demonstrate that however delayed, partial, or allegorized, the social identity of Filipino Americans forces a reckoning with the past, a revisiting of U.S. empire. The situated knowledges of Filipino Americans mediate the history of U.S. empire *through* the memories of "differential inclusion" as immigrants or foreign nationals and as a *racialized* labor force within the United States. All too often, the periodization of immigration to the United States presumes Anglo-European immigration as the nation's originary past, while racialized immigration is temporalized as if it is a recent event, following the Immigration and Nationality Act of 1965. The history of Filipinos in the United States demonstrates, to the contrary, that the long-standing phenomenon of racialized Filipino immigration is indeed, along with U.S. empire, part of a longer history of the development of modern U.S. capitalism and democracy, a longer, more notorious past in which a nation intersected over and over again with the international contexts of not only the Philippines, but also Puerto Rico, Mexico, Samoa, Guam, Korea, and Vietnam. I have argued elsewhere that the material legacy of America's imperial past is borne out in the "return" of immigrants to the imperial center. A number of the essays collected here suggest that memories of U.S. imperialism are refigured as alternative modes in which Filipino immigrants to the United States are the survivors of empire, its witnesses, its testifiers.

Thus, the essays here presume that the legacy of U.S. colonialism in the Philippines can be "read" in the circumstances of Filipino immigration to and settlement in the United States. Furthermore, numerous essays also discuss how Filipino Americans have been constituted as an object of disciplinary knowledge, and many frame the question of the intelligibility of Filipino American formation as a pressing question for students of race, culture, law, and labor in the U.S. university. They specify the immigrant history in which Filipinos had been "included" as subjects of U.S. colonialism, then excluded and repatriated as "aliens," and then "differentially included" in the United States as racialized labor. Yet the essays are directed asking why the Filipino American racial formation continues to be relatively illegible within traditional scholarly disciplines in the university, like history, anthropology, sociology, law, or literature, and even somewhat still obscure in emergent interdisciplinary fields like ethnic studies, American studies, and Asian American studies. And with respect to the discourses in which Filipino Americans are legible, these authors query the reasons that the status of Filipino American formation is often one of analogue or duplicate, treated as similar to rather than distinct from other Asian American or other U.S. minority or immigrant groups. Why is Filipino American formation not treated as an object of knowledge that requires a transformation of the methods and the research questions customarily employed by disciplinary formations? These essays boldly insist on this transformation. They ask different research questions than those previously asked of other racialized and immigrant groups, and their means of answering do not merely uncover and document "new" facts about Filipino Americans as a social identity, but also contribute significantly toward the reworking of existing methods and objects within the traditional fields of knowledge in which Filipino Americans have been either previously studied or previously obscured.

With respect to Asian American studies, the field within which the study of Filipino Americans has often fallen, I have commented that the force of recent work in Asian American studies has not been aimed exclusively at the restoration of a cultural heritage to a social identity. Rather, I understand much of the most important work to argue that the historical specificity of Asian immigrants within the history of the United States highlights a series of convergences in which U.S. nationalism has been exercised through racial exclusion, gendered violence, and labor exploitation. The "case" of Asian Americans, in other words, provides a set of historical materials that enables us to consider the changing institution of U.S. citizenship in terms of the history of racialized labor immigration. The essays in *Positively No Filipinos Allowed* pursue a similar hermeneutic, that is, reading and interpreting the specific case of Filipino Americans, and underlining the manner in which its *difference* contributes to, and inaugurates a revision of, the critique. The authors ask what the specificity of Filipino Americans—as former U.S. colonized subjects who immigrate to the United States to become a racialized and gendered labor force—brings to the "table" of Asian American studies, what this formation adds to that critique. They demonstrate that the differently gendered experience of Filipino men and women in the United States sheds light on a general understanding of the intersections of race, work, gender, and sexuality. In the work collected here, the impact of legislation on the Filipino immigrant to the United States—from the Alien Land Laws and the Tydings-McDuffie Act to antimiscegenation laws and the Immigration and Nationality Act of 1965—not only reveals the role of the state in determining race, gender, class, and labor in the development of the United States, but also testifies to the ongoing effects of U.S. colonialism in the Philippines on the lives of immigrants in the United States. Studies of men and women of Little Manilas—in Stockton, Los Angeles, or Seattle—or in popular youth culture today, tell us much about community memory as a force of unrecorded unofficial history, and the role of work and play in Filipino political movements and community building. Taken together, the essays in *Positively No Filipinos Allowed* vigorously pursue Filipino American critique. They insist that the forgetting that renders the Filipino American "lost to history" must be made visible and intelligible. They direct the student and scholar to locate that intelligibility institutionally, and they query what forms of practice must necessarily issue from its emergence into intelligibility.

Acknowledgments

First and foremost, we want to thank the contributors for sharing their work and their patience throughout this process. It has been a privilege and pleasure working with all of you. Thanks also to those at Temple University Press who worked with us: Janet Francendese for her invaluable editorial advice, and Jennifer French for production assistance. We also thank series editor Michael Omi for his unwavering faith in the project, and Bobbe Needham for copyediting assistance. We are especially indebted to Rick Bonus, Oscar Campomanes, and Martin Manalansan IV for their seminal works that laid the groundwork for this project. Lastly, we would like to thank our families for the love and support at every stage of the project.

ANTONIO T. TIONGSON, JR.

Introduction

Critical Considerations

U.S. Filipinos and their indeterminate forms critically pose the problem of
"unassimilability" and unrepresentability to a range of U.S. discursive fields,
or more importantly, cannot be so "assimilated" without these discourses
themselves being disrupted or transformed altogether.
—Oscar V. Campomanes

FOR MANY FILIPINOS TODAY, the phrase "positively no Filipinos allowed"
continues to resonate, a reminder of the anti-Filipino practices and sentiments the
manong generation encountered at a particular historical moment in the United
States. Displayed prominently on doors of hotels and other business establishments
throughout California in the 1920s and 1930s, it was a sign Filipinos frequently encountered in their day-to-day lives symptomatic of their racialization—as nationals
and aliens through state-sanctioned practices and policies, and as cheap labor by
capital interests and imperatives—that resulted in their disenfranchisement and
disempowerment. As a consequence, Filipinos were denied not only public accommodation but also access to rights and entitlements, including citizenship, the
franchise, and property ownership. In this regard, *Positively No Filipinos Allowed*
lends itself to a reading of Filipino history that evokes the historic exclusion of
Filipinos from the U.S. national polity and their location outside the cultural and
racial boundaries of the nation.

But in titling the anthology *Positively No Filipinos Allowed,* we seek to provide
an alternative reading of Filipino history in the United States as a way to think
through the main concerns of this volume and put into focus the kinds of interventions we hope to accomplish with it. More to the point, we deploy "positively no
Filipinos allowed" to signify the ways Filipinos endure the burdens and legacies of
empire past and present, which cannot be understood simply in terms of exclusion
but more in terms of the coerced incorporation of Filipinos into the nation, underwritten by the violence of conquest, empire building, white supremacy, and global
capital.[1] Additionally, we wish to underscore how Filipino social formations are
not coextensive with U.S. national borders, just as "the United States" is not commensurate with a nationalist focus but determined by the international dynamics
of empire and global capital. Thus, the racialization of Filipinos as nonwhite (or,

just as problematic, "Asian American") cannot be properly addressed by merely referencing the internal dynamics of any one nation or by considering the United States as a discretely bounded entity.

As a number of scholars have noted, in the United States an inability and unwillingness to account for its imperial legacy has given rise to cultural aphasia in relation to the enduring and pervasive effects of empire on colonized peoples and its significance to the self-definition of the nation.[2] Notwithstanding the centrality of imperialism to the national formation, this history has effectively been expunged from the historical record and the collective memory of the nation and constructed as antithetical to the U.S. experience. William Appleman Williams, for example, has noted the elision of U.S. imperialism within dominant U.S. historiography, while Amy Kaplan has noted the elision of U.S. empire building from the study of U.S. culture and the United States from studies of empire.[3] This elision is also evident in the use of qualifiers such as "insular," "sentimental," or "benevolent" to refer to U.S. imperialism, with the effect of mitigating U.S. complicity and sanitizing its effects.[4] U.S. culture, therefore, is characterized by a repression of its imperial history that obscures the link between freedom and expansion and the formation of an American identity and the violent conquest of nonwhite peoples.[5]

The historical amnesia surrounding U.S. imperialism has proven to be deeply consequential not just for the United States but also for those colonized by the nation. For Filipinos, it has come to mean grappling with the "spectre of invisibility" themselves, precisely because a full accounting of their presence necessitates a full accounting of a largely unthinkable history.[6] Just as the notion of the United States as an empire has not fared well in dominant U.S. historiography, neither has the notion of Filipinos as colonized subjects. Within standard historical accounts, for example, Filipinos have all but disappeared, as evidenced by the erasure of the Philippine-American War and Filipino insurgency against U.S. imperial rule; if Filipinos appear at all, it is usually as objects of derision—savages unfit for self-government, economic threats displacing white labor, sexual deviants obsessed with white women, or ungrateful recipients of U.S. beneficence.[7] It has also come to mean being made to fit into a discursive framework and narrative like that of immigration and settlement that serves to elide the historical and material specificities of Filipinos and to efface the very processes and relations that have shaped Filipino subject and community formation.

At the same time, *Positively No Filipinos Allowed* is intended to mark the tenuous position that the study of Filipino social formations occupies in the academy. As Lisa Lowe comments in the Foreword: "Filipino American racial formation continues to be relatively illegible in the university within traditional scholarly disciplines like history, anthropology, sociology, law, or literature, and even somewhat still obscure in emergent interdisciplinary fields like ethnic studies, American studies, and Asian American studies." Within Asian American studies and Filipino

American studies, for example, empire has yet to be integrated as a critical frame, while U.S. imperialism has been conspicuously absent from the purview of post-colonial studies.[8] In both traditional and emergent disciplines, then, the study of Filipino social formations on its own terms has yet to materialize, remaining outside the disciplinary focus and scope of these fields.

Put another way, Filipinos constitute a disturbing presence to be contained or effaced because of the challenge they pose to the coherence of these fields that revolves around a refusal to know. A case in point is the 1998 Association for Asian American Studies (AAAS) annual meeting, when Filipinos literally became a disturbing presence, at least in the eyes of the AAAS executive board members, in the wake of the granting of the Best Fiction book award to Lois-Ann Yamanaka for *Blu's Hanging*, notwithstanding criticisms leveled at the book for its purported racist representations of Filipinos. While some see the award and ensuing "controversy" as matters of artistic freedom and censorship, we see them as symptomatic of a broader dynamic, a reflection of the marginalized status of Filipinos in the association and, more generally, in Asian American formations, and as yet another manifestation of Filipino illegibility, as evidenced by the inability or unwillingness of board members to come to grips with anti-Filipino racism in the association.[9]

Oscar V. Campomanes has also written about this issue, alerting us to the illegibility of Filipino social formations in various academic fields and linking the marked absence of Filipinos in both academic and popular discourse to the profound silence and denial surrounding the history of U.S. imperialism. He reflects on the issue of Filipino unassimilability and unrepresentability in both traditional and emergent disciplines and in particular on how the specificities of Filipinos defy disciplinary paradigms and categories. But rather than focus on Filipinos themselves, he directs our attention to historical and institutional conditions that render Filipinos and their forms unassimilated and unrepresented in the first place. In other words, the issue has less to do with Filipinos themselves and deficiencies in their constitution or culture than with a particular set of social relations and historical circumstances that define their terms of intelligibility, but only at the cost of a certain epistemic violence that elides their particularities.

Lowe's reflections on the kinds of challenges that a critical consideration of Filipinos and their formations poses to the constitutive basis of Asian American studies and related disciplines and Campomanes's work on the imbrications of empire, disciplinary production, and Filipino social formations have proven to be tremendously productive in terms of making sense of the unassimilability and unrepresentability of Filipinos. They problematize the narratives of Filipino history and subjectivities and the inscription of Filipinos as "national" subjects or an "immigrant" group because of the way this kind of formulation fails to exhaustively account for the realities of empire and global capital. Together, these critics foreground the stakes involved in the production of knowledge and the complicity of disciplinary formations in the erasure of empire and the illegibility of Filipino social formations.

But as both Lowe and Campomanes suggest, Filipino intelligibility demands more than incorporation in already established frameworks; it necessitates a reconfiguration of grounding assumptions (based on the frame of nation) and foundational narratives (based on the narrative of immigration and settlement) of various disciplines. In other words, a critical and substantive consideration of Filipino social formations is not simply a matter of "recovery" or "inclusion," for that leaves in place the same practices of historical narration of Filipino subject and community formation that have proven problematic. Instead, Filipino assimilability is predicated on the disruption and dissolution of these disciplines as presently constituted. What is at stake, therefore, is not simply integrating Filipinos as objects of study into preexisting disciplinary paradigms but questioning the terms of their production and inscription and calling into question the coherence and constitutive basis of various fields of study.

A central focus of this volume is the study of historical and contemporary Filipino social formations in various realms—political, economic, cultural, juridical, academic—as well as the historical and social conditions out of which they emerge. By "social formations" we are alluding not only to the ways Filipinos have been historically constituted—fashioned into a particular kind of subject in order to fulfill U.S. imperialist, white supremacist, patriarchal, and capitalist context imperatives—but also to the contradictory ways Filipinos themselves have negotiated the very terms through which they have historically been defined, acknowledged, and recognized. Moreover, the volume puts into focus the competing claims made on Filipinos and the various interests they serve, as well as how these claims figure in broader debates about national identity, citizenship, and culture.

Additionally, this volume grapples with a key problematic conceived around the term "Filipino American," in particular, the troubled and uneven coupling of these two signifiers and their emergence into being under conditions characterized by extreme imbalances of power. As E. San Juan, Jr., points out: "The Filipino American subject-position cannot be defined without elucidating what the problematic relation is between the two terms which dictates the conditions of possibility for each—the hyphen or nexus which spells a relation of domination and subordination."[10] It is this historically determined relationship we wish to highlight in this volume as continuing to loom large in the lives of Filipinos in the United States and around the globe and indispensable to understanding the formation of Filipino subjects and communities.

Rather than look to "Filipino American" as a neutral or innocent descriptor of Filipinos in the United States, we locate and read this signifier within a much broader historical context, in imperial and global terms that take into account the imbrication of U.S. national formation and its imperial history. Our aim, therefore, is not to insist on the commensurability of the two terms, to engage in what Kandice Chuh and Karen Shimakawa describe as "a politics of claiming legitimacy and rights as Americans," for doing so just ends up reinforcing the myth of exceptionalism that underwrites the United States and disavowing the very conditions that made possible its emergence.[11] Instead, in placing these terms alongside one another and in quotes, we wish to shed light on those historical and material conditions that underpin their incommensurability, as well as on the specificity of each term.[12]

Taken together, then, the essays in this volume set out to provide a theoretical and historical understanding of the emergence of Filipino subjects and communities and the forces that shape and constitute them. Investigating a number of sites and contexts—the 1896 Filipino Revolution, Stockton's Little Manila, and Balik-Aral (Back-to-Study) summer programs, to name a few—the book brings together scholars grounded in a wide range of disciplines, including ethnic studies, history, literature, and legal studies. The volume also brings together scholars who engage with emerging themes that have yet to be taken up substantively in the academy and that touch on ongoing sites of tensions and debate, including comparative racializations, the constitutive powers of law, and genocide as an analytic frame.

By the same token, contributors to this volume demonstrate that a critical consideration of the collective experience of Filipinos not only deepens our comprehension of their social and historical formation but also points to intriguing analytic possibilities that extend beyond the specificities of their history. In an interview included here, Rick Bonus describes the broad social and theoretical relevance of the study of Filipinos this way:

> It is about American empire, about wars and colonization, about popular culture and representation, about global capitalism and the recruitment of particularized labor, the processes and consequences of racialization, the productions and use of gendered and sexualized subjects, the formations of collectives and solidarities, the building and maintenance of communities of resistance—all using the complexities and specificities of Filipino/Filipina experience as both products and productive of uneven relations of power.

Building on Bonus's insight, a critical consideration of the specificities of Filipinos is crucial and needed precisely because the history of this group has become paradigmatic of the majority condition in today's late capitalist age. The collection of essays and interviews we have gathered in this volume aims to illuminate this history and its broader resonance in terms of the theoretical positions they stake out, the analytic frames they utilize, and the kinds of questions and lines of inquiry they put into focus.

Despite addressing a varied set of concerns, common to them all is their interrogation of conceptual frameworks and dominant narratives that have historically informed the study of Filipinos and the articulation of emergent paradigms better suited to make sense of the specificities of Filipinos. This volume, in other words, aims to more than just fill a gap, that is, to compensate for the dearth of scholarship on Filipinos, which usually takes the form of uncovering Filipino "accomplishments" or, just as problematic and insidious, documenting Filipino "firsts" (what Campomanes describes as "insignificant although comforting fictions"), as in the notion that Filipinos are the first Asian American group to settle in the United States via the Manila galleon trade between Mexico and the Philippines. Instead, it aims to engage in the more difficult but necessary task of delineating the contours of what it means to exhaustively account for the specificities of Filipinos.

This means continuing to be a disturbing presence by placing the burden on institutional formations and practices to begin to consider Filipino social formations on their own terms, and frustrating institutional and disciplinary expectations by looking to other institutional spaces and arrangements—Chicano studies, Puerto Rican studies, Native American studies, and Pacific Islander studies—and exploring the potential of aligning with these fields of study and the kinds of possibilities these alignments open up. That this volume is being published as part of a series on Asian American History and Culture has not escaped our attention. It reflects the institutionalization of the category "Asian American" and the subsumption of Filipinos within this category. But as Bonus notes in his contribution to this volume, it also reflects the expectation that Filipino scholars draw upon Asian American scholarship, or at least have a conversation with it.

Our aim, however, is to frustrate this expectation, for to continue to conceive of "Filipino American" and "Asian American" as commensurate at this historical juncture overlooks not only the arbitrariness of placing Filipinos within the Asian American category but also connections between Filipino subjects and other colonized subjects, which have yet to be adequately considered and theorized.[13] Filipinos may indeed share some affinities with Asian American groups, but because of their status as colonized subjects, it makes more sense to group them with Chicanos, Puerto Ricans, Native Americans, and Pacific Islanders. Conflating "Filipino American" and "Asian American," therefore, forecloses the potential of generating alternative ways of narrating Filipino history and subjectivities informed by the histories and situated knowledges of other colonized groups that speak to the violence of conquest and empire building and the realities of globalization and that, ultimately, better illuminate the particularities of Filipinos.

IMPERIAL LEGACIES AND FILIPINO SUBJECTIVITIES

The anthology is organized in four sections, each of which addresses a particular theme. The first part, "Imperial Legacies and Filipino Subjectivities," theorizes the significance of empire as a core category of analysis. The history of U.S.

imperialism constitutes a particularly important site for understanding the subjectivity and self-activity of Filipinos. It created cultural, military, economic, and political ties between the United States and the Philippines, inaugurating, in E. San Juan, Jr.'s words, "this long, weary, tortuous exodus from the periphery to the metropolis with no end in sight."[14] U.S. imperialism also transformed the Philippines into a major source of cheap labor and raw materials, paving the way for the incorporation of Filipinos within the circuits of global capital. In short, U.S. imperialism set in motion a process that structures the lives of Filipinos today, a process that reaches into their lives "not so much like a shadow as like a chain."[15]

Tracing the varied articulations of empire in different sites and contexts—the 1896 Filipino Revolution and its resonance with Filipinos today, the figure of the Filipino savage in the late nineteenth and early twentieth centuries, and the experiences of manongs in the 1920s—contributors in Part I demonstrate how U.S. nation building and U.S. empire building are inextricably linked and mutually constitutive, how genocide, conquest, and expansion have been pivotal to the formation of the nation. In doing so, they deepen our understanding of the ways purported "national" categories of race/ethnicity/gender have been shaped by the "international" dynamics and logic of empire building. Empire building, therefore, does not constitute a "tragic but exceptional" episode in U.S. history. At the same time, "the United States emerged not simply through a break with European imperialism but through the establishment and elaboration of its own imperial cultures."[16] In their consideration of the social and historical formation of Filipinos within the context of empire, contributors show in compelling and powerful ways that imperialism is not a social phenomenon of the past. Rather, imperial practices past and present continue to structure social relations today, despite the deep and pervasive denial of the imperial history of the United States.

Jody Blanco's essay, which revisits and reconsiders the legacy of the 1896 Filipino Revolution, starts off this section. In it, Blanco looks to the centennial as an opportunity for reflection on Filipino identity, history, and agency and explores the relevance of this period to the struggles of Filipinos today. According to Blanco, the revolution provides us with a prism to view not only the past but also the future, to consider the changing inflections and elaborations of the term "Filipino," what it meant to nineteenth-century Philippine-born intellectuals, and what it means to contemporary Filipinos. He goes on to assert that a careful and critical reading of the revolution illuminates the interrelated histories of Filipinos and other marginalized groups and anticipates later social movements. This history, then, is significant because it points to what Blanco describes as "new ways of seeing and speaking," to possibilities and prospects for social change as Filipinos continue to grapple with the legacies of imperialism and the machinations of global capitalism.

Blanco's essay is followed by an interview with Oscar Campomanes, who discusses the implications of the self-effacements of empire, which he characterizes not so much as profound and far-reaching but as obvious. Directing our attention to the specificity of U.S. imperialism, Campomanes makes the point that it is this obviousness that makes possible the self-effacements of empire in the first place. He also delineates the ways U.S. imperialism constitutes a particularly important site for understanding the subjectivity and self-activity of Filipinos, including their struggle for "independence" and engagement in a politics of recognition and representation. Finally, Campomanes discusses the limitations of narratives and paradigms that have historically informed the study of Filipinos and points to alternative accounts, including those developed by Chicanos, Puerto Ricans, Hawaiians, and Pacific Islanders that situate their analyses of social formations within the context of empire.

In her essay, Nerissa S. Balce contextualizes the emergence of the figure of the Filipino savage during the late nineteenth and early twentieth centuries. Examining discourses of degeneracy and savagery coded in the language of the U.S. Empire, Balce links the figure of the Filipino savage to earlier grammars of American otherness. She elaborates on the notion of the phenomenon of reciprocity, delineating the ways racialized and gendered representations of black and red savagery prefigured and structured representations of Filipino savagery. Balce concludes with a consideration of what she calls postcolonial African American critique, writings of black women writers and ordinary soldiers that illuminate the connection between empire and lynching, between imperial domination abroad and racial violence at home, as a means of establishing and maintaining white supremacy "over the darker races."

In the final selection in Part I, Ruby C. Tapia theorizes the experiences of manongs in California during the early twentieth century in her attempt to illuminate the workings of power and patriarchy and the convergence of race, class, gender, and sex in the lives of this marginalized group of men within the context of European/American imperial discourse. Elaborating on and engaging with feminist critiques of masculinity and nation building, Tapia examines the form that this convergence took in both popular and political discourse and suggests that the mode of racialization specific to manongs cannot be understood in isolation from other social categories but only in relation to them. She is particularly concerned with the violence that it produced, as evidenced by the representation of manongs as an economic threat and sexual menace, which served to consolidate national and racial boundaries and maintain domination. She ends with a discussion of how the history of manongs "reminds us that this nation—and the intersectionality of race-class-gender-sex that reinforces it—always possessed the qualities of its (now postmodern) ghost."

Public Policy, Law, and the Construction of Filipinos

Part II, "Public Policy, Law, and the Construction of Filipinos," is concerned with the constitutive powers of political institutions and social policies, as well as the historical conditions which give rise to them. Considering a range of public policy issues and their broader implications and significance, it documents how a series of acts and judicial rulings are implicated in shaping the contours of Filipino subjectivities and communities. Filipinos have been subject to immigration quotas, citizenship restrictions, alien land laws, antimiscegenation legislation, and urban renewal policies that helped define and consolidate their nonwhite status. Filipinos, in other words, have been subject to what Sharon K. Hom describes as law's violence: "Through immigration and citizenship narratives, a system of state-sanctioned death, and an impoverished and partial vision of welfare and social security, law and legal discourses define community and belonging, dignity and survival, and life and death."[17]

To think of law and legal discourse solely in terms of sanctions and prohibitions, therefore, denies and obscures their constitutive powers. In uncovering the historical subjection *and* construction of Filipino subjects on the basis of debates on and enactments of social policies in different historical and social contexts, contributors in this part of the book trace the various manifestations of law's violence on Filipino bodies, lives, and communities—the construction of Filipinos as a racial and sexual menace, as inhabitants of "blighted" neighborhoods, and as a foreign presence. They are especially concerned with the ways social policy, in the form of particular pieces of legislation and court rulings, has served as a central locus where the racialization and the sexualization of Filipinos have taken place, a vehicle for both consolidating and undermining dominant meanings associated with particular notions of difference. In their readings of pieces of social policy, these works not only shed light on the relationship among and between law, culture, identity, race, gender, and sexuality—as well as on the contradictions and arbitrariness inherent in the establishment of these categories—but also alert us to the role of law as a generative and legitimating social force.[18]

Dawn Mabalon assesses the impact of urban policies after World War II on a section of downtown Stockton, California, known as Little Manila, home to the largest number of Filipinos outside the Philippines for most of the twentieth century. Little Manila residents created a neighborhood that thrived until urban redevelopment projects, "slum" clearance, and freeway construction decimated the community beginning in the 1960s. Mabalon documents how the community responded to demolition, pointing out that in the absence of organized opposition, two Filipino immigrants spearheaded efforts for the construction of a Filipino center that eventually became the focal point of the community. Incorporating personal narratives of Little Manila residents in her analysis, what she describes as "personal stories of loss and grief," Mabalon notes how the ongoing struggle over Little Manila is a battle not just over space, power, and policy but also over history and memory.

In the final selection in Part II, Angelo Ancheta examines the color lines that have shaped discrimination against Filipino Americans. Ancheta is particularly interested in historical and contemporary manifestations of what he calls "foreigner discrimination" along the lines of race, national origin, language, culture, and citizenship that have served to reinforce a norm of racial exclusion rather than inclusion and to mark Filipino Americans as foreigners excluded from full membership in the nation and the national community. Scrutinizing a number of key court decisions and pieces of legislation, he focuses on major forms of anti-Filipino discrimination—immigration and naturalization restrictions, citizenship-based and language-based discrimination, and the racialization of Filipinos as "perceptual foreigners"—to elaborate on the notion of foreigner discrimination and demonstrate problems associated with it.

RECONFIGURING THE SCOPE OF FILIPINO POLITICS

Part III, "Reconfiguring the Scope of Filipino Politics," delineates the broad contours of Filipino politics and maps their implications. Precisely because of a long history of political exclusion and institutional neglect, Filipinos have pursued a wide range of political activities and practices that exceed conventional notions of politics. These include participating in anticolonial struggles, labor movements, radical politics, student movements, and homeland politics, as well as engaging in cultural politics in their effort to negotiate with, challenge, and reconstitute power.[19] In doing so, Filipinos show that politics cannot be considered within a narrow framework that reduces the political to a particular mode (e.g., through middle-class institutions or organizations), a limited set of activities (e.g., electoral politics), a fixed geographic space (e.g., the domestic), or a particular site of contestation (e.g., the state or the everyday).[20]

In documenting the ways Filipinos have engaged in various forms of political activities and practices—namely, those that encompass both national and international contexts, look to culture as a site of political critique and intervention, and take into account multiple colonial histories—the contributions in this section broaden and reconfigure the scope of what is considered political. Additionally, contributors in Part III provide a critical evaluation of Filipino politics, elucidating oppositional possibilities but also collusions and complicities, while at the same time demonstrating that Filipino political activities and practices cannot be understood simply in terms of dichotomies like domination and resistance precisely because of the complexities and contradictions that constitute the political.

This section starts out with an interview in which Theodore S. Gonzalves interrogates the politics of Filipino youth culture, speaking to both the reactionary and the liberatory potential of culture. Given the elision and distortion of Filipino history in conventional historical accounts, Gonzalves specifies how expressive forms of culture take up this burden and serve as important vehicles for the enactment, narration, and expression of history. He also discusses the importance of culture as a generational marker, a way for Filipino youth to negotiate with the values and worldviews of their parents, as well as to claim their own distinct identity. Moving away from celebratory and uncritical readings of cultural forms and practices, Gonzalves makes sense of the participation of Filipino youth in a wide range of expressive forms, including Pilipino Cultural Night and theater and their attendant politics, and reflects on the long history of Filipino involvement in black and Latino cultural forms such as the blues, jazz, hip-hop, Latin jazz, and Latin rock.

Dean Itsuji Saranillio examines Filipino "American" politics in Hawai'i—more specifically, the way it serves to both maintain and disrupt the colonial system there and the colonial status of Native Hawaiians—through his analysis of contrasting visions of Hawai'i and Filipino settler history. Situating his critique within the history of the U.S. conquest of Hawai'i, Saranillio contends that in their efforts to assert their Americanness, Filipinos unwittingly align themselves with the U.S. colonial state. He calls for a critical consideration of the position of Filipinos in Hawai'i, in relation not just to haoles but also to Native Hawaiians, and recognition of U.S. colonization not just of the Philippines but also of Hawai'i. He ends his essay with a discussion of the collective efforts of a group of Pinays engaged in a form of anti-imperialist activism that recognizes the intimate link between the colonization of the Philippines and Hawai'i without losing sight of the very different relations of Filipinos and Native Hawaiians to the colonial state.

RESIGNIFYING "FILIPINO AMERICAN"

Part IV, "Resignifying 'Filipino American,'" provides a critical interrogation of the term—the historical and material conditions that made its emergence possible, the complex forms of negotiations and identifications taking place, and the various contexts in which it is mobilized to designate a wide range of social formations, subject positions, and cultural practices. Notwithstanding the currency of the term and its ahistorical and acontextualized deployments, "Filipino American" constitutes a fluid and contingent social formation with shifting boundaries and meanings. In the same way, "Filipino" is not reducible to a constellation of traits with the Philippines serving as the originary and privileged site of Filipinoness. Instead, it is a signifier that evokes a multiplicity of positions that cannot be construed in the singular.

Taking as the starting point of their analysis the normative claims and boundaries of "Filipino American," contributors in this section demonstrate that the production, deployment, and redefinition of "Filipino American" continues to be conditioned by a history of U.S. conquest and empire building, U.S. racial formations, and diasporic displacement. They foreground the contingent and discursive nature of "Filipino American," its various inflections and elaborations, and the ways these are inextricably bound up with questions of empire, nation, race, gender, and class. In doing so, contributors provide us with frameworks whereby we can have a deeper and more theoretically and historically specific understanding of the term "Filipino American" and its usage as a signifier of identity, culture, and community.

Dylan Rodríguez's essay, which analyzes the constitutive basis of Filipino American studies, begins this section. Taking as his starting point the U.S. genocidal conquest and colonization of the Philippines, Rodríguez aims to map what this encounter means for the field of Filipino American studies in terms of its theoretical and structural coherence. He contends that it is precisely this historical condition that is elided in the field's conception of "Filipino American" relation and subjectivity. Instead, Rodríguez argues, the field is implicated in and relies on the production of a kind of sentimentality that effaces Filipino American studies' originary location in genocide for the sake of continuity and coherence. He goes on to make the point that a critical consideration of white supremacist genocide in the Philippines entails a rupturing of the logic of the field that disavows the very conditions that made possible the emergence of the "Filipino American."

Next, in an interview, Rick Bonus maps the contours of Filipino American studies, a field he characterizes as "heterogeneous, multiply defined, and relationally constructed." Bonus notes the standard assumptions, categories, and analytic frames that inform Filipino American studies, as well as the many shifts taking place in Filipino American scholarship, including the move beyond the United States as the principal locus of identity and community formation and the framework of immigration and settlement as a way of making sense of the historical realities of Filipinos. He also addresses the basis of the vexed and contentious relationship of Filipino scholars to the institutional formation of Asian American studies, which, for Bonus, is as much a matter of identity as of power, as much a question of stronger identifications with other groups as of the marginal status of Filipinos within Asian America. Putting into focus the creation, processes, and consequences of categorization, Bonus concludes the interview with a discussion of the many ways we can understand the signifier "Filipino American" while recognizing each term's and each combination's inflections and elaborations.

An essay by Elizabeth Pisares explores the skepticism over Jocelyn Enriquez's racial authenticity and loyalty and what this says about the racialization of Filipinos in the United States. Interested in theorizing Filipino invisibility, Pisares contends that the racial ambiguity surrounding this popular Pinay freestyle artist is actually a condition familiar to Filipino Americans, who, as she points out, "are seen as everything and anything but Filipino." Enriquez had to deal with accusations of passing first as Latina, then as black, but rather than center her analysis on the question of Enriquez's culpability, Pisares focuses on the broader context wherein this dance-music artist's racial fidelity becomes an issue. She argues that Filipinos' invisibility stems from their classification as Asian American, while their experience of racial ambiguity stems from not conforming to others' perceptual expectations of Asian Americans. Pisares concludes with a discussion of the ways Filipinos counter invisibility, examining different modes of Filipino self-representation.

Concluding this section is an essay by Lily Mendoza that focuses on the ambiguities of homeland "re-turnings" among college-age second-, third-, and fourth-generation Filipino American youths, what she describes as "the phenomenon of a different breed of *balikbayans* or homeland returnees." Looking into Balik-Aral (Back-to-Study) summer programs designed to take Filipino American youths to the Philippines to learn about Philippine history, society, and culture, Mendoza examines what it means for these youths inspired by the Philippine indigenization movement to undertake not merely a symbolic but a literal return to a place they have never set foot on yet consider "home." She asserts that these programs serve as the basis for the reclamation of a previously disavowed history and the emergence of a newfound Filipino subjectivity. As Mendoza notes, however, this process is far from straightforward and unproblematic, providing possibilities for both reproducing and disrupting commonsense identifications with the signifier "Filipino."

"FILIPINO AMERICAN" CRITIQUE

In putting this volume together, we included contributions from established scholars who have profoundly shaped the scholarship on Filipinos, but the bulk came from emerging scholars. This cohort of young scholars is producing what we consider exemplary scholarship, which bodes well for the future of the study of Filipino social formations precisely because they are in a position to shape the contours and trajectory of this scholarship. We consider their works exemplary for placing under careful and close scrutiny disciplinary formations and epistemologies and highlighting their limitations. In the process of doing so, these scholars are producing works that not only generate new theoretical insights but also suggest new directions and analytic possibilities. We consider their work to represent the best of an emergent body of scholarship that suggests what it would look like to exhaustively account for the specificities of Filipinos.[21]

The publication of this volume takes place as Filipino social formations, as well as the historical and social conditions out of which they emerge, remain largely illegible in both academia and the larger culture, and as Filipinos themselves continue to grapple with the spectre of invisibility. This elision is neither innocent nor benign but symptomatic of a kind of cultural aphasia that operates in various fields of study and underwrites the theoretical and structural coherence of these disciplines. Nonetheless, we hope that in its vigorous pursuit of "Filipino American" critique, this volume will provide the kinds of critical engagements necessary to render Filipino social formations intelligible on their own terms.[22]

I.

IMPERIAL LEGACIES AND FILIPINO SUBJECTIVITIES

1 Patterns of Reform, Repetition, and Return in the First Centennial of the Filipino Revolution, 1896–1996

"It was morning when the Spanish long boats sailed from Cebu to Mactan."
She paused, looked thoughtful, and went on: "Everything in this country happens in the morning."

Shocked, Clarissa could only ask: "Why?"

And the child replied: "Because it is a country of beginnings."

—N. Rosca, *State of War*

DR. JOSÉ RIZAL didn't like the United States. Like most travelers who came from across the oceans to see the young North American nation, one that had recently celebrated its first centennial as a national republic (1876), the future national hero was certainly impressed by the vastness of the Nevada desert and the Nebraska prairie, or the gentle beauty of the New England countryside and the "gigantic and imposing" force of Niagara Falls. The brief journal of Rizal's first and only tour across the United States conveys the fragmented impressions of the crowds at the docks of the New York harbor, the majesty of the Statue of Liberty, the wild horses grazing on the hills of Colorado, all with a great degree of admiration. Speaking of the Hudson River, he even remarked: "The landscape is beautiful and compares favorably with the best of Europe" [El paisaje es hermoso y no tiene mucho que envidiar a los mejores de Europa].[1] Still, that old "demon of comparisons" characteristic of colonial intellectuals in the nineteenth century (and even the present) led Rizal to conclude that this same river was too solitary, compared to Luzon's own Pasig River in the Philippines; and that even the awesome rush of Niagara Falls lacked the beauty of Los Baños.[2] Leaving the New York harbor on 16 May 1888, he went on to become the most recognized and admired national hero of the Philippines.

Of course, few pause to recall Rizal's brief, seemingly insignificant U.S. stopover, particularly given the exciting details of his eventful life. Who cares what the young author of *Noli me tangere* (1886) thought about the United States in the aftermath of his first exile from the colonial archipelago? He was en route to a destiny of brilliance and tragedy, a brief but intense period of scientific and humanistic education, social and political agitation, novel writing, organizing, exile, betrayal—and execution on 30 December 1896, four and a half months after the outbreak of the first national revolution.

One hundred years later, Filipinos in the United States and Filipino Americans have every reason to ask what Rizal—along with the revolution he inadvertently inspired some seven thousand miles across the Pacific Ocean—has to do with student and academic communities in the United States today. They certainly won't appear in most classes on U.S. history, or Asian American or U.S. ethnic studies for that matter. Why should Americans (even U.S. minorities) concern themselves with Filipino—or for that matter any extra– or anti–United States—nationalism?[3] If anything, Filipino immigrants taking the Immigration and Naturalization Service (INS) exam might find more compelling reasons to know the importance of Abraham Lincoln and Martin Luther King, Jr., than the likes of Rizal, Marcelo H. del Pilar, or Graciano López Jaena—three Filipino intellectuals and publicists who wrote mostly in Spanish, had conflicting loyalties between mother Spain and their native Filipinas, and didn't have much of an opinion on the United States by the time they died in 1896. Even if thousands of U.S.-based Filipinos and Filipino Americans continue to commemorate Rizal's execution on Rizal Day (30 December), celebrated with food and formal dress everywhere from Alexandria to Detroit, how many of us know or care that del Pilar and López Jaena died of poverty and tuberculosis (the same year Rizal died), neglected and forgotten by everyone, as a new generation of Filipino thinkers and revolutionaries braced itself for a war against the past and future empires of the Western world? And if we did know the history of those who inspired an entire generation to go to war against the superior arms and resources of that vast and powerful North American country, would we care?

Let's pursue these rhetorical questions a bit. It might be argued, for instance, that U.S.-based Pinoys have more pressing concerns than the study or commemoration of the 1896 revolution. As Filipinos and Pilipino Americans anticipated becoming the largest declared "Asian" population in the United States by the year 2000, our painful invisibility or virtual nonexistence in public office, on academic faculty lists, or in public culture, largely overshadowed any concern in the United States for the veneration for Filipino national heroes.[4] And even if our invisibility did not serve to deter us from the study of Filipino history and culture, the heated debates of intellectuals on both sides of the Pacific complicated any easy search for heroes and villains in the tangled, dark romance of U.S.-Philippine relations. To this day, there seems to be little consensus on who ought and ought not to be considered a Filipino national hero to begin with—or for that matter, when and where the 1896 revolution actually began, or if it actually did begin; and at what point it could be legitimately called a national revolution. Still others ask whether the revolution did in fact end; or whether, as Ninotchka Rosca's novel *State of War* seems to suggest, it never ended, but merely changed masks.[5]

Closer to us than the memory of Rizal and Andrés Bonifacio's revolution, it would seem, are the memories of teenage Filipino girls whose numbers comprise the highest suicide rate among U.S. ethnic groups.[6] In contrast to the quiet classrooms where we might read novels about forgotten wars or debate the separation of church and state, we hastily skim the newspapers and email briefs that tell us all we need to know about the ideology of "structural adjustment." Time to study Filipino and Filipino American history, or debate why the distinction is or isn't necessary? Between the rally and the teach-in, we are busy signing petitions seeking to override the institutional discrimination at work in the refusal of the U.S. government to grant the Filipino veterans of U.S. wars the same compensation granted to every other American soldier.[7] Every now and then, perhaps, the eager Pinay student would like to stay behind, dally a moment to read a downloaded poem by revolutionary Gregoria de Jesus. But as we watch the steady decline of Filipinos and Pilipino Americans at universities, which has resulted in Filipinos and Pilipino Americans comprising, for example, less than .02 percent of the UC Berkeley student population, our education more often than not proceeds by way of the slogan and the student organization, rather than any directed (or directionless) investigations into the study of conflict and grief that we commemorate as the 1896 Filipino revolution.[8]

These are some reflections that frame the moment of our U.S. Filipino and Filipino American student communities at the centennial mark of this central yet constantly displaced event. At UC Berkeley, it is common knowledge that students don't learn Filipino and Pilipino American history in a classroom. They learn it from the exiles and veterans of the anti-Marcos, anti–martial law movement, who have gone into nonprofit organizing in health, legal, and educational services throughout the San Francisco Bay Area. They learn it from attempts to devise an argument that will convince the university to invest in a ladder-rank faculty member knowledgeable in the fields of U.S. Filipino and Pilipino American history and cultural studies.[9] They learn it on breaks between dance practices for the annual Pilipino cultural night (also called Samahan, Pagdiriwang, among other names)—a four-hour extravaganza of music, dancing, and theater that attempts to compensate for our collective absence in U.S. mainstream mass media, public opinion, and education. What need, then, for the patient task of education concerning a distant archipelago and a diasporic population that have always claimed to be both *more* and *less* than one country and one people—an amalgam of ethnolinguistic groups, indeterminate mixtures, transculturations from Europe and mainland Asia? What do any of us here and now owe to a commemoration of 1896? Understanding why Rizal refused to openly support the 1896 Filipino revolution, or why the president of the first Philippine Republic had two other leaders executed under false pretexts, or why General Artemio Ricarte spent almost the entire first half of the twentieth century plotting to finish the republican revolution of 1896, which the world's memory had long cast into oblivion—these historical tidbits cannot alter the realities of a U.S.-based ethnic group that has never ceased to be defeated by and subordinated to a world history written by the great European and U.S. intellectuals and magistrates, and enforced by acronyms like the IMF, the WTO, GATT, and the INS.[10]

Still, the historical coincidence of centennials gives us pause to reflect on the possibility that the gestures of half-forgotten dramatis personae who once filled the theatrical stage of a noble idea—the idea that people had the power and right to determine how they were or were not to be governed—may tell us something about our today. Let us pose one example of this possibility in the form of our earlier question: why didn't Rizal like the United States? Perhaps it had to do with the quarantine of his boat off the coast of California, perhaps Angel Island, for seven days before he and 643 Chinese emigrants were allowed to set foot on U.S. soil. Perhaps, too, it had to do with Rizal's conviction that the quarantine was issued because it was election time in the United States, and the party in power held the boat in quarantine to placate the widespread xenophobia in California.[11] In a well-known letter to his friend (and later secretary of the Filipino revolutionary government in exile) Mariano Ponce, Rizal expands his critique of America:

> La América es indudablemente un gran país, pero tiene aún muchos defectos. No hay verdadera libertad civil. En algunos estados el negro no puede casarse con una blanca ni una negra con un blanco. El odio al chino hace que otros extranjeros asiáticos, como los japoneses, sean confundidos por los ignorantes y sean también mal mirados. Las aduanas son excesivamente severas. Sin embargo, como dicen bien, ofrece una patria para el pobre que quiera trabajar. Hay además mucha arbitrariedad.

> [America is undoubtedly a great country, but it still has many defects. There exists no true civil liberty. In some states a black man can't marry a white woman nor a black woman marry a white man. Hatred against the Chinese leads the Americans to foolishly confuse them with Japanese, who also end up ill looked upon. Customs is excessively severe. However, as they rightly say, America offers a native land for the poor person who wants to labor. (But) there is, besides, a great deal of arbitrary rule].[12]

In fact, U.S. contempt for the immigrant masses that shaped it from within turned out not to be confined to immigrants at all. As Rizal's journal a year later shows, Americans had occasion to prejudge and denigrate Europeans as well. Listening to an American passenger complain about Europe and Europeans, Rizal becomes convinced that the passenger is a U.S.-constructed "automaton," "an artificial man," Rizal remarks of the American, "created and launched into the world by Americans with a perfect inner mechanism designed to discredit Europe to the triumph of the great [American] republic; a machine that would feed on the very steam of locomotives" [un hombre artificial creado y lanzado al mundo por los americanos con un perfecto mecanismo interior para desacreditar la Europa y hacer triunfar la gran república; una máquina que se alimentaría con el vapor mismo de las locomotoras].[13] The American automaton, in Rizal's mind, emblematized both the advanced industrial and technological force of the new republic and the arrogance of its people, to the diminution of the rest of the world.

Perhaps, then, it should come as no surprise that Rizal's misgivings about the future of U.S. technology and U.S. republican institutions led him to identify with another side of America—the Native American side, one precisely obscured by both racial segregation within U.S. borders, and industrial and commercial arrogance outside them. As is well known, the name of Rizal's group of friends in Europe, "los indios bravos," hearkened to the Native American Lakota and Cheyenne peoples, led by Sitting Bull, who defeated General George Custer at Little Big Horn (also in 1876). In 1891, Rizal's novel *El filibusterismo* characterizes the protagonist-turned-antihero Simoun as a "redskin" who sharply criticizes mob violence and the practice of lynching in the United States.[14]

These fragments of Rizal's work present us with a blurred version of the first critique of U.S. institutions by a native-born, self-proclaimed Filipino intellectual toward the end of the nineteenth century. Yet are the two operations so discrete? Is it not more likely, rather, that Rizal has left us with *both* legacies—the articulation of a national cultural identity and a critique of U.S. institutions—insofar as they are in fact related? In the pages of Rizal's memoir, the performance of a Filipino identity and the awareness of the interrelated histories of dominant and subaltern groups just prior to and during the heyday of U.S. imperialism resonate and overlap with one another. For it is Rizal's double consciousness as a colonial subject that allows him to see himself as both a denigrated *indio filipino* in the eyes of the Spaniard, *and* a Native American, a segregated black man, or a quarantined Chinese immigrant in the eyes of a Filipino. This resonance, this "structure of feeling," this Filipinoness or haecceity, does not necessarily begin in the Philippines, or even in Spain.[15] It begins with the world, as a name for a historical agency that arose toward the end of the nineteenth century—at times separate from, but at other times intimately linked with, historical currents as disparate as the extermination of the Cherokees, the legalization of racial segregation in the United States, and the greater struggles of imperialist countries over the future of Asia in the epoch of advanced capitalism.

From this perspective, 1896 provides us with an important point of dispersion for summing up and elaborating the many articulations of this haecceity that pass through Asia, Europe, and the Americas in unprecedented ways. At the bottom of Rizal's perception, his speech, and the controversial word he ceaselessly wielded—*Filipino*—a web of historical events and interpretations implicate and interpellate us in unexpected ways. I'll have to save those investigations for another day: suffice it to say, for now, that the celebration or commemoration of the 1896 centennial invites us to consider a time when the word "Filipino" was still relatively new. Whatever other historical legends or political processes have been distorted, imagined, or bastardized in the hundred or so years between the cry of Balintawak (was it Balintawak?) and the cries of balikbayans at the Aquino International Airport, the signifier "Filipino" was then, and remains, our first and most lasting plebiscite—a public forum that opens itself to the kaleidoscope of interpretations based on the day-to-day experiences of a half-imagined population, speaking at least 172 different languages and their multiple dialects in the Philippines alone; living in the most ecologically biodiverse region to be called a nation in the entire world; or expatriating by the thousands every year to countries across the world; or living a life of perpetual instability framed by prostitution around U.S. military bases or the "care chain" of domestic workers across Europe, the United States, and the Philippines.[16]

How did the word "Filipino" sound to the champions of modern democratic republicanism condemned to live and die in a perpetual state of emergency throughout the latter half of the nineteenth century and the opening years of the twentieth? A cross-section of nineteenth-century intellectuals born or raised in the archipelago may help us here. For Padre José Apolinario Burgos, the invocation of "Filipino" was a political act that bound native-born creoles and indios in the archipelago together, identical in their possession of ethical virtue and human dignity. For Rizal, the Filipino was a subject of knowledge, who saw herself or himself in every other colonial subject victimized by arbitrary rule. For Graciano López Jaena, to be Filipino meant to love the freedom, equality, and fraternity affirmed in the years of the first revolution in France—a country at that very time commemorating its own first centennial by reflecting on the legacy of those daring and uncompromising ideals in a century of restorations, state compromises with elite interests, and the rise of modern European imperialism.[17] Behind the machinations of Spanish political parties, Catalonian and Basque regionalism, and the cynicism of the Spanish constitutional monarchy, López Jaena asserted simply that Filipinos were Filipinos insofar as they loved the freedom, equality, and fraternity that only a democratic and constitutional republic could guarantee. It may have been the utopian dream of a disenfranchised bohemian youth who faced a future of exile on the European continent, but it was a dream that opened the door to new ideals and radical initiatives.

In retrospect, we may smile at the willful ingenuousness, the determined innocence of the past century's sentenced youth, as we recall their lives during the first centennial of the Filipino revolution that we commemorate today. After the deaths of these figures in 1896, it became increasingly impossible to imagine what

Filipino revolutionary premier Apolinario Mabini called the "national life" of an integral Filipino people. Before 1896, it was still possible for Graciano López Jaena to declare that Las Filipinas would soon form the axis of world trade between Asia and Europe. Before 1896, it was still possible for Rizal to spend the final hours of his life in the heroic composition of a poem that still nurtures us with its reflective and contemplative beauty—we Filipinos, López Jaena would say, we lovers of freedom, equality, and fraternity, whoever and wherever we are today.

Does a reflection on history, then, lead us to our own, weak revival of cosmopolitan hero worship—here, in the United States, one hundred years after the outbreak of the Filipino revolution? Let us recall one of the central tenets of Mabini's great testament to the Filipino revolution: individual heroes always merely embody the desires and insights of collectivities. Our commemoration of these Filipino heroes in the United States, then, should lead us not to the nostalgia of lost heroism, but rather to a deeper joy and participation in the imagination and becoming of greater collectivities and notions of a common good heralded by such figures throughout the twentieth century. The revolution materialized that participation on a radically new level at the turn of the century: it made possible our first contact with Chinese revolutionary Sun Yat-Sen and Afro–Puerto Rican revolutionary Ramón Emeterio Betances.[18] It made possible our first conversations with Afro-Americans, drafted to fight for a society that discriminated against them as much as it did against Filipinos.[19] And it forced the early U.S. imperialists to recognize that their nation's drive toward world hegemony would have to be fought every step of the way by unseemly, outmatched, scrappy opponents, armed with little more than the ardent belief that the future was not determined all the way to the end, and that ordinary people (without riches, without guns, and without diplomacy) have the power to participate in the making of that future as active and willing agents.[20] These contacts and solidarities did not occur solely by coincidence: they involved an active will and agency bent on shaping the contours of radical republicanism and democratic thought in the twentieth century.[21]

Nor are these small achievements to the Filipino or Filipino American student who sets aside an afternoon to read of them. Narratives give meaning and coherence to later struggles, impacting movements as diverse as religious messianism, socialist internationalism, Latin Americanism, ecological and feminist utopianism, and U.S. agricultural labor unionism. From our view in the United States, these intersections anticipate Filipino involvement in the civil rights movement, just as much as the civil rights movement inspired the Kilusang Demokratikong Pilipino (Filipino Democratic Movement, or KDP) that helped short-circuit U.S. support of the Marcos dictatorship in 1986.[22] They give us a way of understanding how the U.S. genocide of Filipino Christians and Muslims at the turn of the century was every bit as cruel and brutal as the German concentration camps and Japanese atrocities committed during World War II. And they teach us that the process of framing and reframing the terms of our constituencies and collective endeavors—our "ethnoscapes," as one critic recently called this process—can and must lead to more than the production of new consumer markets: they must lead to enduring movements for political and social change.[23]

"No uprising fails. Each one is a step in the right direction."[24] For every official celebration of Filipino national heroes, most likely to be sponsored by AT&T and the Ayala Corporation, an "underside" of history narrates a counterpoint vision—a world that aspires to the right to (re)imagine and bring into being a concept of human and equal opportunity over the regime of flexible capital and the mortgaging of the Filipino population as cheap unskilled and semi-skilled labor. And for every representation or strategic use of Rizal to support a religious conservative or bourgeois liberal agenda, let us celebrate the radical, uncontained Rizal who shaped the imagination of the future generation of U.S. Filipino migrant workers. Carlos Bulosan certainly read Rizal in this light, as can be seen from his comparison of Rizal to Russian proletarian writer Maxim Gorki, both of whom (to Bulosan's mind) were opposed to "those who do not work at all, those rich bastards who kick the poor peasants around; . . . we can still have a nice country without money and politicians. We just need workers."[25]

In our attempts to read the signposts of identity politics, mainstream multiculturalism, the suppression of affirmative action policies in the university, and the unchecked growth of the military arms and prison industries in the United States at the expense of health care, education, and social security, let us pause to hear the cacophony of voices that inhabit the plebiscite in session whenever one pronounces the word "Filipino." Stirring restlessly beneath the veneer of colonial politics before 1896, it has since then never ceased to rage against the colonial legacy that limits the horizon of our understanding. Above the din, we may perhaps catch strains of the French and Spanish revolutions in the democratic republicanism of our *ilustrado* patricians; we may hear the bombastic reverberations of U.S. Manifest Destiny from their origins in the 1848 U.S. seizure of Mexican territory. Perhaps a discussion comparing Jim Crow legislation in 1883 and 1896 with antimiscegenation laws against Filipinos in California during the 1930s might have just begun.[26] Certainly, the plebiscite would have to include those voices of messianic movements that plagued the U.S. invading army and Philippine constabulary for more than ten years after Teddy Roosevelt declared the "official" end of hostilities between U.S. troops and the Filipino revolution.

Listen well. For it is in these conversations that we discover, reflect, multiply, and improvise new ways of seeing and speaking our way past the gatekeepers and automatons of historical amnesia and institutional invisibility.[27] In this endeavor, we join the Graciano López Jaenas of the past century, who with grace and inspiration explored the ways of seeing and speaking through the prospects and limits of our divergent modernities. It is time we meet one another again, introduce ourselves, and see how or if we can help each other, teach ourselves and each other what the university will not (or may not want to) teach us. Centennials, after all, do not only say: "Well enough! All this has come to pass." They also say: "Begin! And what has been stopped, suppressed, or interrupted, go on and begin again!"

ANTONIO T. TIONGSON, JR.

2   On Filipinos, Filipino Americans, and U.S. Imperialism
Interview with Oscar V. Campomanes

TONY TIONGSON: How do you conceive of U.S. imperialism? As a tragic or "exceptional" episode in U.S. history? As a matter of economics or diplomacy, or something much more? For example, do you think it has an embodied presence in the lives of individuals from colonized nations today?

OSCAR CAMPOMANES: To frame U.S. imperialism in terms of William Appleman Williams's controversial thesis on "the tragedy of American diplomacy" (actually the title of his pathbreaking book published in 1959) or of the hegemonic and uncritical historiography on the U.S. Empire which draws from a protean and extended tradition of discoursing on "American exceptionalism" is, immediately, to capitulate to enduring but ultimately dissatisfying analytic conventions and debates on the topic. Indeed, to get caught between the "economistic" analysis of U.S. imperialism by Williams or his influential students (the "revisionists" Walter LaFeber, Thomas McCormick, etc.) and the realist predilections of U.S. diplomatic historians/international relations scholars—the shadow cast by George Kennan, Williams's vaunted *antagoniste*, is very long—is to fall into a trap within which one can only suffer from a self-reproducible kind of conceptual and critical asphyxia. This is not to say that I don't admire—indeed, I thoroughly do—the conceptually idiosyncratic and solidly empirical work of Williams; I believe that apart from *Tragedy*, his *Roots of the Modern American Empire* (1969) and that fabulous set of essays, *Empire as a Way of Life* (1983), should be required reading for anybody interested in the problematic of U.S. imperialism. But as Amy Kaplan and a few astute others have pointed out, Williams's work does not pay enough radicalizing attention to the cultures of U.S. imperialism and the terms by which this imperialism has been customarily framed by its observers, students, apologists, and, not least, by Williams himself in the kinds of critical research and commentary that he produced so prolifically on the subject for much of his career.

    The important thing to note about U.S. imperialism is that its economic motors—especially in the expansion, after 1898, into the Philippines and East Asia/Pacific, the Latino-Caribbean zone, and the Americas—remained unspecified, or continued to be discussed as if these were comprehensible only in terms of an "economistic" analysis such as that developed by Williams (which by itself did indeed offer much explanatory power). But the limitations of this approach became evident in the ease with which his detractors could dispute it or overemphasize its problems by mere recourse to the culturalist alibis of the empire or also to what historians would call "counterfactuals." U.S. empire building in these regions, in the view of one counterfactual hypothesis, did not prove to be as profitable to the modern U.S. economy as early ideologues and advocates had fantasized. The power of these counterfactual arguments is evidenced in the bathetic career of "the China markets thesis" as an explanation for the rise of the U.S. Empire, and the stale or deadlocked debates to which it gave rise, after Marilyn Young's and Thomas McCormick's otherwise solid research and arguments for its truth claims!

Also, the political forms that the U.S. Empire took—the sheer novelty and the improvisational or highly pragmatic expressions of both its constitution after 1898 and its Philippine colonial experiment, given the inexperience of the United States in extracontinental expansionism and the decline of formal colonialism in due course—made this imperialism easily assimilable into a "diplomatic" or statist paradigm; the nature of this "New Empire" became easily reducible into what some of its more conservative students cleverly formulated, categorically, as "an imperialism of suasion."[1] That is to say that it could be claimed with a straight face by most as hardly an imperialism at all, simply the highly contingent maneuvers, the realpolitik, of pragmatic U.S. statesmen who were concerned not to build or sustain an empire, formal or informal, but to exercise and claim U.S. national power and secure U.S. national interests on a "global" scale. With the onset of U.S. cold-war politics and perspectives later, amidst the full-blown unfolding of post–World War II decolonization, U.S. imperialism could thus be neutrally nominated by its unimaginative and apologetic historians or scholars as "globalism" or "internationalism," extremely meaningless euphemisms. Yet the work is already clearly done: diplomatic historians or foreign policy scholars, that particular species that studies U.S. imperialism not as imperialism but as statist politics, are able to vaporize the empire into nothingness (the singular exceptions to my mind are Louis Perez, Emily Rosenberg, Akira Iriye, and Michael Hunt and their always evolving work). Critical historians like Williams had to struggle heroically to give it a density, a history, and some discernible form so as to make it accountable at all; and I mean "accountability" here, with respect to U.S. imperialism, both in the sense of being capable of narrative or recounting, and of being made available as an object of critique and political contestation.

We already know the story. The bulk of the literature produced by diplomatic historians or scholars of U.S. foreign policy/international relations simply worked to counter and dispute work like Williams's, or to assimilate and contain it (as happened to the work of some of his students) into essentially self-conservative and largely realist paradigms obtaining in these fields. Gareth Stedman Jones once termed and satirized this hegemonic literature correctly, in my view, as "State Department historiography." In a prolegomenon of sorts that I wrote for one section of a special issue of the journal *Radical History Review*, I pointed to the pressing need to meditate upon and investigate the peculiar and highly novel form of imperialism practiced by the United States after the disaster of 1898 and its Philippine colonial interventions/experiment.[2] I argued, for instance, that its economic underpinnings are amalgamated and strange in their provenance and conjunctions (drawing, for one, from a strain of business/corporate-sector antiexpansionist sentiments), its cultural politics and political/organizational expressions both hegemonic and diffuse (drawing, for another, from the constitutional and old-guard strains of the Anti-Imperialist League and similar or affiliated movements or citizen protests). In short, what I discerned in my own attempts as U.S. "imperialism," following Williams's lead, was a slippery political beast, an elusive critical object, a tough nut to crack. Williams could only name it, oxymoronically and variously, as "imperial anticolonialism" or "anticolonial imperialism"!

It is a miracle that we could even learn from the iconoclastic anti-imperialist critiques of Edward Said, Gore Vidal, Noam Chomsky, Gabriel Kolko, Samir Amin, et cetera, given the incredible animus heaped upon their writings by conservatives for the baldness that is their hallmark in delineating the U.S. Empire's otherwise unrecognizable forms. But we are fortunate, at this point, to have the bounteous fruits of the critical research/writing undertaken within the last ten years by the comparatist Lisa Lowe (UC San Diego); the Yale historian Matthew Allen Jacobson; the "new Americanists" Amy Kaplan (University of Pennsylvania) and John Carlos Rowe (UC Irvine); the legal scholars Leti Volpp (American University), Edilberto Roman (Loyola-Chicago), and Efren Rivera Ramos (Puerto Rico); the University of Michigan historians Kevin Gaines and Penny von Eschen; the cultural critics Robert Lee (Brown), Melani McAlister (George Washington University), Viet Thanh Nguyen (University of Southern California); Laura Briggs (University of Arizona), Mari Yoshihara (University of Hawaii), and Vicente Diaz (University of Michigan); the sociologists/anthropologists Rick Bonus (University of Washington), Martin Manalansan (Illinois), Lanny Thompson (University of Puerto Rico), and James Loewen (Catholic University); the feminist scholars Gail Bederman (Notre Dame) and Louise Newman (University of Florida); the "new" historians of the U.S.-colonial Philippines Michael Salman (UCLA), Vince Rafael (UC San Diego), and Paul Kramer (Johns Hopkins); the singular scholars Reynaldo Ileto (National University of Singapore) and Resil Mojares (University of San Carlos); the prodigious archivist Jim Zwick (BoondocksNet.com); and the exciting new work of an entire cohort of young Filipino American scholars: Kimberly

Alidio (University of Texas-Austin), Cathy Ceniza-Choy (UC Berkeley), Cynthia Tolentino (University of Oregon), Sunny Vergara (San Francisco State), Allan Isaac (Wesleyan University), Victor Bascara (University of Wisconsin-Madison), Theo Gonzalves (University of Hawaii), Arleen de Vera (SUNY-Binghamton), Nerissa Balce-Cortes (UMass Amherst), Jody Blanco (UC San Diego), Sarita Echavez See (University of Michigan), and so on. I should also not fail to mention the critical and political writing of Neferti Tadiar (UC Santa Cruz). All of them not only bring a trove of new material/archival evidence and pose startlingly new questions to U.S. imperialism and its aftermath as phenomena with long lives and as critical objects, but also produce new and pointed studies of the intersections, in varying degrees, between U.S. imperialism and U.S. nation building in the late nineteenth century and by the twentieth. This new work gives me immense hope!

Does U.S. imperialism have "an embodied presence in the lives of individuals from colonized nations today"? Let me rephrase the part of your question "from colonized nations" into "U.S.-neocolonized nations" to make our discussion more specific. Needless to say! If you are asking me about post/neocolonial migration and immigration from the Philippines, and from nations within the effective ambit of U.S. "spheres of influence" (which is just about the entire planet), most certainly. Every Filipino migrant and immigrant, for example, bears the brand of the U.S. Empire on his or her forehead, its unmistakable imprints on his or her body. To bowdlerize Fanonian discourse a bit, empire is epidermized in Filipino brownskins, encoded in their cultural genes.[3] Make that true for Puerto Ricans who end up in New York or elsewhere in the different states because to remain in Puerto Rico, the longest-running (in)formal neocolony in the world, is to be cursed, both formally and constitutionally, with a third-rate (because statutory) and heavily compromised kind of U.S. citizenship. Think of American Samoans, Guamenians, all those Pacific Islanders whose habitats remain shanghaied, like Puerto Rico, into that official designation "U.S. Possessions" (often tagged as an obsolescent afterthought to the full-fledged "States"). To a different but no less significant extent, this embodiment of the neocolonial is just as descriptive of migrants/immigrants from Central America, the Middle East, the Korean peninsula, Vietnam, and so on—wherever the exercise of U.S. "globalism" resulted and continues to result in massive economic displacements and tumultuous political upheavals for these peoples, and the maintenance of informal relations of subordination of their countries of origin/affiliation into U.S. strategic interests and imperial geopolitics.

TT: Do you consider U.S. nation building and U.S. empire building historically coterminous and mutually constitutive? What is the significance of empire to the formation of the U.S. nation and identity?

OC: In answer to the first question: Absolutely. Of the small handful of U.S. historians who had stood pat on this argument, Williams was the most exacting. Marilyn Young, in a posthumous conference to honor the legacy of Williams, was correct to summarize his work as one big argument for U.S. imperialism as *fundamental,* not peripheral or exceptional, to U.S. nationalism and nation building. In *Empire as a Way of Life,* Williams exhorted his fellow U.S. citizens to look hard at the centrality and constitutive dimension of imperialism and empire building to their national history and way of life "without blinking." Few Americans, citizens or politicians/intellectuals, gave heed to his warnings that failure to do so would risk reproducing "the tragedy" of U.S. diplomacy or relations with other countries, especially after the Cuban debacle of the late 1950s and early 1960s (when the United States ultimately faced down Cuba and the Soviet Union in a near brush with mutual, and planetary, nuclear annihilation). In many ways, that tragedy, which Williams characterized as fundamentally predicated upon the national reflex—developed since the Spanish- and Philippine-American wars—to export and project the domestic crises of U.S. capitalism and society abroad so as to manage them or resolve their endemic contradictions (no matter how fitfully) continues to be reproducible today with even more and more macabre twists (consider 9/11 and the cynical warmongering against Iraq). We are not sure, in other words, that the long "American Century"—after its inauguration by the neocolonial conquest of the Philippines, Hawai'i, and other former Spanish territories—has truly ended. To extend and tweak a bit the triumphalist rhetoric of that scandalous avatar of U.S. imperial conservatism, Francis Fukuyama: the United States, with the millennial turn and its vaunted victory over the USSR in the cold war, has not so much "ended history" as commenced it upon a path that few people in the world with an ounce of critical intelligence would entertain as "progress" or even as a thinkable future/fate.

The mutual imbrication of U.S. nation and empire building was something that many U.S. statesmen from the early Republic at least through Theodore Roosevelt had little trouble accepting (unlike the historians and scholars of this country since 1898 who contrarily discourse/d about a "denial of empire," to borrow that deadly phrase from Whitney Perkins). In fact, it was something that these statesmen articulated with disarming candor and ritually celebrated in their policy making and pronouncements. Arguably, it is from William Howard Taft's and Woodrow Wilson's presidencies (both deeply implicated in the Philippine neocolonial experiment of the United States) up to the present that we begin to have U.S. statesmen who would believe, with increasingly alacrity, in the fiction that the building of a powerful/prosperous nation is *not* the building of a new and formidable kind of empire, only the building of a nation self-appointed or destined to serve as the global gendarme and political/economic exemplar for all other peoples on the planet (representing, as it presumably did, an exceptional kind of national development, and informed only by the most benevolent intentions and motives).

William Appleman Williams noted one significance of empire to the formation of U.S. national identity, one which alarmed him and was his constant lament: the way in which what he called "the strategic mind" and imperial self-entitlement became less an exclusive province of statesmen and opinion leaders and more a generalized mentality and disposition among U.S. citizens themselves as empire became the very scaffolding of their way of life and the fount of their renewable opportunities. What alarmed him and he lamented was that the more empire became a popular Weltanschauung—the more, that is, that U.S. citizenship and membership in the U.S. nation became *imperial* (as the American Century wore on)—the less engaged citizens became in matters of state, essentially abdicating their decision-making powers and responsibility to unscrupulous political leaders and tendencies the disastrous consequences of whose unchecked actions or agendas are everywhere in plentiful evidence. For Williams, while empire increasingly gave prosperity and a sense of well-being to Americans, it was at the tremendous cost of degenerating the essence of U.S. democratic governance itself and of leaving the power or potency of U.S. citizenship diminished and defanged (the very spectre prophesied and feared by the anti-imperialists during the contentious national debates over the Philippines from 1898 through the early 1900s).

As a historian, Williams was concerned to *historicize* U.S. imperialism, which is to show it as the product of a particular kind of political or social evolution and development, with particular consequences and a discernible future that might yet be significantly altered or reoriented by enlightened citizens and leaders. I am more inclined, however, to agree with the observations made by a long tradition of outsider commentary on what I called in one essay the "genetic imperiousness" of the United States.[4] Both in the nineteenth century and the twentieth, we have a long line of the finest intellects whose fascination with (or even admiration for) what they considered the radical modernity of the United States and the future-orientation of Americans was tempered with a sense of portentousness (at times, with a dose of ressentiment) about what this kind of nation might mean and do for the world of the future and the future of the world. I am thinking of the nearly half century of exchanges between Karl Marx and Friedrich Engels on determinate and related developments in U.S. capitalism and nation building, from early in the antebellum period (peaking at around the time of the Civil War and postbellum economic upheavals) through the untimely death of Marx in 1883 (Engels up to the 1890s continued to keep close tabs on U.S. developments); of the interested commentaries on the United States made by the Cuban Jose Martí, or closer to home, our very own José Rizal or Apolinario Mabini; in the twentieth century, you have everybody from Antonio Gramsci ("Americanism and Fordism") to Octavio Paz (whose fabulous essay "Imperial Democracy" just about says it all) and our own Nick Joaquin (on *sajonismo*) to the pithy and enigmatic statements of Deleuze and Guattari in *A Thousand Plateaus*. One might say, although perhaps they would not countenance it, given their quickness to catapult toward the "future" as the very American nation whose "imperialism" they have now consigned to a mere stage and an immediate past in the development of "their" empire, that Antonio Negri and Michael Hardt were, in fact, *exclusively* discoursing about the United States in their best-selling book, *Empire*.[5]

Risking reductionism or even caricature, I would say that all these observers/commentators (it helps that they are outsiders except for the American Hardt) both ratify and shear away in fear from the implications of something like what that true visionary and early architect of the U.S. Empire, William Henry Seward (Abraham Lincoln's bellicose secretary of state), once imperiously declared: "The story of American [national] development [is] the most important secular event in the history of the human race."[6] If the secular and the modern are now identified with the very conception of the American nation itself, and if this is something that would be affirmed and then puzzled out by its most perspicacious critics or students, then empire must be radically, if embryonically, present at the birthing of the U.S. nation itself. I find Seward's conceit the very basis for saying that for one to be *identified* as American is right away to *become* the privileged citizen of a peculiar and therefore powerful kind of imperium. (Indisputably, a statement like Seward's is believed truly by many from the beginning and across the generations—in various ways and said differently throughout different periods in U.S. history, this imperious statement about the exceptionality of the United States, as you may well know, can also issue from the speech acts of Americans on the streets and in boardrooms.) This statement, in its continued iterability and as the fundament of an entirely recognizable discourse or a practical language spoken widely, is simply *imperious,* breathtaking in its *genetic* imperiousness, almost mandatory, beyond dispute. "America is the greatest country on earth." Once uttered, its power to hail imperial citizens, to reproduce U.S. imperialism as a disposition among all kinds of people in this country, is simply remarkable; and this, to me, is already wagering a major understatement.

TT: William Appleman Williams has noted the elision of U.S. imperialism within the dominant U.S. historiography, while Amy Kaplan has noted the elision of U.S. empire building from the study of U.S. culture and the elision of the United States from studies of imperialism. I wonder if you could talk about the profound and far-reaching implications of these multiple effacements.

OC: I used to think that these "multiple effacements" of U.S. imperialism across U.S. historiography, U.S. culture studies, and international postcolonial critique do hold "profound and far-reaching implications" for those neocolonized by the United States, like Filipinos, and for Americans themselves. But having spent much of my picaresque career (and I see no end or relief in sight) divining these mysteries, I am now of the opinion that these "implications" are not so much "profound and far-reaching" as *obvious*. And it is this obviousness, even of the self-effacements of U.S. imperialism, that allows such "implications" and U.S. imperialism itself to be elided—indeed, to be blissfully ignored for the longest time—by historians, Americanists, and postcolonial critics working in U.S. research universities and institutions. In "Anthropology's Interlocutors: The Colonizer and the Colonized," which was originally an address he delivered to a Modern Language Association convention, Edward Said castigated U.S. humanist scholars for their readiness to talk about all kinds of imperialisms and postcolonialities except that of, or associated with, the United States. This perhaps explains why Indian/Caribbean scholars, writers, and critics have little problem finding comfortable niches in the highest academies of the U.S. Empire (in addition to the superlative quality of their work and the rich intellectual traditions that fortunately sustain them). In the United States, you can prattle all you want about imperialism for so long as it is that of the British or the French!

Some might say though, with much optimism, that this dismal situation is now changing, but that is thanks, in large part, to the initiatives of people like Said and all the others I mentioned earlier who remained undeterred by the institutional neglect of U.S. imperialism as an object of critique and research in several disciplines. If the outlook for U.S. imperialism, Philippine, Filipino American, and U.S.-postcolonial studies is collectively improving now, this is *not* due to the magnanimity or liberalism of prevailing regimes in the fields concerned. I won't repeat myself and tire you out by invoking my familiar spiel on how the history and politics of the self-invisibility of U.S. imperialism (at least since 1898) had everything to do with the *conspicuous* invisibilization—in academic and public culture conversations—of the Philippines, Filipinos, Filipino Americans, and all other peoples and territories imperialized by the United States (for this you can revisit, if you wish, the series of agonistic essays I wrote on the topic within the last decade). I'd simply qualify, as a form of additional critique: what is curious in something like international postcolonial criticism (which is heavily cultural studies in orientation) is that if there is any consideration of U.S. imperialism at all, say in the work of somebody like Gayatri Spivak, it is of this imperialism as late capitalism incarnate, as an economic beast or machine superseding that of the classical empires; and that just as curiously, in U.S. historiography, this economic cast to U.S. imperialism is airbrushed out of existence, and this imperialism becomes almost exclusively a matter of culture (or civilizationist discourse)! Of course, I am being caricaturish here with respect to these fields, but I hope the point is made. Perhaps it is a case of fearful symmetry, then, that American studies (at least until very late and until the emergence of the so-called New Americanists), which as an interdiscipline should have been the meeting ground for reconceptions of U.S. imperialism as *both* material and ideal formation, paid the question of U.S. empire no or little attention at all!

The question, it seems to me, is what exactly allows U.S. imperialism to *elude,* and not just to be elided by, the characteristic periscopes of these various fields of study. If it eludes the grasp of the most sophisticated minds in the U.S. academy or research apparati (Said's MLA address made this point obvious), we must pose the difficult question of its nature, its modalities (again, I refer to my formulations in my 1999 *Radical History Review* [*RHR*] essay which, admittedly, are only inchoate). Let's go back, for example, to Williams's oxymoronic description: imperial anticolonialism/anticolonial imperialism. He was onto something, no matter how immediately problematic his phraseological act was. William Pomeroy, that U.S. leftist who flirted with the Huk communist movement in the Philippines (one might say he married it) and became the favorite whipping boy of reactionary U.S. Filipinist scholars, wrote and published a book on U.S. neocolonialism in 1970 (it is actually a very solid book—I'd add it to the mandatory reading list on the empire). In it he said: "the anti-imperialism of [yesterday] is the neocolonialism of today."[7] When I first read that, I was really struck dumb. What a transformation that must have entailed, what reversal!—and we have no comprehensive critical account, as of yet, of the process by which this might have occurred. Indeed, with the "liberation" of Cuba, Puerto Rico, and the Philippines by the U.S. Army/Navy in 1898 and immediately thereafter, it would not be difficult to find self-certain pronouncements that such inaugural imperial crusades of the United States *abroad* were not imperialism but were, in fact, anti-imperialist, anti-colonial. You fast-forward to the late-lamented cold war and the Free World struggle to liberate or keep the rest of the world from the evils of Soviet social imperialism—the discourse holds fast. All the proxy wars fought, the counterinsurgency campaigns throughout the decolonizing world, the CIA coups and interventions in many regions, from the Iran of Mossadeq's time to the Chile of Allende—these were not to be classed as imperial but precisely anti-imperialist!

Add to this the popular and long-running conceit of the American Revolution as the first anti-imperial or anticolonial struggle and one, moreover, that succeeds so beautifully, and you have the United States becoming the prototypical postcolony itself.[8] Well, at least *The Empire Writes Back* critics had no problems upholding this idea of the United States as the first modular example of postcoloniality—think, also, of the similarly problematic claim made by the Harvard literary historian Laurence Buell.[9] Little wonder that our ever-vigilant antipostcolonial neocolonial critic Epifanio San Juan, Jr., would bristle at this suggestion and would in short order produce a series of indignant essays and at least three books (and counting) debunking this outrage! Rather than be pushed into a reactive position though, one might wish to follow the lead of Marilyn Young, who observed that Williams's oxymoron wonderfully captured the paradoxes of U.S. imperialism, that what Williams did (and now, maybe Pomeroy) was to find a formulation that "reconcile[s] America's righteous rhetoric with its venal practice" in the field of neoimperial/colonial politics. I added, in my *RHR* essay, that rather than characteristic of U.S. imperialism, this happy "reconciliation" of the polar terms of U.S. imperialism was less characteristic (which Young seemed to imply) than symptomatic. At this point, I'd say that the first problem in delineating U.S. imperialism and the first step in appreciating its power, its self-invisibility, its protean shapes, might lie in the need to generate a different deconstruction of its "righteous rhetoric" or its formidable language (the "venal practice" is easy to document and critique). And by "different" I mean, negatively, nothing of the sort of deconstructivist analyses done so far of comparable and older imperialisms and, positively, a deconstructivist analysis whose terms and maneuvers we have yet to make thinkable, no matter how liminal, this late.

TT: In what ways does the history of U.S. imperialism constitute a particularly important site for understanding the subjectivity and self-activity of Filipinos?

OC: I say you should wait for the manuscripts of Kimberly Alidio, Allan Isaac, Nerissa Balce-Cortes, and Arleen de Vera to get published for full and highly informative answers to this sharply formulated question. Eric Reyes has also recently completed a dissertation at Brown, under the guidance of Neil Lazarus, that speaks directly to this concern (I am also thinking of Lily Mendoza's unusual *Between Homeland and the Diaspora* [2002]). But I am glad you are raising it. The Guamenian Lawrence Lawcock completed this voluminous UC Berkeley Ph.D. dissertation, "Filipino Students in the United States and the Philippine Independence Movement, 1900–1935," in 1975. It is chock-full of precious documentation of the "subjectivity" and "self-activity" of a particular and much-neglected population, the *pensionados,* that small and select cohort of U.S.-Philippine colonial government scholars who were sent, between the early 1900s and the late 1920s, to the highest academies of the empire to apprentice in U.S. "ideals" and cultural/political administration. It is a pity that we have not heard from Lawcock since or that he did not see fit to revise his work for publication. But I speculate that such was the fate of anybody doing Philippine-themed dissertations in U.S. universities for the longest time: *oblivion,* with their research output eventually covered over with thick films of dust in the musty shelves of university repositories (and the list is long; the Australian Filipinist Paul Matthews once compiled an extensive dossier of such dissertations in U.S. universities and nearly all these projects sound great, but we never heard from or about their authors again).

Anyway, Lawcock was practically making the emergent argument (he did not theorize it, unfortunately) that the nationalism that these first Filipino colonials discovered and recovered from their extended stints in the metropole (the exact opposite of the effect intended and desired by this colonial government project of co-optation) directly extended and recontexualized within the United States as the new terrain of struggle the nationalism of the *ilustrado* generation. More, he effectively argued that the U.S. imperial conquest of the Philippines, with these pensionados among its first bastard offspring, furnishes a case where emergent Filipino nationalism was radically reoriented toward the very modernity that was its object of desire in the age of José Rizal, Marcelo del Pilar, Graciano López Jaena, et cetera, given the compulsive U.S. claim, in contrast to "medieval" Spain, of precisely embodying in itself the secular and the modern. The consequences of this reorientation, the reengineering of the Filipino national subject toward the U.S. ideal and with the "recognition" of the United States as his or her goal, are enormous and should make us appreciate the kinds of self-limiting and limited activities to which Filipinos from that moment onward would devote their energies in quest of "independence."

Benedict Anderson, in his problematic but enlightening essay "Hard to Imagine: A Puzzle in the History of Philippine Nationalism," makes a point similar to Lawcock's but sharper: for him, U.S. imperialism, through the English language and cultural Americanization, transformed Filipino subjectivity and nationalism (as their "self-activity") in ways that would elude the conscious scrutiny of Filipinos themselves; not only was their nationalism reoriented toward a U.S. model, but also it was now reoriented from native territory to ethnic identity as its obsessive object of desire (from the territorial "Philippines" to "Filipino" ethnic/national identity)—as Filipino diasporic dispersal in the late U.S. colonial period, first to Hawai'i and the Pacific Coast states (as an army of cheaply waged and mobile reserve labor for the burgeoning agribusiness estates and canneries), begins to happen on a scale never before possible in Philippine history and still and now accelerating, with a global reach that observers say is simply epical and unprecedented.[10] Or rather, as Anderson pretty much argued: this diasporic turn induced by U.S. neocolonial displacement by the 1930s furnishes, in many ways, the dim template for the Filipino global dispersal we have recently been experiencing on such an epic scale, that is, from the time of Marcos (and Blas Ople—this Teflon politician is said to be the architect of the warm-body export policy) to the present day.

I am in substantial agreement with both Lawcock and Anderson, although I would add that the "subjectivity" and "self-activity" of Filipinos emerging from the historical striations of U.S.-Philippines neocolonial relations also got immediately and effectively predicated upon what I termed, in an invited lecture before the Department of Literature at UC San Diego in 1995, "a politics of recognition and representation." Much energy has been and is spent seeking the integration of U.S. Filipino history and literature into the U.S. national literary and historiographic canon; for the longest time, on the part of Filipino writers and intellectuals in the Philippines, much energy was devoted to a similar kind of assimilation into U.S. national and cultural history of the history and texts of Americanization during the colonial era and in the postindependence period—both to little avail, as we all know. Hence the level of obsessiveness to which these quests have attained and the corresponding sense of "failure" or "lack" to which such quests seem congenitally doomed (I mean the integration or "assimilation" *happens* and *can come* but not to the extent desired by Filipino advocates; one need only recall the analogous fates of the Filipino independence movement and missions from the time of Governor-General Francis Burton Harrison to the Commonwealth).

In an aside to my 1995 UC San Diego lecture, the ever-generous David Lloyd alerted me to a series of regnant statements made on precisely this kind of condition by the decolonizing Martinican intellectual Frantz Fanon in his famous chapter, "The Negro and Recognition," in *Black Skin, White Masks*.[11] The mother statement, paraphrased from Fanon's cryptic language and oblique metaphors, is this: "recognition can *lead* to representation, but there can also be representation *without* recognition." If you revisit that section of this powerful book, you will find Fanon's imaginative rendition of the otherwise impossible quest to which our subjectivity and self-activity as Filipinos might be committed (it is the sort of rendition that a philosopher like Alexandre Kojève, glossing Hegel on the self-emancipatory labor that the slave performs for and against the master, would have found eminently apt): the good white master, "one day," and "without conflict," deciding to invite and "allow his slaves to eat at his table." Does this constitute the recognition from the master that the slave wants? Fanon asks; to which we are only given the absolute answer, "But the former slave wants to make himself recognized." For the white master/colonizer might have given us a place to eat at his table but not an equal place to roost in his mind and heart. In short: you have here representation without recognition, for if it is recognition at all it is "without conflict." What a prescient language on the perils and strategies of containment of U.S. multiculturalism and political liberalism!

Because it is the master/colonizer who holds the prerogative and power to recognize (for it was him who, with violence and unbending will, put the other in the stranglehold of unrecognizability and subhumanity), the slave/colonial who craves this recognition after a long, drawn-out struggle of asserting his or her humanity and equality to the Other is, in fact, left only to desire true recognition from the Other as an absolute precondition toward authentic emancipation from colonial bondage. As the Fanonian persona articulates, in ways that could have spoken for other colonized peoples like Filipinos (and here I will quote at length, please bear with me): "As soon as I *desire* I am asking to be considered. . . . I demand that notice be taken of my negating activity insofar as I pursue something other than life; insofar as I do battle for the creation of a human world—that is, of a world of reciprocal recognitions. . . . He who is reluctant to recognize me opposes me. In a savage struggle I am willing to accept convulsions of death, invincible dissolution, but also the possibility of the impossible. . . . The other, however, can recognize me without struggle: [quoting Hegel] 'The individual, who has not staked his life, may, no doubt, be recognized as a *person,* but he has not attained the truth of this recognition as an independent self-consciousness.'"[12]

This obsessiveness about the master's recognition is, as the speaking ex-slave in Fanon's text himself recognizes, something impelled by its impossibility. For the colonizer to recognize the colonized truly—to imagine a reciprocal humanity with the Other—is for the master/colonizer to destroy the very principle of inequality and hegemony that underwrites his mastery and colonial privilege; it is, in effect, to destroy the otherwise self-impregnable bond between colonizer and colonized, master and slave. Perhaps the most insidious aspect of this bondage is that the slave/colonial is thereby oriented exclusively to and must perform forever for the master, whose recognition is promised as a reward for this obsessiveness but is really never forthcoming. So when "the other can recognize me, *without struggle,*" one has to wonder, as the speaking slave does, about the quality and substance of that act of recognition from the master. The slave/colonial is left only to desire "the possibility of the impossible," to struggle for it "in convulsions of death" as if he could only "pursue something other than life." For he who "has not staked his life" on this "savage struggle" to make the impossible possible—the self-destruction of the master/colonizer in the act of recognizing the slave/colonial in the radical terms by which the latter desires "to make himself recognized"—is doomed never to attain to "the truth of this recognition as an independent self-consciousness."

Fanonian thought has helped me immensely in my effort to understand both the obsessiveness of my own projects and the radical edge of what otherwise would be dismissed so easily these days as the limited self-activities and political subjectivities of Filipinos who continue to practice recognition and representation (what some economically determinist critics would scoff at as "identitarian") politics.

TT: Could you talk about the central narratives and paradigms that have been traditionally or historically deployed to make sense of Filipino subject and group formation? For example, does it make sense to think of Filipinos as an immigrant group?

OC: I'd take the shorthand approach here because it's truly a tiresome and ultimately unrewarding task to survey the "central narratives and paradigms" usually used to recount Filipino subject and community formations, not the least for their theoretical impoverishment and repetitiousness (by and large, these are orientalist in Said's sense, and because of their perpetual reaffirmations, neo-orientalist—I remain skeptical about the claims for the general possibility of a post-orientalist account being made by scholars like Vince Rafael, Anne Stoler, etc.). I prefer to talk, in other words, about what is common to all or recurs as determinate refrains/axioms in these forms of knowledge production about Filipinos and Filipino Americans.

One such central narrative or paradigm is what I termed in a critical essay "cultural determinism," which is indisputably colonial in origin and tenor. This cultural determinism model cuts across both U.S. area studies of the Philippines (the handful that exists) and U.S. ethnic/Asian American studies of Filipino Americans (although this strain is fast being discredited or, better and in radical fashion, *displaced,* by the theoretically sharp and empirically sound work of the young Filipino American scholars I have mentioned). The line of descent of this model is very long, from the U.S. colonial scholars of Dean Worcester's time (and later Ralston Hayden's) to Howard Brett de Melendy, Stanley Karnow, Al McCoy (although he is more sophisticated than the rest of the pack), and Glenn May by the late twentieth century, including that deranged and highly controversial account by the pseudoanthropologist James Fallows on our so-called damaged culture. The most powerful critiques/accounts of this kind of scholarship and writing that I have seen are those by the Australian scholar Rodney Sullivan (on Worcester) and the eminent Filipino historian Reynaldo Ileto (on U.S. orientalist social science on Philippine political history and political practices/institutions).

What this cultural-determinist narrative does, at bottom, is give new dress or costumery, each time it threatens to wear out, to the much-rubbed colonial alibi that the Philippines, because of its history of multiple colonizations, is culturally transparent and predictable. (When this argument is extended to Filipino American cultural forms and formations, which it always is, a great deal of the specificity of U.S. Filipino cultures and community histories is simply subjected to considerable epistemic violence.) In the Philippines, you have careless local social science scholars and in the United States you have unreflexive U.S. historians and political scientists on the Philippines replaying this cultural determinism from essay to essay and monograph to monograph, albeit with seemingly "novel" theoretical ramparts whenever some form of "innovation" is necessitated (the "patron-client" model has long been discredited with respect, for example, to India, but its career in U.S. Filipinology is simply obdurate). In the same essay, I refer to this cultural determinism as an unwitting inverse of the "culture of poverty thesis" used by War on Poverty scholars and policy makers in the United States to explain African American personal and social "pathologies." In our case, then, it seems worse: the problem presumably is "a poverty of culture" itself—how these various proponents of cultural determinism do not see their family of resemblances and line of descent to U.S. civilizationist discourse on the Philippines is much cause for astonishment (but perhaps not). It's certainly caused a great deal of defensiveness and generated a reactive literature of positive self-stereotyping among Filipinos, from the time of Lawcock's pensionados during the colonial period to the self-nativist tunes played no end by indignant Filipinos "abroad" in our own moment. When it is not inducing an unreflexive defensiveness and politics of negation among us, the power of this cultural determinism actually recruits or realigns many Filipinos and Filipino Americans in their own thinking and auto-critiques, especially when they are compelled to confront personal dysfunctions or to account for endemic problems in community organizing/politics in the context of struggles for "recognition and representation" abroad or in the United States.

Another such narrative, for lack of a better term, is the "immigrant model." You are familiar with my own critique of this as a paradigm to study Filipino American formation, especially in Asian American literary history and social science literature. I'd only add that Filipino American formation is probably best and more fully understood through comparisons with and new insertions into alternative accounts, such as those developed for Chicano/as, Puertorriqueño/as, Hawaiians, and Pacific Islanders (and what binds all of them is the common subjection to a history of U.S. imperial expansion; we belong to this history more than to the history of Asian Americans). I mean, who really buys all these insignificant although comforting "fictions" about Filipinos as among the founding settlers of Los Angeles or as Manilamen developing the Louisiana bayous? Not only is the research not developed for these sorts of claims, but the founding questions are not even problematized, even posed! So after we are able to say that we were among the first Asian settlers and immigrants, does this redress the problem of bad and faulty Asian American historiography or sociology of immigration with respect to Filipino Americans? Will it alter or seriously modify the very narrative and the very immigration mythography that must first be questioned as a paradigm with respect to our own development as "Americans" of a kind, whether as neo/postcolonial subjects or neo/postcolonial "immigrants"?

Technically speaking, you cannot consider the movements of Carlos Bulosan's generation (Pinoys/Manongs) and the pensionados to the United States as immigration! As the Chicano scholars would say with respect to a formative period in the Americanization of their communities, and as we should say with respect to ours, it was the borders that moved and not people alone. From the establishment of colonial government in the Philippines to the time of the Commonwealth, Filipinos moved to the continental states not as nationals of a sovereign nation but as *U.S. nationals* of a territory "appurtenant to" but considered as "belonging to" the United States. It is kind of like the movements Puerto Ricans make now from the island to New York, or American Samoans or Guamenians to Hawai'i or California, with their indeterminate status as neocolonial Americans. Even with the postindependence period, "immigration" from the Philippines has to be seriously qualified by its undeniable neocolonial inflections. Until the abrogation of the Mutual Defense Treaty and the bases agreement and the eventual clampdown on immigration through recruitment into U.S. national security institutions like the U.S. Navy, where have you seen a case where the nationals or citizens of an already supposedly sovereign country like the Philippines could actually be allowed, by special dispensation, to move into and work for such strategic spaces and institutions of another, especially for a security-conscious nation like the United States? And we have not discussed yet the case of Filipino medical or health professionals, especially our ever-precious nurses, and how immigration law is massively tweaked to facilitate their deployment in nursing-starved U.S. hospitals and caregiving industries!

I am thrilled to see some immigration scholars now, like the University of Chicago historian Mae Ngai or our own Kimberly Alidio and Cathy Ceniza-Choy, making these kinds of categorical critiques and producing alternative accounts of Filipino migrant histories in light of our neocolonial past, present, and futures. I am quite envious of the Puerto Ricans, who have a whole array of their finest minds devoted to the study of the equally peculiar case of Puerto Rico's neocolonial integration and territorial displacements, especially the status studies, and the sophisticated investigations now being conducted (with help from eminent U.S. legal scholars and law-school professors) on the Insular Cases and their continuing relevance to the pressing status and statehood questions that confront the island and its inhabitants/migrants (these cases just as equally concerned us but, alas, no Yale Law School conferences and novel U.S. university-press anthologies for us, as there have been for the Puerto Ricans). I am also grateful for the effort of somebody like Leti Volpp, who has broached the question of Filipino American inclusion into the "Latino" coalition and has deployed the particularity of the Philippine/Filipino question in her exhaustive work to challenge and interrogate even the most progressive terms of U.S. citizenship and critical-legal studies in such a prominent circuit as the LATCRIT network. I say Filipino Americanist scholars should start reaching out to alternative coalitions and engagements with U.S. constituencies/scholarships with which we have much more in common, in terms of searching questions to pose and urgent answers to search. Think, for example, of how much we would profit from looking at the prolific results of Pacific Islander studies of the past few decades!

TT: How does an "internationalist" framework which takes into account U.S. imperialism and genocide confound the signifier "Filipino American" as well as distinctions between "Filipinos" and "Filipino Americans"?

OC: Your question is way too overdetermined for me to answer in full or with reasonable adequacy, especially concerning "genocide." We might want to be a little more careful when using that term in reference even to the genocidal tenor of the war that inaugurated our Filipino "American" history, in deference to the Native Americans and other peoples whose implication in that kind of imperialist expansion or settler colonialism dwarfs our extracontinental experience in scope and consequences. You might want to pose a question like this to the feisty and controversial young Filipino American scholar/activist Dylan Rodríguez, who, I believe, has been paying this kind of conjunction and articulation between our own particular situation and those of Native Americans and others scrupulous and sensitive attention, with expansive concern for larger ethical and political questions in respect to the United States and its continuing practices as a nation in power brokerage both as an empire and as a machine/regime of capital accumulation.

My answer is very brief—you might have noted how, regarding your indeterminate use of "Filipinos" in your questions to refer both to Filipino Americans and Filipinos in the Philippines/elsewhere, I have actually sought to "distinguish," with respect to the "internationalist" history of U.S. imperialism, even as I have desisted from challenging or asking you to subdivide it in consideration of specificities and particular histories. For as you say, it is a matter of confounding. I prefer to work from this confounding, as you apparently do, rather than insist on particularity and disarticulation all the time, as now seems to be the reflex. I have always maintained the position that the term "Filipino American" is a redundancy (and not just an apparent oxymoron): to be Filipino is already, whether you move to the United States or remain where you are, to be American. The term "Filipino American," in spite of its anchorage in a history of U.S. identity politics, can be a signifier just as descriptive of the modern and U.S. colonial period formation of Filipinos as it is of an emergent and self-empowering political subject in U.S. multiculturalism. For me, the term to privilege is "Filipino," for it is the truly plastic term with the capacity to authorize a whole series of valences, historically speaking (from Spanish colonial times to the diasporic moment of the present). But to expand on this is grist for a longer-grinding mill and will veer us away from the focus here on U.S. imperialism.

3 Filipino Bodies, Lynching, and the Language of Empire

AS A RESULT of the Philippine-American War and their long history of labor migration, Filipinos, the second-largest Asian immigrant population in the United States, figured prominently in the U.S. popular imagination during the late nineteenth and early twentieth centuries.[1] In his autobiography, *America Is in the Heart* (1946), labor activist and writer Carlos Bulosan chronicles the lives of Filipino farmworkers during the Great Depression. A substantial part of the text is set in California in the 1930s, when an increase in the state's Filipino immigrant population provoked anti-Filipino sentiment and Filipino farmworkers were the subjects of racial violence and discrimination.[2] The book depicts this violence in vivid terms, nowhere more graphically than in a scene where three Filipino farmworkers are lynched. The narrator, Carlos, is preparing union materials with two Filipino labor organizers in a restaurant when five white men with guns barge in and force them into a car:

> We entered the woods and in five minutes the car stopped.... The man on my right got out and pulled me violently after ... hitting me on the jaw. I fell on my knees, but got up at once, trembling with rage. If only I had a gun! Or a knife! I could cut these bastards into little pieces! Blood came out of my mouth. I raised my hand to wipe it off, but my attacker hit me again. I staggered, fell on my face, and rolled on the grass....
>
> Painfully I crawled to my feet, knelt on the grass, and got up slowly. I saw them kicking Millar in the grass. When they were through with him, they tore off Jose's clothes and tied him to a tree. One of them went to the car and came back with a can of tar and a sack of feathers. The man with the dark glasses ripped the sack open and white feathers fell out and sailed in the thin light that filtered between the trees. Then I saw them pouring the tar on Jose's body. One of them lit a match and burned the delicate hair between his legs. "Jesus, he's a well-hung son-of-a-bitch!" "Yeah!" "No wonder whores stick to them!" "The other monkey ain't so hot!" They looked in my direction. The man with the dark glasses started beating Millar. Then he came to me and kicked my left knee so violently that I fell.... Another man, the one called Jake, tied me to a tree. Then he started beating me with his fists.... A tooth fell out of my mouth, and blood trickled down my shirt. The man called Lester grabbed my testicles with his left hand and smashed them with his right fist. The pain was so swift and searing.[3]

The scene keeps faith with the historical experience of Filipino farmworkers terrorized by white mobs who regarded them as an economic threat to white male workers and as a sexual threat to white women, and at the same time viewed them as bestial savages (thus the racial epithet "monkey").[4]

This scene and other acts of racial violence against Filipinos in Bulosan's text can be read through the lens of "race," gender, and empire.[5] The Filipino farmworkers had stepped out of line by organizing unions and threatening the economic order. They had also violated the boundaries of the color line in their supposed and real relationships with white women.[6] Angry whites justified this brutality as a way to maintain the economic and racial order, with the discipline centered on the Filipinos' sexual organs. This scene in the book recalls the efforts of Ida B. Wells in the late nineteenth century and of African American journalists at the turn of the century to call attention to lynchings as physical and symbolic acts of controlling emancipated black bodies. The lynching and other brutalities depicted in Bulosan's *America* can be read as acts of discipline imposed on unruly, savage male bodies—bodies that were subjects of the U.S. Empire.

In 1899, African American soldiers were sent to the Philippine Islands to the Philippine-American War (1899–1902), and black journalists across the nation were warning that the lynching of black men, women, and children in the South was the same kind of violence being committed against Filipino men, women, and children in the war. As William Loren Katz notes, at the height of U.S. overseas expansion, the lynchings at home escalated. From 1899 to 1902, "almost 2,000 black men, women and children were lynched, often with unspeakable brutality."[7]

My essay focuses on two theoretical ideas: the phenomenon of reciprocity (a term coined by Oscar V. Campomanes) in late nineteenth-century discourses on the Filipino savage as the new colonial Other; and the formation of what I call post-colonial African American critique against U.S. imperialism, whose genealogy we trace to the protofeminist works of black women writers of the mid–nineteenth century and the writings of W.E.B. DuBois. The phenomenon of reciprocity exists in racist discourses in which black, red, and Filipino or "brown" savagery were rearticulated and recirculated after 1899, the beginning of the Philippine-American War. As Etienne Balibar reminds us, imperialism is an "extreme term" for a nationalism that seeks to "subjugate" and rule by "might."[8] In studying empire as a language, I recognize Balibar's observation that there exists between discourses an "ideological symmetry" based on racism's power to represent and commit violence. My study of the language of the American Empire recognizes the palimpsest of the past or earlier forms of racism—what Balibar describes as the "presence of the past" (38) and the "repetition of themes" (41) in imperialist and anti-imperialist discourses. The "past in my discussion refers to earlier representations of black and native subjects and how these stereotypes merged and coalesced in the figure of the Filipino savage.

The second theoretical idea, which examines early African American anti-imperialism, departs from the accounts of historians such as Stuart Creighton

Miller who cite the founding of the Anti-Imperialist League of Boston in 1898 as the origin of organized political opposition to U.S. imperialism.[9] I recognize an earlier anti-imperialist tradition, albeit an informal or unorganized one, in the writings of African American women in the mid–nineteenth century and of black soldiers sent to the Philippine Islands to fight in the Philippine-American War. My ideas on lynching and empire were especially influenced by literary critic Hazel Carby's discussion of a nineteenth-century black feminist anti-imperialist tradition.[10] U.S. imperialism for Frances Harper and for Anna Julia Cooper was "unrestrained patriarchal power" exercised by white males. Both associated U.S. imperialism with the gendered myth of the founding white fathers as a narrative of "rampant lust, greed and destruction," and white male rule as "bestial in its actual and potential power to devour lands and peoples."[11] For black women writers of the era, U.S. expansion was the expansion of U.S.-sponsored racial violence around the globe. Lynching was a violent act that occurred locally, while imperial conquest was a violent act that occurred globally or in other lands.

In this essay, I contend that popular discourses on Filipino savagery, the rise of lynchings in the South, and the emergence of a U.S. imperial policy in the Pacific are the historical milieu of the term "Filipino." Long before the arrival of thirty thousand Filipino migrant laborers immortalized by Bulosan in his novel *America Is in the Heart,* the term circulated at the moment of the emergence of the U.S. Empire. After 1898, Filipinos were racialized as savage black bodies, and this idea of Filipino savagery would affect the lives of Filipino migrant workers in the 1920s and later decades.

"HALF DEVIL AND HALF CHILD": THE FILIPINO'S SAVAGE BODY

In 1898, the United States became involved in the Philippines, then a Spanish colony, as an offshoot of the U.S. war against Spain. On 13 August 1898, U.S. troops took over the city of Manila in a sham battle negotiated with the Spaniards, who preferred to surrender to the Americans rather than to the Filipinos, who had revolted against them and who were also poised to take over the city. During the mock hostilities, however, Filipino revolutionaries managed to occupy some of the capital's suburbs, which they refused to hand over to the Americans and which later became the first battle zones in the Philippine-American War. On 10 December 1898, Spain and the United States signed a peace treaty in Paris that ceded the Philippines, along with Guam and Puerto Rico, to the United States for twenty million dollars. On 4 February 1899, shortly before the U.S. Senate ratified the treaty, hostilities broke out between Filipino troops and U.S. soldiers when an American private fired at Filipinos who refused to obey his command to halt. That shot marked the beginning of the Philippine-American War.

While economic and imperialist motives largely drove the decision to control and occupy the Philippines, and hence to fight the war, Kristin L. Hoganson notes that U.S. imperialists anchored their support for colonizing the Philippines on what she terms "Filipino degeneracy" or savagery. This notion was based on and reinforced by racialized and gendered stereotypes of the Filipino that were disseminated in the popular media shortly after the Americans moved into the country: Filipinos as dark "savages," as "children," and as "feminized" subjects. In essence, Filipinos were viewed as a backward people "lacking the manly character seen as necessary for self-government."[12]

The war was thus the originary moment for the recirculation of domestic grammars of Otherness that informed discourses on Filipino savagery. Imperialists and anti-imperialists, while vigorously disagreeing on the issue of Philippine colonization, agreed that the Filipino was a "savage." On the one hand, University of Chicago professor Harry Pratt Judson wrote in favor of colonizing the Philippines as an "annexed territory" without extending citizenship or constitutional rights to "inferior races." Yale professor Theodore S. Woolsey, on the other hand, pointed to the backwardness of the country to make his argument that colonization would entail "the burden of administration and responsibility for the conduct of seven millions of half-civilized or savage Filipinos."[13]

While U.S. essayists debated their nation's empire building, non-American writers took on the issue as well. A popular poem by Rudyard Kipling, "The White Man's Burden," romanticized and encouraged the imperial project of colonizing the Philippines, describing Filipinos as "fluttered folk and wild," as "sullen peoples, / half devil and half child." Kipling described empire building as an affirmation of U.S. manhood that, up to that moment of 1898, had been unavailable to the "young" republic:

> Take up the White Man's burden!
>   Have done with childish days—
> The lightly-proffered laurel,
>   The easy ungrudged praise:
> Comes now, to search your manhood
>   Through all the thankless years,
> Cold, edged with dear-bought wisdom,
>   The judgment of your peers.[14]

Ever the cheerleader for Anglo supremacy and expansionism, Kipling encouraged the United States to join other imperial powers who had taken on the "white man's burden" and to turn for models to the older and more established colonial powers, who could pass on to the fledgling imperialist the "judgment of your peers."

Parodies of Kipling's pro-imperialist poem appeared in other publications; the London *Truth* published the anti-imperialist "Brown Man's Burden," which viewed colonization as the gratification of "greed" that entailed clearing away the "niggers," the epithet used by U.S. soldiers for Filipinos.

> Pile on the brown man's burden,
>   Compel him to be free;
> Let all your manifestoes
>   Reek with philanthropy.
> And if with heathen folly
>   He dares your will dispute,
> Then in the name of freedom
>   Don't hesitate to shoot.
>
> Pile on the brown man's burden,
>   And if his cry be sore,
> That surely need not irk you—
>   Ye've driven slaves before.
> Seize on his ports and pastures,
>   The fields his people tread;
> Go make from them your living,
>   And mark them with his dead.[15]

In this parody, imperial expansion is deromanticized by exposing the hypocrisy and greed behind its facade of a civilizing mission and philanthropy. The author reminds U.S. readers that Americans encouraged Filipinos to throw off the yoke of Spanish imperialism, then sarcastically advises them to shoot the "brown man" if he dares to question U.S. military rule.

In Ernest H. Crosby's anti-imperialist poem in the *New York Times*, vice and disease are not innate to the degenerate tropics but brought over by the "sturdy sons" of the United States:

> Take up the White Man's burden;
>   Send forth your sturdy sons,
> And load them down with whisky
>   And Testaments and guns.
> Throw in a few diseases
>   To spread in tropic climes,
> For there the healthy niggers
>   Are quite behind the times.

The writer also advises the United States to assimilate the native through modern methods of discipline:

> Take up the White Man's burden,
>   And teach the Philippines
> What interest and taxes are
>   And what a mortgage means.

> Give them electrocution chairs,
>   And prisons, too, galore,
> And if they seem inclined to kick,
>   Then spill their heathen gore.[16]

Editorial cartoons conflated Filipino savagery with "blackness." In one Canadian cartoon, titled "His Point of View," Uncle Sam or the Union is about to swallow a black figure in a loincloth (Figure 3.1). The cartoon, in which a colonial native "speaks" in a black vernacular, presents both a representation of savagery popular in the late nineteenth century and an unflatteringly critical representation of two empires. The Spanish Empire is a "shark" and the U.S. Empire is an "alligator" ready to consume what the shark has not.[17]

Another cartoon, "The White Man's Burden" (a reference to the Kipling poem), suggests that colonization is the burden of the United States because it is a "civilized" nation (Figure 3.2).

Cartoons typically represented former colonial subjects of the Spanish Empire as black men. "Our Awkward Squad" shows a "Puerto Rican," a "Cuban" and a "Filipino" as dark-skinned, thick-lipped persons. That the Filipino is wearing a grass skirt and hoop earrings instead of military attire suggests that Filipinos are a people still in the primitive stage (18 [12]: 331).

Further examples of brown savagery can be read in the discourse of representations of the "native." "Filipinos Must Be Taught Obedience," an article in the *Washington, D.C., Star,* described Filipinos as "treacherous, arrogant, stupid and vindictive, impervious to gratitude, incapable of recognizing obligations." Further: "Centuries of barbarism and subjection have made them merely cunning and dishonest. We cannot safely treat them as our equals, for the simple and sufficient reason that they could not understand it. They do not know the meaning of justice

FIGURE 3.1. "His Point of View." The cartoon caption reads: "Ex-Spanish Colonial Native: 'By de Great Yaller Hoodoo, what's de advantage ob gettin' cl'ar ob de shark if I'se got ter be swallered by de American yallergator?'"
Source: Literary Digest, Vol. 18, No. 5:141.

FIGURE 3.2. "The White Man's Burden."
Source: Literary Digest, Vol. 18, No. 7:180.

and good faith." The article's author advocated more brutal conduct in the war against Filipinos, who after all were not "moral equals" of Americans (18 [7]: 181). The rules of civilized warfare did not apply when fighting savages.

In an editorial, "How Far Shall We Go?" the *Detroit News* recommended suppressing all Filipino dissent against U.S. military rule, describing the Philippine Revolution against the U.S. Army as merely an "insurrection": "The insurrection [that] began under Spanish rule must be suppressed under American rule. The men that defied the authority of Spain must be punished for transferring their defiance to the authority of the United States. The patriots of a year ago have become savages to be treated after the manner of savages—and more power to the Krag-Jörgensen rifle that does the treating" (18 [7]: 181). This passage reflects how the terms of the discourse on Filipinos had shifted. In 1898, just after the outbreak of the Spanish-American War, the United States recognized Filipinos as "patriots" for their revolution against Spanish imperialism. But less than a year later, when they continued their war for independence, this time fighting the U.S. Army, they became "savages" who deserved brutal treatment, an image that would display remarkable staying power.

Filipinos were viewed not only as savages but also as simianlike and treacherous:

It is impossible for the United States to hold themselves responsible for the acts of half-wild peoples. . . . I sometimes think that this people are nearer the monkey than the man. Conceive, if you can, a people made up of individuals without the least consistency of character—anything to anybody at any time. One day, a Filipino may be your sworn friend, and the next day he may stab you in the back, and that without provocation. This character is not due to volatile weakness of character, but to a total absence of character, for the Filipino is phlegmatic and unemotional in the extreme. (18 [11]: 297)

Such depictions of Filipinos as monkeylike reprise the popular stereotypes of blacks as "savage" and "beastly," more animal than human, as well as of the treacherous and inscrutable "Oriental." In a *Harper's Weekly* editorial, Frank D. Millet compares Filipino treachery to the "uncivilized warfare" of North American Indians (18 [13]: 358–59).

In other news accounts, the leaders of the Philippine Revolution exemplify Filipino treachery. An account in the *New York Independent* by the Belgian consul to Manila, Edward C. André, described Filipino general Antonio Luna as "the leader of the radical independents,... both bloodthirsty and unprincipled." For André, however, the most dangerous elements of the Filipino revolutionary army were not its middle-class leaders but those, like lawyer Apolinario Mabini, from humbler origins, because "the radicals...have no property. They have nothing to risk or lose, but everything to gain in a revolution" (18 [13]: 357, 358).

Infantilizing the Filipino, or representing the Filipino as a child, was the theme of an editorial cartoon that depicts Uncle Sam laughing at a small person marching in a large helmet and asking the "little native," "Where did you get that hat?" The helmeted figure, who holds a sword with the name "Aguinaldo" on the scabbard, represents the Filipino revolutionary general Emilio Aguinaldo, who led the Filipino revolutionary armies (18 [6]: 152). Other caricatures of Aguinaldo represented him as a wild, savage child with dark skin and Uncle Sam as a paternal figure. "Holding His Own" shows Uncle Sam holding Aguinaldo in a rocking chair with another weeping savage baby, whose shirt carries the word "Iloilo," a province occupied by Filipino revolutionaries (Figure 3.3). In "Philanthropy Up to Date," a small dark boy with two pistols fires at Uncle Sam, who holds a bayonet to the boy's throat (18 [9]: 260).

While these cartoons suggest that the Filipino revolutionary armies were Davids fighting the Goliath that was the U.S. Army, other accounts of the war show that the Filipinos offered fierce resistance. As early as February 1899, during the first few days of the war, some international newspapers predicted that the Philippine army would resort to guerrilla warfare. The *Vienna Tageblatt* and the *Hong Kong Telegraph*, respectively, predicted that "a guerrilla war may be carried on for six years," even if the Philippine fighters were defeated, and that Filipinos "would be able to carry on a most trying guerrilla warfare for a long period."[18]

During one battle in the first week of the war, 160 Filipinos died and 87 were mortally wounded, and an Associated Press report mentions that members of the U.S.

FIGURE 3.3. "Holding His Own."
Cartoon caption reads: "Uncle Sam:
'This isn't exactly pleasant, but these
children have got to be brought up right,
and I'm not backing out on the job.' "
Source: Literary Digest, Vol. 18:240.

Hospital Corps were shocked to discover "several women, in masculine uniform, and with hair cropped" among those killed in action (18 [5]: 180). U.S. publications such as the *Literary Digest* ran translations of Filipino revolutionaries' statements of their determination to continue the Philippine Revolution. Quotations such as this one from the *Republica Filipina* reflect a character far different from the U.S. image of the quaint "little native boy": "We want independence at any price, and will not recognize the transaction by which we are sold like so many cattle. The Americans have over and over again asserted that the only object of their war with Spain was to give independence to the Spanish colonies, and the Philippine people will not rest until they have won that independence. The yoke of the new master will not be as irksome as that of the old, we are informed, but chains are hateful to us tho they be gilded" (18 [5]: 260).

As the war dragged on for months, U.S. general Elwell Otis ordered U.S. defeats censored. In July 1899, Manila correspondents for various U.S. newspapers disseminated a letter of protest, complaining that their dispatches were modified to present an "ultra-optimistic view" and that hospital reports of the numbers of killed were suppressed. Editorials across the United States demanded the government tell the truth about the war (19 [5]: 121–23, 143–44).

Meanwhile, racialized images of Filipinos continued to appear in editorial cartoons and news reports. In November 1899, the *Chicago Inter Ocean* reported that more than a hundred generals and officers in the war were "Indian veterans" who knew how to defeat "Indian tactics," compared the war to the "Indian campaigns," and predicted that U.S. victory was inevitable since the soldiers were experienced fighters and successful in the campaigns against "the Cheyennes, Arapahoes, Comanches, Modocs, Apaches, Nez Perces, Utes, Sioux and the Piutes" (19 [22]: 633–34). The allusion to the "Indian wars" recalls Amy Kaplan's idea that wars "continue each other" through cyclic discourses that generate symbolic meanings which transpose and reinterpret earlier wars.[19] Like the U.S. frontier, the Philippines would become a conquered territory of the Union.

Cartoons continued to depict Aguinaldo and the Filipino colonial subject as black males: one shows Aguinaldo as a bird-man with a dark face and thick lips; in another, set in a classroom and captioned "Keep right on studying, boys; don't mind the noise outside," Aguinaldo appears as a young student with other young wards of Uncle Sam who must learn the "ABC's of self-government" (19 [22]: 634; 20 [7]: 204). A December 1901 cartoon titled "Another Stocking to Fill" shows Aguinaldo as a pickaninny with "Philippines" written on his shirt as he hangs a Christmas stocking, near which hangs a sign that reads: "Funds for maintenance of government in the Philippine Islands" (23 [25]: 793). In a final example, two black figures smoke; the larger, "Cuba," holds an oversized cigar from which issues the smoke of "independence" as he tells the smaller "Philippines": "Yo' watch me, chile, mebbe yo' hab a chance yo'se'f some day" (24 [21]: 703).

African Americans struggling with their own war against white supremacy and racism would read and interpret such discourses on empire and race differently.

Racial Violence at Home and Abroad: Reading Lynching and Imperialism

Critiques against racism and imperialism are part of a long-standing tradition in African American political discourse. In 1846, Frederick Douglass attacked the U.S. war against Mexico, and black journalists opposed the Spanish-American War of 1898 as unjust.[20] The *Salt Lake City Broad Ax* claimed on 30 April 1898 that the "Negro's main enemy is Southern lynchers," not the Spaniards, and the *Iowa State Bystander* contended on 6 May: "White America's cruelty equals Spain's" in the lynchings of men and women "murdered by the American white people in the past 25 years." Black communities, concluded Kansas's *Coffeyville Journal* the following day, were not "spoiling for a fight" for a country that could not protect its "colored" citizens, and the *Parsons Weekly Blade* of 11 June argued that even as "Uncle Sam can find time to shoot Spaniards for their cruelty to Cubans," the United States continued to ignore lynchings in Louisiana, Texas, Maryland, Missouri, and Arkansas.[21]

In 1899, critical voices in the Negro press suggested that for many black Americans, the Philippine-American War was an effort to enforce Jim Crow laws on another dark race. A common theme of editorials in proexpansion newspapers was imperialism as "assimilation." Statesmen eager to claim the Islands for the U.S. flag portrayed Filipinos as "orphans" separated "from their Spanish fathers and desired by other European powers," as Vicente L. Rafael writes. To protect them, the United States annexed the Philippines. Rafael describes this colonization as founded on racial ideas of white supremacy and the racializing discourse that constructs the natives as the dark "beloved," a form of "white love"—a "benign" version of Carby's description of U.S. expansion as "white rape."[22]

Black intellectuals and ordinary soldiers in the late nineteenth century challenged the very processes of Anglo or white hegemony bent on establishing and maintaining the U.S. racial and economic status quo at home and abroad—that is, lynching and war—by linking lynching and empire as attempts to dominate the darker races. Their interpretation elaborates the shared histories of racial violence and economic oppression of black Americans and colonized peoples in Asia and the Caribbean, a "third-worldist perspective" in the early writings of DuBois that Pan-Africanist intellectuals would take up in the 1950s.[23]

As literary critic Sandra Gunning notes, and as we have seen in the contemporaneous cartoons, an antiblack message in discourses at the turn of the century deemed the darker races unassimilable, an "inferior human species." For Americans, these darker races included Filipinos. As Gunning observes, Theodore Roosevelt in 1899 referred to Aguinaldo as "the typical representative of savagery, the typical foe of civilization of the American people." Historian Paul Kramer writes that U.S. colonial officials and anthropologists faced with "making racial sense of the population" drew on the discourse and racial ideas of the "Negro Problem."[24] I believe that discursively representing the Filipinos' "savagery" justified to the nation the savage conduct of the Philippine-American War, just as lynching was justified as a solution to the "Negro Problem."

The tenor of the debate over a U.S. Empire in Asia and the conduct of the war can be gleaned from a 7 October 1899 editorial in the African American *Indianapolis Freeman*, which supported U.S. annexation of the Philippines: "Those papers and prominent citizens, who said that the Negro was a fool if he espoused the cause of our government as against the Philippines, have some considerable crow to eat, or in order to be consistent, prove to be the fools themselves. The strife is no race war. It is quite time for the Negroes to quit claiming kindred with every black face from Hannibal down. Hannibal was no Negro, nor was Aguinaldo. We are to share in the glories or defeats of our country's wars, that is patriotism pure and simple."[25] By proving their zealous nationalism, proexpansionist African Americans believed they would eventually receive fair treatment under the law and enjoy civil liberties. But pointing out that Aguinaldo was "no Negro" also emphasized a simple truth: some African Americans at the turn of the century saw through the hypocrisy of Philippine annexation as a civilizing mission.[26] Thus, while the dissemination of the racial image of Filipinos in mainstream and black proannexation newspapers was a hegemonic racial project in support of imperialism, the same racial image became a counter-hegemonic racial project in "Negro papers" that maintained anti-imperialist and antiracist positions regarding the war.

Editorialists and reporters in these newspapers took a strongly anti-imperialist position, emphasizing "the interconnection between the government's domestic and foreign policy in dealing with dark-skinned people"; their editorials contended, writes Marks, that the United States "was not wise, just and democratic enough to govern people of a darker hue in the Philippines or anywhere."[27]

On 10 December 1898, a few days before the ratification of the Treaty of Paris, a *Parsons Weekly Blade* editorial noted that Uncle Sam "steps in and takes the children [Spanish colonials, in this case, Cubans] under his arm for protection" yet on the other side of the globe "gobbles up another small kingdom"—the Philippine Islands. The *Blade* concludes: "All this highway robbery is done in the name of humanity and is done by a nation that shows by its actions at home that the principles of humanity are an unknown factor when the treatment of the American Negro is taken into consideration."[28] The *Cleveland Gazette* on 7 January 1899 quoted Ida Wells Barnett, the black journalist who exposed the horrors of lynching in the South, as saying that all black citizens should oppose expansion until the U.S. government could "protect the Negro at home" from white mob violence (109).

On the first day of the Philippine-American War, 4 February 1899, the *Washington Bee* reported that "a majority of the negroes in this country are opposed to expansion," since most blacks believed that a government that could not protect its citizens from racial violence at home had no business invading another country; the status of an "American protectorate" was "nothing more than political and physical oppression," and expansion was a fraud (112). A week later, on 11 February 1899, a *Bee* editorial entitled "Negroes Opposed to the Treaty of Paris" claimed that the "consensus of opinion among the negro citizens of this government was naturally opposed to a ratification of the treaty" because black citizens were denied their rights in the United States, a circumstance the editorialist suggested that Filipinos in the Philippines would share as subject peoples of the United States (114).

The same day, the *Coffeyville American* opposed U.S. annexation of the Philippines, an issue not confined to the right of the U.S. government to acquire land "by purchase or conquest" but one that affected all "people who belong to the dark-skinned races." The *American* pointed to the historical treatment of Indians, Chinese, and Negroes by "white Americans" and concluded not only that the Filipinos would be equally mistreated but also that U.S. civilization had "very little to commend it" (114–15). The *Indianapolis Recorder* on 18 February 1899 described the Philippine-American War not as the "war for humanity" depicted in the mainstream papers but as a "slaughter" and a war of greed. During its first month, "6,000 natives" were killed; what was being established in the Islands was "the dominating mastery of the Anglo-Saxon asserting itself; humanity—never!" (115–16). The *Recorder* reported on 4 March that Filipinos were being "civilized" by the U.S. Army just as the North American Indians were "civilized" through war and violence (116). Two weeks later, on 18 March, the *Recorder* describes the "bayonet-imposed civilization" of the United States: "The Americans are determined to make the Filipinos accept civilization at the point of the bayonet. The officers in command of the American forces are old Indian fighters, who owe their success to the close adherence to the theory that 'a dead Indian is the best Indian.' They will employ the same methods in dealing with the Filipinos" (117). In fact, of the generals who served the U.S. Army in the Philippines from 1898 to 1900, 87 percent had fought in the "Indian wars."[29]

Among the black press's admirers of the Filipino insurgents, the *Washington Bee* on 11 March 1899 wrote that Filipinos exhibited "the spirit of heroism" and that their struggle for independence proved that "all people who are oppressed will fight, and if need be, die for their liberty." The *Bee* linked the Filipinos' struggle for independence from the United States with the struggle of black citizens for constitutional rights; "hence a bond of sympathy naturally springs up" (116–17).

In the *Salt Lake City Broad Ax* for 25 March 1899, an editorialist expounded on the continuum of violence of U.S. expansion, from the frontier to the Pacific:

> When the Pilgrim Fathers landed at Plymouth Rock, they came into contact with the law-abiding and peaceful Indians; and the blood stained pages of history record their hellish plots. The Fathers robbed, plundered the Indians and outraged their wives and daughters and murdered them, so that they could acquire their land without compensating them for it.... The same fate awaits Aguinaldo and his subjects if they permit themselves to be conquered.... For if they submit, the same treatment is in store for them which has been meted out to the Negro for over two hundred and fifty years.
>
> What right has this or any other nation to interfere with the inhabitants of those islands? What right has it to foully murder innocent women and children?...This war is simply being waged to satisfy the robbers, murderers, and unscrupulous monopolists who are crying for more blood! This country is not invested with any valid title to those islands. (118)

Journalists for black newspapers invoked the supposed savagery of Filipinos and the actual savagery of the war against them in commentaries on the lynch law. A *Broad Ax* editorial on 25 April 1899 contended that the American people were deceived into believing that U.S. soldiers were sent to the Islands "on a mission of love and goodwill, and to carry the torch liberty and freedom to those benighted savages." Instead, U.S. soldiers had killed over "6,000 of the natives— more than the Spaniards have killed in fifty years," although the slaughter may have been a "blessing," since Filipinos were not considered civilized "by the people of this country who believe in mob and lynch law." The policy of annexation was "inhuman, blood-thirsty," and "wrong"; the U.S. government was willing to "wade in human blood and gore up to their knees in order to fasten a new policy upon the people" (124). Similarly, the *Iowa State Bystander* on 28 April 1899 criticized the

U.S. government for its inaction on the lynchings in the South and its continuing violence against the Filipino people:

> The recent lynchings in the Southland, especially in Georgia and the Carolinas, of colored people who are accused of a crime without a trial, evidence, or facts except the mere accusation, has become a stench upon our civilization and damnable curse on our vaunted humanity.... Is this civilization? Is this America's justice? Is this humanity? Are those white people insane?... Were Americans fighting the Spaniards to free Cuba from barbarous treatment of Spain; what thinks Spain of our barbarous treatment of our own citizens? Why are we now fighting the natives 10,000 miles away in the Philippine Islands, trying to force our flag and banner over them to civilize them? If the action of the Southern States is civilization, then away with such a government.

The *Bystander* concluded that the U.S. government had no right to ask its black citizens to serve in the Philippine war if the government could not protect them from racial violence (125).

Black soldiers in the Philippines wrote about the war in letters home and to newspapers. The editors of the *Salt Lake City Broad Ax* on 16 May 1899 vehemently opposed annexation because of "race prejudice": it was a common practice among white soldiers to call Filipinos "niggers." Black soldiers wrote that white soldiers also had "an utter contempt 'for the niggers which they are engaged in slaying.'" The *Broad Ax* advised blacks with any conscience to conclude "that the war is being waged solely for greed and gold and not in the interest of suffering humanity" (126). The *Omaha (Neb.) Progress* extended the *Ax*'s sentiment: "Every soldier in the Philippines who uses the term 'nigger' does so with hell-born contempt for the negro of the United States, and it is our one desire that he be cured of his fiendish malady by a Filipino bullet" (128). The *Helena (Ark.) Reporter* on 7 February 1900 castigated black soldiers in the war:

> Every colored soldier who leaves the United States and goes out to the Philippine Islands to fight the brave men there who are struggling and dying for their liberty is simply fighting to curse the country with color-phobia, jim-crow cars, disenfranchisement, and lynchers and everything that prejudice can do to blight the manhood of the darker races, and as the Filipinos belong to the darker human variety, [it is] the Negro fighting against himself. Any Negro soldier that will cross the ocean to help subjugate the Filipinos is a fool or a villain.... May every one of them get ball-stung is our sincere prayer. (167)

Not just the black press but Filipinos themselves compared the racist treatment of African Americans in the United States with that of Filipinos in the Islands. A letter by a black soldier, William Simms, that appeared in the *Indianapolis Freeman* of 11 May 1900 quoted a Filipino child's question: "Why does the American Negro come from America to fight us when we are much friend to him, and me all the same as you. Why don't you fight those people in America that burn Negroes, that made a beast of you, that took the child from its mother's side and sold it?" (169). Simms expressed surprise at the boy's candor and knowledge of race issues in the United States.

A placard in Spanish nailed to a tree near a U.S. military camp implored black soldiers to protest the lynchings in the South earlier that year by refusing to fight in the war. Several hundred copies of the placard were addressed specifically to the colored regiment of the Twenty-fourth Infantry. The *Richmond Planet* published a translation of the placard on 11 November 1899:

> To the colored American soldier. It is without honor that you are spilling your costly blood. Your masters have thrown you in the most iniquitous fight with double purposes, in order to make you the instrument of their ambition; and also your hard work will make soon the extinction of your race. Your friends, the Filipinos, give you this good warning. You must consider your situation and your history, and remember that the blood of your brothers, Sam Hose and Gray [lynched in the United States earlier that year], proclaims vengeance.[30]

This psychological warfare was successful in some cases and even led to desertions by African American soldiers to Aguinaldo's army. The most famous of these, David Fagan of the Twenty-fourth Infantry, became a general in the Filipino revolutionary army and fought for two years before the U.S. Army captured and beheaded him.[31]

The anxiety of soldiers who read the placard is reflected in a letter by Michael H. Robinson of the Twenty-fifth Infantry published in installments in the *Colored American* on 17 and 24 March 1900:

> I will say that we of the 25th Infantry feel rather discouraged over the fact that the sacrifice of life and health has to be made for a cause so unpopular among our people. Yet the fact that we are American soldiers instills within us the feeling and resolve to perform our duty, no matter what the consequence may be as to public sentiment. . . . We have been warned several times by insurgent leaders in the shape of placards, some being placed on trees, others left mysteriously in houses we have occupied, saying to the colored soldier that while he is contending on the field of battle against a people who are struggling for recognition and freedom, your people in America are being lynched and disenfranchised by the same people who are trying to compel us to believe that their government will deal justly and fairly by us.[32]

The *Wisconsin Weekly Advocate* on 17 May 1900 published a black soldier's unsigned letter that recounts the mistreatment of Filipinos by white soldiers, who

> cursed them as damned niggers, steal [from] and ravish them, rob them on the street of their small change, take from the fruit vendors whatever suited their fancy, and kick the poor unfortunate if he complained, desecrate their church property, and after fighting began, looted everything in sight, burning, robbing graves. . . . But I have

seen carcasses lying bare in the boiling sun, the result of raids on receptacles for the dead in search of diamonds.... On upbraiding some fellows one morning,... the reply was: "Do you think we could stay over here and fight these damn niggers without making it pay all it's worth? The government only pays us $13 per month: that's starvation wages. White men can't stand it." Meaning they could not live on such small pay.... They talked with impunity of "niggers" to our soldiers, never once thinking that they were talking to home "niggers" and should they be brought to remember that at home this is the same vile epithet they hurl at us.... I want to say right here that if it were not for the sake of the 10,000,000 black people in the United States, God alone knows on which side of the subject I would be.[33]

The author implies here that perhaps only the potential repercussions of his desertion—the possibility of even more lynchings if black soldiers were to leave their posts en masse—keep him from joining the Filipino rebels.

What these editorials and letters outline is a history buried in the larger narrative of U.S. expansionism and imperialism. This moment of U.S. empire is also the origin of an African American anti-imperialist paradigm that recognized the connections among violence against Native Americans, African Americans, and colonized peoples such as Filipinos. As a shared burden, U.S. imperial expansion meant an increase of racial violence against emancipated blacks and a brutal war of colonization against Filipinos who had barely ended their war with Spain.

THE LANGUAGE OF EMPIRE AND DUBOIS

The year 1898 was the originary moment of the circulation of racialized ideas constructing the discourses of "empire" and the "Filipino." Visions of a U.S. empire appeared early in the political life of the nation with pronouncements like those of geographer Jedidiah Morse on a U.S. empire "that will comprehend millions of souls" west of the Mississippi.[34] With the interconnected discourses on race, gender, and power in the late nineteenth century, the ideology of empire took root and materialized as both a policy and an aesthetic. By 1893, Frederick Jackson Turner's thesis on the necessity and the natural order of expansion had taken on such force that many later politicians and writers echoed his ideas on U.S. expansion as innate to the American nature. Turner's violent "vision and ideology" was softened around the edges by notions of "tradition," "nature," and the "natural" order of things.[35] Simultaneously, discourses appeared on the savagery and inferiority of the "darker races" such as Filipinos, who were subjects of the new empire. The "natural" order of things required the subjugation of lesser races through laws, policies, or lynching.

In the early twentieth century, this new language of empire was disseminated and propagated by not only Anglo-American politicians but also popular literature. In *Tarzan of the Apes* (1914), Edgar Rice Burroughs's main character embodies white masculinity as a result of both his Anglo-Saxon heritage (his British parents) and his jungle boyhood, during which he was raised by apes. Tarzan is an icon of white male hegemony and empire. As Gail Bederman has shown, he also represents white supremacy, as he is "a one-man lynch mob, a proud murderer of African men," introducing himself to his love interest, Jane, as "TARZAN, THE KILLER OF BEASTS AND MANY BLACK MEN." Burroughs wrote this description in upper-case block letters and consistently celebrated Tarzan's racial violence as an essential component of his masculinity. According to Bederman, for Burroughs, "the impulse to kill black men" was also "a racially superior man's inherent masculine instinct."[36]

While authors like Burroughs romanticized the discourses of empire and white supremacy, others chose to challenge and expose their violence. W.E.B. DuBois's multigenre 1920 text, *Darkwater*, for example, is an American literary work that incorporated an African American anti-imperialist perspective with incisive analysis of a history of racism shared by colonized peoples in Asia and black Americans. While *Darkwater* has been described as "a less successful sequel" to DuBois's popular and critically acclaimed autobiography, *The Souls of Black Folk*, it is an important text because of its anticolonial perspective and experimental form.[37]

In *Darkwater*, DuBois locates the colonial world as central to history (29), anticipating the writing of subaltern scholars decades later. Indeed, the text is an early example of a modernist, anti-imperialist aesthetic. Critic John Carlos Rowe observes that DuBois was one of the first U.S. intellectuals to critique "Euro-American imperialism's reliance on hierarchies of race, gender, and class" in *The Souls of Black Folk* and *Darkwater*.[38] *Darkwater* is an autobiography informed by two twentieth-century African American political formations, liberalism and Pan-Africanist Marxism.[39] As a multigenre narrative of "many strands," the text exemplifies DuBois's "anti-colonial thinking."[40]

What I highlight here is DuBois's notion of a world color line that "binds together not simply the children of Africa, but extends through yellow Asia and into the South Sea," a vague concept of a shared "nationhood" of people of color united by the "common disaster" of being nonwhite and by "one long memory" of racism—which raises issues of racial essentialism and nationalism.[41] However, what I find illuminating is *Darkwater*'s unapologetic attack on imperialism, racism, and capitalism; I read the book as the experimental autobiography of an anti-imperialist intellectual. For DuBois—as for Anna Julia Cooper, whom DuBois quotes in the book, and black journalists at the turn of the twentieth century—lynching and empire were bitter fruits of the same tree.

In *Darkwater*, DuBois describes whiteness as "the ownership of the earth forever and ever, Amen!" He views imperialism as "this new religion of whiteness" and as "conquest sugared with religion; mutilation and rape masquerading as culture" (498, 501). Elsewhere, he discusses the way "white culture" disseminates the notion that " 'darkies' are born beasts of burden for white folk" and members of the "darker world" (503). Predating Edward Said's notion of a modern or "American Orientalism" by sixty years, DuBois outlines the theoretical concerns of a discourse in support of U.S. empire: "The supporting arguments grow and twist themselves in the mouths of merchant, scientist, soldier, traveler, writer, and missionary: Darker peoples are dark in mind as well as in body; of dark, uncertain, and imperfect descent; . . . they are fools, illogical idiots,—'half-devil and half-child' " (504). The allusion to Kipling's "White Man's Burden," an ode to the civilizing mission of the United States, recalls the image of the Filipino as "half devil and half child." Natives or "darkies," then, were the "idiots" in need of U.S. civilization. In imperial discourse, race is a significant marker in establishing superiority and degeneracy. DuBois argues that "everything great, good, efficient, fair and honorable" is associated with whiteness, while "everything mean, bad, blundering, cheating and dishonorable is 'yellow'; a bad taste is 'brown'; and the devil is 'black.'" Further, in the United States, "changes on this theme are continually rung in picture and story, in newspaper heading and moving-picture, in sermon and school book" (505).

In DuBois's text, Filipinos are, like black Americans, Mexicans, Asian immigrants, and other nonwhite peoples, the "savage half-men," the "dogs of men" (505). DuBois links racism in the United States with imperial expansion in an alternative history of that nation:

> For two or more centuries America has marched proudly in the van of human hatred,—making bonfires of human flesh and laughing at them hideously, and making the insulting of millions more than a matter of dislike,—rather a great religion. . . . Instead of standing as a great example of the success of democracy and the possibility of human brotherhood America has taken her place as an awful example of its pitfalls and failures, so far as black and brown and yellow peoples are concerned. . . . Absolutely without excuse she established a caste system, rushed into preparation for war, and conquered tropical colonies. (508)

In this radical history, racial hatred, violence, and colonial expansion replace democracy. Filipinos share this history with other subjugated peoples, and so the U.S. context of the term "Filipino" emerges from the matrix of discourses on "U.S. empire" and race from the late nineteenth century. The language of empire was a celebration not merely of whiteness and power but of the violence of power on bodies that were liminal subjects of the U.S. Empire.

4   "Just Ten Years Removed from a Bolo and a Breech-cloth"

The Sexualization of the Filipino "Menace"

CONTEMPLATING POWER, Andrea Dworkin asserts that it is "men [who] have the power of naming, a great and sublime power. This power of naming enables men to define experience, to articulate boundaries and values, to designate to each thing its realm and qualities, to determine what can and cannot be expressed, to control perception itself."[1] Here, I employ Dworkin's insight to aid my own contemplation of power and naming, located at the specific point(s) of U.S. imperial contact with the Philippines, to identify the wielder of the "power to control perception itself" as a subject much more specific and more historical than the biological male. Thus appropriately complicating our notions of patriarchy and power, we can address Yen Le Espiritu's important critique about the "failure of feminist scholarship to theorize the historically specific experiences of men of color."[2] In this essay, I attempt to do this by examining the experience of the *manongs* in California during the early twentieth century—specifically, the naming of their maleness, their sex, their bodies, and their work by European/American discourse.[3] Through examining how the Filipino "first wave" experienced the intersection of race, class, gender, and sex within the domains—labor, laws, and love—that Espiritu discusses in her own work on Asian Americans, we can productively elaborate feminist critiques of masculinity and nation building, and the violence that these formations produce for immigrant communities of men and women alike.

Affirming Lisa Lowe's observation that "race [is] not a fixed singular essence, but the locus in which economic, gender, sex, and race contradictions converge," I discuss moments of this (often violent) convergence in the experiences and representations of the manongs in the United States during the early twentieth century.[4] I choose specific sites of this convergence—as they have been identified in previous historical accounts—and reexamine them for the "origin" of what Avery Gordon terms the "ghostly matter" of modernity.[5] This matter, which takes and maintains form in racialized popular and legal discourse, in narratives of citizenship and nation, and within the cultural memory and production of "others-within," is, I argue, what haunts much "post"-modern theory, rendering it incapable of processing power/knowledge as a white male supremacist "truth" that seems to have been before everything. My attempt to theorize the historically specific experiences of the manongs, then, is an attempt to illumine the sites of intersection of economics, race, and gender that are the structural "joints" of the modern *and* postmodern nation-state. I am interested in how the imperial nation has historically constructed these joints via the labor and bodily material of oppressed racialized groups, and how these constructions have in turn produced "structures of feeling."[6]

According to Honorante Mariano, images of U.S. democracy and freedom, and the belief that annexation had made these things a reality for Filipinos, beckoned the manongs of the early twentieth century "to see for [themselves] the conditions, to visit the places and to work and sojourn among the people and in the land that claimed [their] allegiance and loyalty."[7] In his own personal narrative, Carlos Bulosan wrote about similar imaginings of the United States, remembering one of the many myths transmitted by a U.S. colonial education that fed young Filipinos' dreams:

> *A poor boy became a president of the United States!* Deep down in me something was touched, was springing out, demanding to be born, to be given a name. I was fascinated by the story of this boy who was born in a log cabin and became a president of the United States.... That evening I troubled Miss Strandon with questions. "Will you tell me what happened to Abraham Lincoln, ma'am?" I asked.
>
> "Well, when he became president he said that all men are created equal," Miss Strandon said. "But some men, vicious men, who had Negro slaves, did not like what he said. So a terrible war was fought between the states of the United States, and the slaves were freed and the nation was preserved. But one night he was murdered by an assassin."
>
> "Abraham Lincoln died for a black person?" I asked.
>
> "Yes," she said. "He was a great man."[8]

Such legends were only part of the colonial project to condition Filipino servitude to capitalist European America and white supremacist ideology. Writing about colonial educational policy in the Philippines, Schirmer and Shalom discuss how "the introduction of the American system was a subtle means of defeating a triumphant nationalism.... The ideal colonial was the carbon copy of his conqueror, the conformist follower of the new dispensation."[9] In the Philippines, then, before the manongs set foot in their new "mother" country, the imperialist project was establishing the "true condition for hegemony," which, as Raymond Williams writes, is "effective *self-identification* with the hegemonic forms: a specific and internalized 'socialization.'"[10] After the islands and their people had thus been "renationalized" via European/American imperial institutions, white economic interests welcomed the opportunity to exploit the illusion of freedom that carried Filipinos to the States. The manongs that constituted the first wave of Filipino immigration and the third wave of Asian immigration—after the Chinese and Japanese—began their adventure in the early twentieth century, and by 1930, more than forty-five thousand of them were living the American reality.[11] They came seeking greater economic opportunity but found themselves employed almost exclusively as domestic and agricultural servants, with some working in canneries. Without the resources of traditional Filipino familial institutions (Filipinos of this first immigrant cohort outnumbered Filipinas fourteen to one), the young manongs were all the more vulnerable to feelings of cultural and social dislocation. Making up 94 percent of the Filipino immigrant population by 1930, most of these single young men (84 percent were in their teens to midtwenties) lived and worked in California.[12]

Sixty percent of Filipinos worked as farm laborers to "fill the need for labor created by the exclusion of the Chinese, Japanese, Koreans, and Asian Indians," and as Ronald Takaki's research documents, western American farm owners confirmed that their nation had gained a superior "stoop labor" class by switching to new "Orientals":[13]

> Special physical fitness is often given as the reason for the Filipino's success in lettuce picking. Their ability to work on wet ground is given as a reason for preferring Filipinos in the Delta Region of the San Joaquin Valley. Being small and agile, they are considered more handy and better able to bear the strain of long continued stoop work than most other groups.[14]

> White men can't do the work as well as these short men who can get down on their hands and knees, or work all day long stooping over.[15]

The Filipino's body was thus racially mutated into an economic instrument, and his presence was welcomed until the Depression compelled the members of white America's working class to perceive it as a threat to their livelihood. During this time of economic hardship, when Filipinos had also become increasingly active in organizing their own labor movements, the racialization of the manongs in popular and political discourse demonstrated Lisa Lowe's assessment of "race" as unfixed, and of "the administration of citizenship [as] simultaneously a 'technology' of racialization and gendering" and, I would add, sexualizing.[16] The manongs that came as wards of the United States—"nationals" under the U.S. flag—had arrived already racially sculpted into an economic asset, but during the 1920s they had slowly "degenerated" along with the national economy into an economic menace because of the threat they posed to white labor. The Depression thus provided a context in which the perception of the Filipino as a subhuman stoop laborer could purposefully transgress its own boundaries to assume the form of a threat to the "purity" of the United States. And the power of racial popular and political discourse "to control perception itself" began documenting this threat with hypersexual, hypermasculine imagery. This imagery, born of the manongs' exercise of the "productive ambivalence" of stereotypes in their own interests, was eventually appropriated by white male nativism and sexualized insecurities as ammunition for anti-immigration and exclusion initiatives.[17]

The fact that the manongs' lives were marked by the absence of Filipinas, and of the familial and cultural institutions that these women represented for many of them, meant that some would acclimate to their new environment, in part, by developing relationships with women outside their national community. They spent much of their free time gambling, and much of the remainder of it in the company of other Filipinos and women (mostly white and of the "lower" class) at taxi dance halls. Although these halls would become a site of frequent racial violence, they were celebrated by the manongs as places to "perform" their bodies into communities of brotherhood and cultural resistance. Linda Espana-Maram writes about the significance of these acts of resistance (both to the manongs and to white male youths and political leaders):

> The counterimage of Filipino workers created by the Filipinos themselves unsettled the dominant culture's assumptions about the brown "hordes." In sporting quality, fashionable attire like McIntosh suits, Filipinos disrupted the stereotypes of asexual laborers in the dirty, tattered overalls of the agricultural fields and the seemingly docile attendant in the uniforms issued by the service-oriented industries. In effect, Filipino laborers appropriated the icons of white middle-class American masculinity, including the ability to dress stylishly, dance well, and exhibit manners appreciated by white women.[18]

Exploiting the economic tension that the Depression brought, white male U.S. leaders read this appropriation for what it might say about their own sexual incompetence, and thus their future (in)ability to reproduce the nation in their own racial image. In popular and political discourse, then, the manongs began to fully assume the form of an American nativist-sculpted sexual beast, equipped with a penis impressive enough to penetrate all of white America, leaving a permanent stain of racial and social inferiority on its people (read: men). Ronald Takaki documents some illustrations of the hypersexual imagery of the Filipinos that spurred and sanctioned anti-Filipino violence and discrimination in the name of driving Filipinos back to the Philippines. He quotes San Francisco Municipal Court judge Sylvain Lazarus's description of the "sexual prowess of Filipino men":

> It is a dreadful thing when these Filipinos, scarcely more than savages, come to San Francisco, work for practically nothing, and obtain the society of these [white] girls.... Some of these [Filipino] boys, with perfect candor, have told me bluntly and boastfully that they practice the art of love with more perfection than white boys, and occasionally one of the [white] girls has supplied me with information to the same effect. In fact some of the disclosures in this regard are perfectly startling in nature.[19]

Takaki also documents a California businessman "put[ting] it more bluntly": "the Filipinos are hot little rabbits, and many of these white women like them for this reason."[20] This convergence of racial discourse between the "everyday" business sphere and the political sphere marked the common ground on which U.S. citizens met to expel Filipinos from the United States. As I discuss later, it also marked the intersectionality of class and gender that allowed these white males to dismiss white women's interest in Filipinos as a "moron" attribute of the lower classes.

Exploiting the economic tension that the Depression brought and the prevalent stereotype of the hypersexual Filipino, California state leaders whipped up a hysteria intended to serve the goal of excluding the "moral and sanitary threat" and "menace to white labor" posed by the manongs' presence. On 10 January 1930, a Pajaro newspaper ran an article detailing a set of resolutions passed by the Northern Monterey Chamber of Commerce and endorsed by Judge D. W. Rohrback, who declared that "the move of the Monterey Chamber of Commerce was but the beginning of an investigation of a situation that will eventually lead to the exclusion of the Filipinos or the deterioration of the white race in the state of California."[21] Judge Rohrback, who had previously described Filipinos as "little brown men about ten years removed from a bolo and a breech-cloth," thus stood strongly by the Chamber of Commerce resolutions' statement that

> we do not advocate violence but we do feel that the United States should give the Filipinos their liberty and send those unwelcome inhabitants from our shores that the white people who have inherited this country for themselves and their offspring might live.... Other Chambers of Commerce have probably passed resolutions endorsing the use of Filipino labor as being indispensable. If that is true, better that the fields of the Salinas Valley should grow weed patches and our wonderful forests be blackened.[22]

Whether or not they explicitly advocated violence, the resolutions lent a state-structured forum to the "Watsonville Riots" that began just nine days after the *Evening Pajaronian* article. They were reminiscent of the Exeter Riot of October 1929, which began with a group of white men harassing Filipinos in the company of white women at a local carnival and ended with the burning of a nearby Filipino labor camp to avenge the stabbing of one of the white rioters. The anti-Filipino violence in Watsonville began on 19 January 1930 and continued until the early morning of the twenty-third, which saw one Filipino, Fermin Tober, dead. He had been shot when "four hundred vigilantes attacked the Northern Monterey Filipino Club."[23] The rioting had commenced with an attack on the Palm Beach taxi dance hall by "decent white boys" who were protesting the Filipinos' fraternization with "their" white women, and the "penetration" of their nation by another race.[24]

By April 1930, California's male leaders had extended this sort of protest beyond state borders, introducing to the House Committee on Immigration and Naturalization a bill to restrict/exclude Filipino immigration "because cheap labor tended to destroy American ideals and racial unity."[25]

The congressional debates surrounding the bill introduced by Representative Richard J. Welch reveal the workings of a national ambivalence in the name of white labor and white supremacy. Thus, I treat the discourse of these debates as data for an analysis of how, in 1930, white male political leaders adopted popular racial images as objective support for their efforts to exclude Filipinos. While I draw from Teun van Dijk's formulations on *Elite Discourse and Racism,* my reading of these debates as a site of a popular-political discursive conversion in the name of white male hegemony contests the top-down view of racist discursive formations which holds that "in ethnic affairs, it is primarily the administration and politicians who define the ethnic situation and set the terms and boundaries of public debate and opinion formation."[26] Instead, I find Raymond Williams's reading of Gramsci's concept of hegemony more useful for understanding white male leaders' discursive (eventually official, legal) reworking of national and racial boundaries to maintain domination. This concept is especially applicable here because the Filipino exclusion movement itself was an example of hegemony, of the relationship between the "whole social process" and "specific distributions of power and influence" that (re)constructed the American nation.[27]

In the hearings on Filipino exclusion on 10 April 1930, one member of Congress asked Welch: "Have you given consideration to the fact that the Philippines are under the jurisdiction of the United States of America?" pointing out the obvious contradiction of excluding people from a country that is "under the American flag." (This problem, which was actually a question of granting independence to the Philippines, was answered in 1934 with the passage of the Tydings-McDuffie Act, which established the Philippines as a commonwealth and provided for independence in ten years. Under this act, Filipinos were reclassified as aliens.) Welch avoided the question, arguing that the social and economic ills that Filipinos' immigration had caused were more than enough to merit their exclusion, whatever their "official" classification. He cited what "other nations do in similar conditions," which was and is, of course, to exclude the "unwanted." He and others throughout the debate referred to a U.S. national "precedent" of excluding Asians—the Chinese and Japanese in 1882 and 1924, respectively—in an attempt to convince the committee that Filipino exclusion was in national, historical order. Most interesting for the analysis at hand, however, was the insertion of popular racist discourse concerning the "sex problem" posed by the Filipino into this official debate.[28]

In his statement supporting the exclusion bill, Representative Valentine S. McClatchy quoted an "expert" on this "most serious phase of the question," Dr. David P. Barrows, "director of our educational system in the Philippines, for four years president of the University of California," and "a friend of the Filipino":

> Their vices are almost entirely based on sexual passion. This passion in the Malay—which includes practically all types of Filipinos—is inordinately strong; and in accordance with native customs it is rarely directed into the right channels or restrained by custom or by individual will. The irregularity of his conduct, and the special problem in American life which his presence aggravates is, in my opinion, entirely based on

this phase of his character. . . . The evidence is very clear that having no wholesome society of his own, he is drawn into [the] lowest and least fortunate associations. He usually frequents the poorer quarters of our towns, and spends the residue of his savings in brothels and dance-halls, which in spite of our laws, exist to minister to his lower nature. Everything in our rapid, pleasure-seeking life and the more or less shameless exhibitionism which accompanies it, contribute to overwhelm these young men who, in most cases, are only a few years removed from the even, placid life of a primitive native barrio.[29]

McClatchy went on to point out that the "Filipino does not bring his females with him," and that "the declared preference of the Filipino for white women and the willingness on the part of some white females to yield to that presence" represented "one of the phases which is at the bottom of the racial trouble in the State of California." He cited the Watsonville riots as evidence of an "inflamed public," then yielded the floor to Representative Free, who told the story of a sixteen-year-old white girl who had been found by the California police at a hotel with her thirteen-year-old sister, both of whom had apparently been in bed with the Filipino who "came to the door in his underwear." The police ascertained that "the Filipino had lived there with them for several days." Using such examples of the Filipinos' horrific sexuality, McClatchy warned that "unless this Filipino immigration is restricted in some way there will be very serious riots in consequence."[30]

Not only did McClatchy warn against the "natural" violence that would continue to arise as a result of Filipinos' rampant sexuality, but also he talked about the frightening future that lay in store for the nation if extensive Filipino-white miscegenation was allowed to occur. This, according to his and others' statements, was already happening, due in great part to the "exclusive dance clubs [taxi dance halls] maintained for Filipinos" where "they hire white girls who live in the club and whom they call entertainers." These white women were, themselves, dangerous accomplices to the ruin of the American seed stock, as they were of the "lower classes." One year after the initial exclusion hearings before the House, the president of the Immigration Study Commission, C. M. Goethe, wrote that "the Filipino tends to interbreed with near-moron white girls. The resulting hybrid is almost invariably undesirable. The ever increasing brood of children of Filipino coolie fathers and low-grade white mothers may in time constitute a serious social burden."[31]

Thus, in the name of "protecting the nation . . . against the peaceful penetration of another colored race," white political leaders engineered what would otherwise be a threat to their masculinity—a more competent Filipino penis, affirmed by white women's preference for it—into a stereotype of white women "morons" who committed a crime against the nation by transgressing the sacred racial boundary. In figuring "their" women thus, they demonstrated that they regarded white and *male* as the only pure ingredients of the U.S. nation. They subsumed (rationalized) the crossing of racist-erected borders by white women within the class-gender border that delineated the U.S. male's own from his disowned, and they therefore remained sexually secure, potent, and empowered to continue the Filipino exclusion process.

Its racist tools having operated effectively to sculpt the first wave of Filipinos according to a white male nativist aesthetic, the U.S. colonial project granted a strategic "independence" (exclusion) to the Philippines and its people in 1934 with the passage of the Tydings-McDuffie Act. The act established the Philippines as a commonwealth and provided for independence in ten years. Filipinos, now residents of an independent country rather than of a U.S. territory, would no longer have the privilege of unrestricted entry into the United States. Instead, immigration from the islands would be restricted to an annual quota of fifty a year, and repatriation campaigns, with both "exclusionist and humanitarian motives," would become part of national policy. In 1933, the chair of the House Committee on Immigration and Naturalization introduced a joint resolution for the repatriation of unemployed Filipinos; its purpose was "to relieve cities, towns, and communities of the United States of the financial and other burdens incident to the care of unemployed and indigent natives of the Philippine Islands who are here and who have fallen into their distressing condition since their arrival in the United States. This object is selfish in behalf of our communities and humanitarian in behalf of these unfortunate Filipinos."[32] It wasn't until 1935 that provisions were actually made for repatriation, and even then, only 2,190 Filipinos were actually sent back to the islands. As late as 1939, Representative Welch—who had introduced the original exclusion bill to the House in April 1930—was asking for an extension of the repatriation law, which was granted.[33]

The United States had waited to simultaneously bestow independence and "alien status" on Filipinos until "they were no longer needed because of the availability of Mexican labor and no longer wanted because of their labor militancy."[34] Having exhausted their usefulness to the service of U.S. capital, those who had come to constitute their own Filipino community within the United States were no longer instrumental in the domestic sphere of European/American imperialism. In fact, the white male erector of boundaries had marked his territory so clearly that Filipinos had come to know, perhaps too well, their place *and* their battleground in the U.S. nation. Besides forming the FLU (Filipino Labor Union), which led successful strikes in California, the manongs expressed their communal consciousness in the organization of "social self-preservation clubs." Royal F. Morales provides an illustration of the Filipino American national identity that the racism of white U.S. institutions helped to create: "The struggle of the Filipino old timers included the formation of 'hard gangs' and social self-preservation clubs. In the Los Angeles area, protective groups developed, such as those coming from towns like Candon, Cavite, and Morong, which served as social escape and sublimation and, at the same time, as self-preservation.[35]

In the name of survival, the manongs embraced what Benedict Anderson might term their own "imagined community," as well as those identity categories that many cultural theorists regard as "fantasy," or reject, or disclaim.[36] Beginning with the U.S. annexation of the Philippine islands, the Filipino experience with/in their country had demonstrated too well the very real, very harmful effects of the U.S. national "imagination." Some seventy or so years before Benedict Anderson would inform us that "nationalism thinks in terms of historical destinies, while racism dreams of eternal contamination, loathsome copulations: outside history," the manongs would bear witness with/upon their bodies of racism's intimate bond with nationalism, *throughout* history. Their experiences proved that—contrary to Anderson's understanding of racism as ahistorical—indeed, "niggers are [not], thanks to the invisible tar-brush, forever niggers" and that Jews, the seed of Abraham, [are not] forever Jews, no matter what passports they carry or what languages they speak and write."[37] Filipinos, while "forever" Filipinos because of always existing just "ten years removed from a bolo and a breech-cloth" were not always the *same* Filipinos. At first they were short, docile, low-to-the-ground, ideal farm laborers, better than the other "Orientals." Then, with history, they became something else. With change in the national economic conditions, change and development of their own communities, change in their practices of resistance, they became "hot little rabbits," hypersexual, slick-mannered, out to get white women and stain America's future brown. Filipinos were not forever Filipinos, but they were forever not white, and—whatever their language or official nation—forever "foreign." No amount of "imagining" could erase the violent markings of nativist borders that U.S. male leaders erased, then redrew at will, repeatedly.

Thus, the liberatory nature of the knowledge of stereotype as fetish[38]—as an illegitimate construction of an illegitimate need for and claim to control—must be complicated in its application to the experience of Filipinos in the United States in the early twentieth century, and to that of all racialized immigrant communities. As Honi Fern Haber asserts, structures of oppression are not designed to circumscribe or exploit individual subjects as such, but rather, "subjects-in-community." Resistance to this oppression, therefore, cannot occur amidst an unreflexive universalization of difference. As Haber puts it:

> The problem with the law of difference as I have stated it is that taken to the extreme (treated as a universal principle), as it is in some present formulations of a politics of difference, it has the unintended consequence of excluding the possibility of oppositional politics. The politics of difference must be reconceptualized to accommodate the fact that if any and all closures are terroristic, then the Other will never be given a chance to form itself as a political force. It will remain unpresented and unpresentable. And since, in fact, political systems (power regimes) which exclude or marginalize otherness do exist, then insofar as the law of difference can be used to keep the Other from articulating itself as a coherent, *even if contingent* identity,

the law of difference serves the dominant and dominating order. It becomes a tool of colonization and keeps the Other defenseless.[39]

The Filipino immigrant experience in the United States illustrates that the "split" produced by racialized differentiation is more easily moved than eradicated, and that this movement is too often instigated by a nation-state whose "legitimate" subjects have no investment in disclaiming their experience of privilege, but who will welcome the oppressed's disclaiming of their own experiences of oppression. As Haber suggests, the adoption of the idea of "universal difference" can be much more dangerous to certain subjects-in-community than to others.

In "Situated Knowledges," Donna Harraway offers an alternative to the idea that "transcendence" of certain national and cultural borders in the postmodern era must be accompanied by a theoretical transcendence of "identity," or difference between "subjects-in-community." With regard to feminist projects, she writes that

> feminists don't need a doctrine of objectivity that promises transcendence, a story that loses track of its mediations just where someone might be held responsible for something, and unlimited instrumental power. We don't want a theory of innocent powers to represent the world, where language and bodies both fall into the bliss of organic symbiosis. We also don't want to theorize the world, much less act within it, in terms of Global Systems, but we do need an earth-wide network of connections, including the ability partially to translate knowledges among very different—and—power-differentiated—communities. We need the power of modern critical theories of how meanings and bodies get made, not in order to deny meaning and bodies, but in order to live in meanings and bodies that have a chance for a future.[40]

This chance—as the manongs recognized in their formation of labor unions and "hard gangs"—is comprised of the sort of "situated knowledge" and experience that derives from having lived, and continuing to live, "in meanings and bodies" that have been shaped inside structures of dominance. The "structure of feeling" that the struggles of the Filipino first wave bequeathed to racialized immigrant communities is one built within, and responsive to, the "hurts of history," one that modernity carries into a would-be afterlife, today. "Would-be" because these hurts still haunt, and because they must for us aggrieved communities to see and feel what forces there are that make and transcend boundaries, that will not be laid to rest by virtue of their own imaginedness, or merely by our imagination. Avery Gordon reminds us that "truth is a subtle shifting entity not simply because philosophy says so or because evidentiary rules of validation are always inadequate, but because the very nature of the things whose truth is sought possess these qualities."[41] And the history of the manongs in the "imagined," "subtle shifting" entity of the modern nation reminds us that this nation—and the intersectionality of race-class-gender-sex that reinforces it—always possessed the qualities of its (now postmodern) ghost.

II.

Public Policy, Law, and the Construction of Filipinos

5   Losing Little Manila

Race and Redevelopment in Filipina/o Stockton, California

AMONG ILOKANA IMMIGRANT Carmen Saldevar's happiest memories are those of her years as a pool-hall operator in Stockton, California's densely populated Little Manila district, which occupied four downtown blocks. The former schoolteacher arrived in Stockton in 1952. "I was so happy!" she recalls. "The people walking around were all Filipinos! When I look at the street from the shop, my goodness, it looks like the Philippines!" All the businesses on El Dorado Street were owned by Filipinas/os, she remembers. "All the buildings there, Filipinos! Downstairs, Filipinos! Upstairs, the Filipinos, living there, who were working the farms, all the way down to Lafayette. All you could see is Filipinos. Walking there. Standing there. Talking there."[1]

Fernando Saldevar, a barber, had traveled to the Philippines in 1949 to find a wife. He was smitten by Carmen, then a thirty-year-old schoolteacher working near her home province in La Union, Ilocos Norte. Under pressure from her parents, Carmen agreed to marry him. Although the couple moved briefly to San Bernardino, where Fernando ran a barbershop, the family scrimped and saved until their return to Stockton with their son, Fernando, Jr. In the early 1960s they bought a barbershop on Center Street in the West End, which they later relocated to El Dorado Street in Little Manila, where they also bought a pool hall.

The postwar years in Little Manila were prosperous and happy as well, Carmen Saldevar said, for her Lolo (grandfather) Ambo Mabalon, owner and cook since 1931 at the humble Lafayette Lunch Counter, a popular diner and bustling center of Little Manila street life, especially for Filipinas/os with roots in the Visayas. The extension of citizenship privileges to Filipinas/os and the relaxation of immigration laws in 1965 allowed Ambo to reunite his transnational family after more than four decades of separation, and the postwar boom had been so good for business that he could buy a three-bedroom home in South Stockton to house its members.

The Little Manila district (bordered by Market, California, Sonora, and Center streets, with El Dorado and Lafayette streets at its center) had been home to the largest community of Filipinas/os outside the Philippines before World War II, and after the war the district bustled with activity as new immigrant families established themselves in downtown apartments and Southside subdivisions. As the city's Filipina/o population continued to mushroom, other *manongs* reunited their families, all beckoned to El Dorado Street by the stories of the close-knit community there.[2]

But the cacophony of falling bricks and the growl of the federal bulldozer would soon disturb the happy atmosphere and bustling street life of the Little Manila neighborhood. After the war, Stockton politicians, developers, business-people, and planners used federal urban redevelopment subsidies to transform downtown's turn-of-the-century landscape and clear its ethnic and working-class neighborhoods. In this essay, I argue that in the rush to remake Stockton's inner city, local officials targeted Filipinas/os (and other racial and ethnic groups, as well as poor whites) for removal from downtown. I document how the city's Filipinas/os weathered redevelopment and displacement, and I explore the community's ongoing struggles over space, power, policy, resources, history, and memory.

In Search of El Dorado (Street): Little Manila, 1920s–1962

In 1972, as the dust cleared from continuous demolitions, only two blocks of Little Manila remained, its manongs scattered throughout the city. On one of those blocks, my Lolo Ambo struggled to keep the Lafayette Lunch Counter open for business. In 1929, more than four decades before the demolitions began, Ambo had arrived in Seattle, along with six cousins, all from the tiny village of Numancia, Aklan province, on the island of Panay. They worked all over the West Coast, sweating in the Alaskan canneries and stooping in the asparagus fields of the California San Joaquin Valley. He and his cousins eventually settled in Stockton, lured by the rapidly multiplying Filipina/o community and job opportunities in that city. He saved his earnings, and in 1931, along with two townmates, he bought the Lafayette Lunch Counter from Ilokana immigrant Margarita Balucas, a local businesswoman who also owned a pool hall. Lolo's business was brisk, as the Lafayette Lunch Counter was located in downtown Stockton near the intersection of Lafayette and El Dorado streets in the heart of Little Manila.

Six to ten thousand Filipinos lived in the neighborhood during its heyday in the decades before and after World War II. Thousands flocked to Stockton annually, some almost immediately upon landing in San Francisco, Seattle, or Los Angeles. Though many traversed the West Coast and Midwest following the crops, many more stayed in Stockton because the area provided work year-round, with pruning in the wintertime, asparagus in the spring, and tomatoes and grapes in the summer and fall.

From 1924 to 1975, city directory records show more than sixty Filipina/o restaurants, auto repair shops, grocery stores, hotels, beauty parlors, newspapers, union offices, community groups, and churches in the six-block area. Among the businesses and institutions were the Lafayette Lunch Counter, Billones

Photography, Juanitas Grocery, Aklan Hotel, Quezon Hotel, Candelario's Restaurant, P. D. Lazaro Tailoring, Hollywood Bath House Shoe Shine Stand and Barber Shop, Philippine Barber Shop, Three Star Pool Hall, Rizal Social Club (a dance hall), Lighthouse Mission (a Protestant mission which served Filipinas/os), and the offices of Dr. Macario Bautista, Stockton's only Filipino American doctor. The numerous though short-lived Filipino American publications based in Stockton in the pre–World War II era included the *Three Stars,* the *Philippine Journal,* the *Philippine-American Observer,* and the *Philippine Yearbook.*

The war left Little Manila's residential and street life largely unchanged. After getting a haircut at one of many barbershops, Filipinas/os might have an inexpensive plate of steaming rice and *adobo* at the Lafayette Lunch Counter, bet on games of pool with friends at the Bataan Pool Hall or Stockton Pool Hall, and then retire to their inexpensive rooms at the Quezon, Bataan, Mariposa, or Lincoln Hotel, or back to their homes in South Stockton. Even those who lived far from downtown or in nearby California cities returned to Little Manila periodically. Veterans and their war brides, as well as new immigrants, who settled in nearby neighborhoods and cities continued to visit the neighborhood to socialize, eat in the Filipina/o and Chinese restaurants, shop for Filipino groceries, or gamble in the Iloilo Circle cardroom, one of many still operating there. Little Manila street life, especially on El Dorado Street, was a welcome relief from the monotony and loneliness of a hotel room or the *campo,* especially in the broiling summers and freezing winters of the Central Valley.

The Saldevars' New Deal Barbershop was one of four owned by Filipinos on El Dorado Street between Washington and Lafayette in the 1960s, and their Stockton Pool Hall was one of several Filipina/o-owned billiard parlors still remaining in the neighborhood by the early 1970s. Carmen Saldevar remembers that her husband's barbershop often hummed with activity until past midnight several nights a week.[3] In the early 1960s, the barbershops, along with the Filipino-owned or -managed pool halls, restaurants, hotels, cardrooms, and grocery stores, served Little Manila's population of elderly manongs, as well as the larger Filipina/o community.

RACE, CLASS, SUBURBANIZATION, AND INNER CITY "BLIGHT"

A number of factors contributed to the postwar rush to redevelop and clear urban America's inner cities, its poorest areas, and its ethnic neighborhoods, including racist and elitist attitudes about the conditions of the urban poor and minorities, ideas about the eradication and prevention of slums and blight, the movement of the white middle class from urban areas to all-white suburbs, and the pressure to squeeze more property-tax dollars out of poor neighborhoods. A pattern emerging in urban centers across the nation in the decades after World War II transformed the city of Stockton: white flight to the suburban subdivisions, the emergence of suburban shopping malls, and massive freeway construction.[4]

The massive movement from urban areas to suburban areas began with a dramatic rise in automobile ownership in the 1920s. The automobile made living far from the city center a more feasible alternative. Nationwide, new homes were built at a rate of more than 800,000 per year.[5] New Deal legislation made home owning cheaper than renting for most middle-class white Americans and systematized the development of all-white suburbs. The privately owned single-family detached home became both American ideal and national policy, to the detriment of residential hotels and dense, mixed-use districts like Little Manila.[6] By 1972, 63 percent of Americans owned their own homes.[7]

In Stockton, "housing complexes sprung up north of the river like mushrooms in the fertile soil" after World War II.[8] A typical deed for a new suburban home contained restrictive covenant provisions prohibiting its sale to blacks and other minorities. These covenants were key to maintaining property values and de facto segregation in Stockton. In fact, the FHA recommended and endorsed such covenants to protect property values.[9] Because FHA lending practices and restrictive covenants barred most newly naturalized Filipinas/os, Chinese, Japanese, Mexican, and black Stockton residents from owning homes in the exclusive north-side housing developments, they bought modest homes or rented apartments in working-class neighborhoods in south and east Stockton or in downtown neighborhoods like Little Manila. Most residents of downtown and the south and east sides were poor people of color; many lived at or below the poverty line, untouched by the prosperity north of the Calaveras River.[10]

Stockton's white middle class and elite abandoned the city's core for new homes in the sprawling north-side subdivisions. City power elites lavished investment and attention on the north side and ignored development and social problems in other neighborhoods, particularly those in the city's south and east sides. In downtown Stockton, more than a dozen city blocks west of the central business district (including Little Manila) were dubbed "Skid Row" by middle-class whites; its residents preferred "West End." Urban historian Paul Groth notes that Americans began using "Skid Row" as a pejorative term in the 1950s for what are more accurately termed "single laborers' zones."[11]

As the suburbs grew, the inner cities, starved of resources, slowly deteriorated.[12] City planners and business leaders argued that if the gritty West End, with its working-class bars, taverns, residential hotels, and ethnic neighborhoods, could be cleared of blight and rebuilt, the city could remake its downtown into a more attractive and economically viable district. The Housing Act of 1949, which provided federal money for public housing and slum clearance, gave elites in Stockton and in cities across the nation the funds and federal go-ahead to clear its downtowns.

The act was the result of a strange conflation of public housing proponents and business interests intent on downtown slum clearance. The legislation, which targeted areas suffering from "physical blight" and "urban blight," authorized more than $1 billion in loans and grants to cities for acquiring blighted land and for redevelopment. Experts defined any area in economic decline as blighted.[13] Though the act purported to be the federal government's remedy for slums, the legislation was backed by influential realtors, bankers, builders, and business groups, all of whom lobbied relentlessly for its passage. In essence, the act authorized federal funding for slum clearance and public housing. Cities nationwide participated wholeheartedly in the program; more than seven hundred cities launched fourteen hundred redevelopment projects from 1949 to 1967.[14]

Policy makers behind the public housing and slum-clearance movements believed slum clearance would improve conditions for the poor, but the federal government did not build enough housing to replace what slum clearance destroyed. Thousands of poor people were displaced. The belief that all mixed-use, mixed-race, working-class neighborhoods were blighted—potential slums—contributed to the misguided clearance of dozens of ethnic neighborhoods nationwide. Downtown sections targeted for clearance included single laborers' zones (such as Stockton's West End), those where ethnic minorities lived, and aging areas. The practice of clearing often vibrant ethnic and working-class communities became so commonplace and so shocking that a chorus of opposition developed against the programs by the early 1960s; but by then, most U.S. cities either already had cleared their downtowns or had begun demolition.[15]

The promise of federal money to clear the city's core galvanized Stockton's power elite of white middle- and upper-class city planners, politicians, businesspeople, and developers, all of whom pushed for downtown redevelopment. In 1952, the Stockton City Planning Commission prepared a report for the City Council advocating the use of federal funds for redevelopment. Pointing to aboriginal Australians and Africans who burned their villages to the ground periodically in order to start clean, the 1952 report advocated a redevelopment plan in downtown Stockton that would clear out the city's "infested" areas, specifically the central business district and the West End.[16]

"Slum clearance and redevelopment has merit from many points of view: citizenship, health, appearance, tax, or property values," wrote Stockton's city planners. "It is better to clear out slums than to continue paying the ever mounting costs both financial and otherwise."[17] Stockton thus followed the pattern of other cities across the nation, which relied on physical restructuring of central cities and working-class neighborhoods to alleviate blight instead of attempting to address its social roots.[18] Police were aggressive and abusive toward the residents of the West End. For example, in the early to mid-1950s, Stockton police arrested unemployed men living in the West End who refused to work as field laborers, prompting the Northern California Chapter of the American Civil Liberties Union to file a complaint with the city in 1955.[19]

One consequence of the planning commission's report was Stockton mayor Dean de Carli's Urban Blight Committee, which saw the West End's working-class and ethnic neighborhoods as eyesores. These blocks of hotels, bars, and small businesses were "a cancer-like growth" that needed to be swept clean. The committee concluded that law enforcement and the justice system had not reduced vagrancy, crime, and drunkenness in the West End. The only answer, the city manager declared in 1955, was clearance.[20]

But where planners and other power elites saw a slum, residents saw a bustling, diverse, working-class community. The area was home to mostly poor and working-class people struggling to survive. Black, white, Latina/o, and Filipina/o seasonal workers who were the engines of the area's agricultural economy had congregated in the West End since the turn of the century. Contractors seeking laborers for farmwork traditionally recruited in the West End's pool halls, bars, restaurants, park, and recreation halls. In the West End's Chinatown and Little Manila neighborhoods, workers and families ate in the cheap Chinese, Filipino, and American restaurants. After a day at work, men relaxed in the bars, cardrooms, diners, and pool halls. Workers and families lived in the hotels, men and women played pool in the Filipino- and Chinese-owned billiard halls, and families and community organizations danced and relaxed in the area's numerous recreation centers. Working-class families from all backgrounds held picnics, religious festivals, and parades in Washington Park, also home to the area's thriving farmers' market. The West End was full of residential hotels and beautiful historic buildings, many of them constructed of locally made red brick, which had earned the city the moniker "the Brick City."[21]

Meanwhile, within the first decade of federal urban redevelopment programs, critics assailed their net effect on U.S. cities. "Blight" had been defined broadly, and, as in Stockton, targets in cities like San Francisco, New York, Boston, Detroit, and Philadelphia were most often black, Latino, and Asian working-class neighborhoods; some anti-redevelopment voices called the program "Negro removal."[22] Critics charged that the programs displaced the poor (especially poor black and Latino families), forced small businesses to close their doors, contributed to unemployment, tore down ethnic and working-class neighborhoods, and left downtown cores empty of street life, community cohesion, and vitality.[23] Nevertheless, most cities pressed on with urban redevelopment into the 1970s.

Among them was Stockton. The result of the elites' push for their view of progress, approved by the City Council in 1955, was the West End Redevelopment Project.[24] In 1956, the council created the Redevelopment Agency and authorized it to carry out urban redevelopment projects in the city.[25] The agency identified three blighted areas in south and east Stockton and targeted nine blocks for clearance. If a building was condemned, the agency could force the land's owners to sell and the building could be demolished. In the summer of 1962, the Redevelopment Agency filed condemnation suits against property owners in the West End who were unwilling to sell.[26]

Demolition began in early February 1964. As buildings fell like dominoes, the area looked like a "war zone," or "a bombed out World War II section of London."[27] At the end, only three buildings remained—the old Nippon Hospital, built in the 1920s to serve Japanese Americans, and two historic warehouses that belonged to the Sperry Flour Mill and the Eureka Grain and Farmer's Union.[28]

THE VICTIMS OF URBAN RENEWAL

Stockton earmarked few funds for relocating businesses, families, and residents, a pattern that emerged in redevelopment districts nationwide: relocation assistance constituted only 0.5 percent of the $2.2 billion federal budget for redevelopment.[29] In April 1964, the Redevelopment Agency's relocation administrator reported that forty-four businesses, fifty-nine single residents, and nine families had relocated. Some residents moved into hotels in other parts of downtown and on the last remaining blocks of Chinatown and Little Manila south of Washington Street, which only exacerbated blight and overcrowding among the poor there. Officials who had believed that most West End residents were vagrants, transients, and seasonal workers learned that many hotel residents had lived at the same address for six to nine years, and most had nowhere else to go.[30] City officials believed they were acting sensitively and in the best interests of both powerful local farmers and the city's laborers by planning the demolitions during the winter, when most of the migratory farm laborers would be away. When the laborers returned in the spring and summer to work the crops, they found they had nowhere downtown to live.

While bankers and real estate developers could measure the success of West End renewal through their financial statements, displaced residents felt grief, sorrow, and loss. (In a study of working-class Italian Americans displaced in Boston's West End, researchers noted that the residents felt extreme hopelessness, anger, and psychological distress.)[31]

The demolitions of the West End Redevelopment Project, which were ongoing from 1964 to 1966, displaced and dispersed much of the Filipina/o community in and near Little Manila. Especially hard hit were the Saldevars. When they received notice of the impending demolition in the mid-1960s, Fernando Saldevar was forced to relocate his barbershop. Carmen Saldevar speculates that the city cleared the area because too many minorities lived and conducted business there, and because it was too noisy. "They said they have to build up the Skid Row place," she remembers. "That's what they say, because the nine-block area is composed of different businesses of the colored, Japanese, Chinese, Filipinos, and Mexicans. . . . The sidewalks are filled up with people."[32]

Preferring to stay downtown among the shop's steady clientele, Fernando and Carmen walked south of the West End in search of a suitable shop. When they found one on El Dorado Street, they were elated. By relocating to Little Manila, they would be in the heart of the city's Filipina/o community. When the Stockton Pool Hall, a Visayan-owned billiard parlor across the street from the barbershop, went up for sale, the Saldevars bought it. Carmen managed the pool hall, and Fernando ran the barbershop.

The Ilokanas/os began to flock to the Stockton Pool Hall, once it was Ilokana rather than Visayan owned. "Everybody I see is Ilokano!" Carmen Saldevar remembers. "And they're happy because we're with our own people." So crowded was it, "you could hardly walk in front of the pool hall. You could hardly get in. Inside, you could hardly walk." Filipinas/os greeted each other with, "Are you Ilokano?" Ilokanos from the town of Abra met Ilokanos from the province of La Union. Their shared heritage and language bound the Saldevars to their clients, and the elderly Ilokano manongs began asking Carmen to act as their translator and representative at trials, the Social Security and Veterans Administration offices, and their visits to Dr. Nicanor Bernardino, the Filipino doctor whose downtown office served the Filipina/o American community. Carmen was happy to oblige.[33]

As the pool hall and barbershop flourished in the late 1960s and early 1970s, Filipinas/os clung tenaciously to the intersection of Lafayette and El Dorado streets and the four blocks of Little Manila that the West End's wrecking ball had spared. Many of the elderly manongs were retiring from farmwork, preferring to spend their last years in the comfort of their hotel rooms, surrounded by familiar faces and businesses, and live on their meager Social Security checks. Some residents had heard rumblings about the impending construction of a freeway nearby, but few knew anything concrete.

Freeway to Nowhere: The Fight over the Crosstown, 1961–1975

From the 1910s through the 1980s, freeway construction went hand-in-hand with the transformation of America's cities and the mushrooming of its suburbs.[34] Soon after the passage of the National Interstate and Defense Highways Act of 1956, the California Highway Commission presented a plan for Interstate 5, which would run from Canada to Mexico via Washington, Oregon, and California and bisect Stockton's west side.[35] Included in the commission plans was a Crosstown Freeway through Stockton's downtown to connect the new I-5 and the state's old north-south mainstay, Highway 99, which bisected the city's east side.

Freeways, most scholars and city planners now concur, accelerated suburbanization and sprawl. In addition, freeway construction destroyed neighborhoods by uprooting and displacing communities, particularly the neighborhoods of poor people of color.[36] As urban historians Andres Duany, Elizabeth Plater-Zyberk, and Jeff Speck note in *Suburban Nation,* the devastation wreaked upon poor neighborhoods by new inner-city highways was so extreme that "a nefarious social intention" could not be ruled out.[37] By the 1960s, massive freeway construction throughout California spurred increased decentralization and the attendant deterioration of the state's downtowns and inner cities. Highway officials, politicians, businesspeople, and urban planners who supported the construction of the Crosstown Freeway through downtown Stockton envisioned the city as the center of a transportation hub linking northern, central, and southern California. Highway planners and engineers claimed the freeway would not divide the city of Stockton but instead revitalize the city. The Crosstown would cut directly through two of the four remaining blocks of Little Manila.

Initially divided over the plan, city leaders eventually became convinced that the freeway would bring more people into downtown and add to the revitalization of the already cleared West End, directly to the north of the planned Crosstown. Expectations were high for the freeway, a $20.7 million project.

THE FIGHT OVER THE FREEWAY

The State Division of Highways proposal for the Crosstown Freeway named three possible routes; of these, engineers identified the Washington-Lafayette corridor as the best in terms of highway user savings and service to through and local traffic. This corridor cut through the struggling remains of Little Manila and Chinatown, and through five other mostly minority neighborhoods, where many families subsisted on less than $3,000 per year, more than a thousand dollars below the identified poverty line in California in 1970.[38] The route would eliminate 461 homes, 126 businesses, six churches, the seventy-year-old Washington Park in front of the venerable St. Mary's Church, a school, and eighty acres of farmland.[39]

The State Division of Highways sponsored a public hearing on the proposed freeway routes on Thursday, 1 June 1961 at the cavernous Civic Auditorium. The proposed freeway plan drew howls of protest from downtown residents. None of the proposed routes garnered any major support, but the route that aroused the most ire was the Washington-Lafayette corridor that bisected downtown, against which more than 175 residents of Little Manila, Chinatown, and the other five affected neighborhoods came to the public hearing to protest.

Although Little Manila lay directly in the path of the freeway, even the largest and most powerful Filipina/o American organizations, such as the Filipino Community of Stockton, Inc., and the Legionarios del Trabajo, failed to muster any kind of organized opposition, leaving business owners and residents of Little Manila without representation at the hearing. But several community members attended and voiced their opposition, and other sectors of the downtown community were vocal in their critique of the proposed freeway.

Opponents came from all sectors of the downtown community—ministers, landowners, businesspeople, community leaders, attorneys, and residents—and included Charles M. Weber, grandson of the city's founder, Charles Weber, who owned Washington Park; members of a Japanese American Buddhist church; and several attorneys representing the Japanese American and Chinese American communities, whose neighborhoods would be destroyed by the freeway. Only two supporters of the Washington-Lafayette corridor attended the public hearing: George Hench of the Greater Stockton Chamber of Commerce, and John Jacobs of the Stockton Redevelopment Agency. For more than four hours, state highway officials and residents battled.

Residents bemoaned the destruction of their community institutions and homes, while business owners felt that the freeway would kill an already deteriorating downtown. Freeway planners seemed motivated by racial prejudice, according to freeway opponents and residents of Little Manila, Chinatown, and Stockton's south and east side neighborhoods, who were mostly black and ethnic Mexican. Residents were suspicious of the freeway's planned location, which would rip through the mostly poor, black, Asian and Mexican American sections of Stockton and displace mostly poor and minority residents. "'Why there?' we asked. Why not through the Mormon Slough, just a few blocks away?" recalled Angelina Bantillo Magdael, who spoke against the Washington-Lafayette corridor at the hearing.[40] Opponents were troubled by the possibility of the freeway becoming a "Chinese Wall" that would divide the city into two camps. Growth would be hindered, too many people would be displaced and affected, and the freeway would be an "eyesore," dissenters claimed.[41] The freeway would also obliterate one of the city's busiest parks, the Weber family–owned Washington Park, which many Filipina/o, Chinese, Japanese, Mexican, and black residents used for leisure, informal gatherings, religious festivals, and picnics.

Despite the vocal opposition, the city's Planning Commission, the Greater Stockton Chamber of Commerce, and the Stockton Merchants Association all favored the Washington-Lafayette route. By December, six months after the public hearing, so did a majority of the pro-redevelopment City Council.[42] When the State Division of Highways chose the Washington-Lafayette Street corridor and the City Council approved the route by a 6–2 vote on 27 December 1971, area residents were incensed but resigned.[43]

MAKING WAY FOR THE CROSSTOWN

In July 1965, the State Division of Highways had created a program that provided between $50 and $200 compensation for families affected by highway construction.[44] Residents of the south and east Stockton neighborhoods that the planned freeway would affect pushed city leaders to begin considering its impact.

Demolitions in preparation for freeway construction began in the winter of 1968. In February, bulldozers demolished the White Hotel, a four-story brick residential hotel at Lafayette and Center streets in Little Manila, although newspaper accounts provide no information on where residents were relocated.[45] In 1970, Division of Highways assistant district engineer Lawrence M. Bjornstad told the *Stockton Record* that the state was attempting to insure that all displaced by the freeway would be relocated "with a minimum of inconvenience and discomfort."[46] Business owners could apply for relocation grants of up to $5,000, and tenants could get up to $1,500 to find replacement housing. This money had been set aside by the state legislature in response to complaints that the state cared little for the people it displaced in favor of freeways. There is little evidence that the Relocation Office assisted a significant number of Filipinas/os in finding replacement housing. According to oral interviews and newspaper accounts, most moved in with friends or relatives.

As the demolition wound down, state highway engineers told the *Stockton Record* in June 1971 that the freeway would enhance redevelopment efforts, reduce blighted buildings, and cause "little or no hardship" for the hundreds it displaced.[47] They were wrong. Most residential hotels in the West End had been razed, and few replacement houses under $50,000 existed in the city. In the spring of 1972, the Highways Division reported that 430 residents and eighty-one businesses had been removed from seven blocks, and the state paid out $605,619 in relocation money.[48] Yet while the state could promise replacement housing and business relocation, it could not replace the community that the Filipinas/os and Chinese populations lost as a result of the Crosstown Freeway.

"EVERYBODY WAS SORRY TO LOSE EL DORADO"

Because almost ten years elapsed from the first public hearings to the first demolitions, few Filipinas/os had a sense of impending doom before they were evicted and the buildings razed. As former colonials accustomed to a long tradition of racial discrimination at the hands of Stockton officials, they probably felt powerless to stop the demolitions. By the early 1970s, Little Manila's days were numbered, and the personal stories of loss and grief that accompanied the demolitions reflect the blow that urban redevelopment and freeway construction dealt to the Little Manila community.

In the early 1970s, Carmen and Fernando Saldevar received notification from the Division of Highways that the freeway would obliterate their businesses, less than five years after they lost their first Stockton barbershop to West End redevelopment. The Saldevar family businesses, the New Deal Barbershop and the Stockton Pool Hall at Little Manila's El Dorado and Lafayette streets, would have to relocate yet again. While searching for a new location, Carmen kept her always busy pool hall open.

One day in 1971, she returned from an errand with a manong to find a puzzled crowd standing in front of the pool hall. Inside, two of her pool tables were missing, taken by a man from the State Highways Division. Carmen first went to the City Council and asked for an extension of her use permit for the pool hall and said she has having trouble finding a new location; the council assured her that they would grant her a new use permit for a new location if there was no opposition from her new neighbors. She went immediately to an attorney who was working with the soon-to-be-displaced business owners, who told her to go to the Highways Division and demand her tables back.

Carmen, barely five feet tall, walked into the Highways Division office and asked to speak to the man who took her pool tables. In his office, "I said, 'I am the owner of the Stockton Pool Hall. I am surprised why you took my pool tables.' He said, 'You have to close the business.' I said, 'Close the business, why? How could I take out the pool tables without a place to put them?' And then he didn't speak up. I said, 'Sir, I need the pool table. Bring it back. I am looking for a place to move my pool tables. Please, bring it back.'"[49] The state highway official was unmoved, and Carmen finally went home.

When she attempted to relocate downtown near Little Manila on Market Street, an Italian American business owner opposed her new use permit, objecting to a Filipino pool hall nearby. The City Council rejected her permit application and suggested that she move her pool hall outside town. "I said to the council, 'Outside town? My customers live inside town! And it's hard for them, and they live in those hotels around the area where I like to be,'" she remembers. She continued to run her pool hall, and dozens of Ilokano old-timers and recent immigrants still flocked to her pool tables. Eventually she found a new location at the Lee Center at El Dorado and Washington streets, a Chinese-themed, low-income residential and commercial building erected by a local attorney on one of the blocks cleared for the West End redevelopment. Its Chinese architectural theme suggested that it was a consolation to the Chinese American community for the recent destruction of Chinatown. After Carmen Saldevar found the new location, the Division of Highways returned her pool tables. Hers was one of the last Filipina/o pool halls in Little Manila, and when it closed in the 1970s after a short stint in the Lee Center, it signaled the end of an era.

Because Stockton's elites were concentrated in neighborhoods north of Main Street, the impact of the Crosstown Freeway on the poor and minority communities of downtown and the south and east sides went largely unnoticed until construction of the thoroughfare was imminent. In May 1971, the *Stockton Record* ran a series of stories on the impact of the freeway on those displaced. Reporter Marjorie Flaherty found that some business owners in Chinatown and Little Manila jumped at the chance to find new locations, while others bemoaned the loss of the Asian American communities that had been rooted in the Washington-Lafayette corridor since the nineteenth century.[50] Several businesses opted for relocation in the area, and the state offered relocation assistance. If businesses could show that relocation would incur a loss, state relocation assistance payments could reach $5,000. The state also offered a going-out-of-business payment. Several businesses took the money, since they could find no suitable place to move.

The *Stockton Record* found that the retired Filipino farmworkers forced to leave their hotel rooms had lived in them for ten to thirty years. Flaherty interviewed two manongs lucky enough to find affordable replacement housing in the downtown area. Santiago Manzig told Flaherty that he was happy with the studio apartment he found in the Lee Center. Magdaleno S. Ybono found a flat in downtown, which he shared with other manongs. Ybono said that he was happy to be near his favorite restaurants, cardrooms, and the bus station.[51]

Without an outlet to express their indignation and outrage at their displacement, Filipinas/os kept relatively quiet during the demolitions. Carmen Saldevar recalls wistfully: "We were so sad, I did not even go and see it. I remember how bad it is, to lose a business. And it's not only the money I'm after—I was helping the Filipinos there with their problems." The close-knit Filipina/o community on El Dorado Street disappeared. "They were scattered," Saldevar says of the old manongs of Little Manila. "No more. They even cried." No longer would she see her elderly Ilokano customers, old-timers who loved to speak the dialect with her and stuff dollar bills into her young son's hands. When she encountered some of the last manongs who remained in the area after redevelopment, "the more I am mad," she says. "I can't sleep. I better go away. I would say [to them], 'I'm sorry. We used to be together here, now we are separated.'"[52]

A year after the state promised to build housing for each family affected by the freeway, inflation hit state and federal budgets and funds for freeway construction began to dry up. A once-flush Division of Highways found its budget slashed; more than $100 million in freeway funds were diverted to other state and federal programs.[53] The July 1972 completion date for the freeway stretch through Little Manila and was pushed back to 1974 when city officials learned that Congress had failed to enact a federal highway bill, though the state would continue to acquire property, evict residents, raze buildings, and clear the area through the early 1970s.

By April 1972, all buildings save one had been cleared.[54] The first stretch of the Crosstown Freeway was finally dedicated in 1976, and it took almost twenty more years to complete. The freeway did not link Interstate 5 and old Highway 99 until 1993.

Though highway engineers had promised that the freeway would be an attractive addition to downtown, the intimidating structure became, and continues to be, a physical barrier between two vastly different Stocktons, separating downtown and the city's affluent, white north side from the poorer, working-class south side, predominantly black, Latina/o, and Asian. One city official referred to the Crosstown as the "Great Wall of Downtown."[55] Hulking, noisy, and gray, it caused businesses and homes to the south to decay further and is detested by many southside residents. It cut off the two remaining blocks of Little Manila from the rest of downtown, psychologically as well as visually.

FILIPINAS/OS AND THE FREEWAY

Little Manila as the Filipina/o community knew it was doomed by 1968, when demolitions began with the White Hotel on Lafayette Street. Only two struggling blocks of Little Manila south of Lafayette Street remained after the construction of the Crosstown Freeway—a few key businesses, such as the Lafayette Lunch Counter, several barbershops and grocery stores, and several hotels.

Decades after the freeway was built, the demolitions continue to haunt Carmen Saldevar.

> I don't know why they moved the freeway close to town.... Imagine those hotels that were demolished. They were still good, good hotels.... Everybody was sorry to lose El Dorado. It's beautiful before. They should not have destroyed that. The state highway should have went farther from the town, but they don't like to destroy houses. How about the hotels, that makes the town more beautiful, and more decent? [Politicians] are not after the community. We should have not elected them. That's how they separated the Filipinos. Some are mad to the Filipinos maybe, how come they do that? They don't remember, they don't think, what the Filipinos have done for California? What made California prosperous? The export products. And who made the export products? The Filipinos, working in the farm. My god. I feel sorry.[56]

Why Filipinas/os brought no organized opposition to the freeway spoke to the factionalism endemic to the community in the postwar years. The large Filipina/o organizations spoke only for their paying members, and after the battles between Filipino laborers and farmers from the 1930s through World War II, and struggles over citizenship, the fraternal orders seemed reluctant to involve themselves in local politics. Mutual aid and hometown organizations proliferated after World War II, but few had more than fifty members; their immediate goals included financial support for those left behind in the Philippines and social networks among new immigrants and established residents. They wielded little political power in Stockton. A Filipino American Chamber of Commerce had yet to be established, and Filipina/o business owners were not organized. Since many Filipinas/os leased rather than owned their businesses in Little Manila, some may have felt that their opinion mattered little. The Filipino Community of Stockton and Vicinity, Inc., a powerful umbrella organization, had tenuous alliances with local politicians that prevented them from taking controversial stances, so they never formally opposed urban redevelopment or the freeway. Most Filipinas/os saw the freeway as a losing battle, for even the most powerful members of Stockton's white elite, even the Weber family, could not stop it.

However, there was a glimmer of hope as the dust cleared from almost a decade of continuous demolitions in the West End. In 1967, two Filipino immigrants, Ted Lapuz and Jose Bernardo, conducted a survey of the housing needs of Filipinas/os there for the Roman Catholic Archdiocese of Stockton. They were appalled at the living conditions in the SRO hotels of Little Manila and Chinatown and were further moved by the massive displacements caused by the demolitions. Relative newcomers to the Filipina/o American community in Stockton, they had a radical new vision for Filipinas/os downtown. Lapuz and Bernardo proposed to buy a newly razed block in the West End from the Redevelopment Agency and build a Filipino Center, the first of its kind in the nation. The center would feature low-income housing, social services, and retail space for displaced businesses. To many Filipinas/os who had grown up in and lived in Little Manila, a Filipino-owned building had been an elusive dream. By 1972, it had become reality. Groundbreaking ceremonies for the Filipino Center on Main Street in downtown were held on 23 July 1971, and the center opened in August 1972.

The Filipino Center became the new focal point of the city's Filipina/o community. The last two blocks of Little Manila gradually decayed as the manongs died and businesses closed, as the Lafayette Lunch Counter did in 1983. A new generation of Filipina/o Americans—I count myself part of this group—was born and raised in Stockton mostly unaware of the vibrant urban landscape that had been home to the most populous Filipina/o community in the nation. Along with the buildings, urban redevelopment and highway construction had wiped clean the historical memory of thousands of Filipinas/os in Stockton and obscured the history of Filipinas/os there. Nonetheless, Little Manila remained a special place in the memories and stories of old-timers and second- and third-generation Filipinas/os born before the 1960s.

When the city of Stockton targeted another block of Little Manila for clearance and redevelopment in 1999, the evictions of some of the last remaining elderly manongs recalled the demolitions of the 1960s and 1970s. Some were evicted from the Fox and Delta hotels. The Gateway Project, as the Redevelopment Agency has dubbed it, replaced the residential hotels, restaurants, and grocery stores that had served the community's low-income residents with a fast-food restaurant and gas station.

Little Manila: History, Memory, and Place

In my earliest memory of Stockton's Little Manila, it is 1977, and I am a precocious five-year-old, scrambling onto a stool to order hotcakes from my indulgent Lolo Ambo at the Lafayette Lunch Counter. Four decades earlier, writer Carlos Bulosan had sat at the same counter, ordered hotcakes, and sifted through his mail at the community mailbox on the counter, usually an old shoebox. Bulosan usually ate free at the Lafayette Lunch Counter because my softhearted Lolo couldn't bear to see Filipinos starve.

In my most painful memory of Stockton's Little Manila, it is May 1999, and I am standing in front of a padlocked, abandoned Lafayette Lunch Counter, shielding my eyes from the sun, squinting to watch the demolition-kickoff festivities for the Gateway Project. Clearing the block that once housed my grandfather's restaurant took more than two months. The prewar brick buildings that had housed generations of tired brown bodies went fairly quickly. The backhoes plucked bricks deftly, and the bulldozers pushed in walls efficiently and ruthlessly. After the dust cleared, almost three-quarters of the block lay in rubble. Now, the downtown exit of the Crosstown Freeway deposits motorists in a landscape that few living in 1930s Little Manila would recognize. On the right sits a mission-style McDonald's and Union 76 gas station and convenience mart. On the left hulks the freeway. Save for the newly installed brown-and-gold corner signs that read "Little Manila Historic Site," few motorists would know that the area was once home to the largest Filipina/o community outside the Philippines.

Little Manila today is a single block of decaying prewar buildings. The Mariposa Hotel, the long-vacant Rizal Social Club at 138 West Lafayette Street, and the Emerald Chinese Restaurant draw more dust than crowds. Few non-Asian Stockton residents know of the area's rich history, and few Filipinas/os younger than I guess that the intersection, long regarded as the city's eyesore, was anything more than a block of tired buildings, drunks, drug dealers, and the homeless.

In less than two months, more than six decades of history were razed. Urban "renewal," in its push for the skyscraper, chain store, and economically lucrative development, cares little for people, history, memory, and community. Old buildings are one generation's home and another's blight, and cheap immigrant labor can always be replaced. We often lament that while other communities have ethnic enclaves, Filipinos lack any physical place on the cultural landscape to claim as ours, as Chinese do a Chinatown or Italian Americans a Little Italy. But before urban redevelopment decimated Little Manila, we had such a haven. Thousands of Filipina/o Americans nationwide can trace their origins to the Little Manila district in Stockton. Understanding the forces and events which destroyed that enclave can encourage us to influence future policies regarding urban redevelopment and historic preservation in our historic Asian American and Filipina/o American communities nationwide.

POSTSCRIPT

In 2000, the Stockton Chapter of the Filipino American National Historical Society lobbied the Stockton City Council for historic site status for the Little Manila area. The Stockton City Council voted unanimously to designate the area as the Little Manila Historic Site, the first city-designated Filipina/o American historic site. In 2002, the newly created Little Manila Foundation dedicated the site in a ceremony that drew almost a thousand Filipinas/os back to Lafayette and El Dorado streets. We placed historic site markers and banners around the site and began a public campaign to preserve the remaining buildings of Little Manila. In 2003, the Board of Trustees of the Filipino American National Historical Society unanimously agreed to locate its planned Filipino American National Museum in the Little Manila Historic Site.

In 2003, a redevelopment proposal to demolish the last of Little Manila and displace most of its Latina/o, Chinese, and Filipina/o residents was brought to the City of Stockton by Bay Area developers. The Little Manila Foundation has engaged in an ongoing campaign to fight displacement of Little Manila's residents and preserve the last historic buildings. In May 2003, the National Trust for Historic Preservation named the remaining buildings on the Little Manila Historic Site to its annual list of the nation's eleven most endangered historic places. That fall, the foundation submitted a competing proposal that would prevent displacement, revitalize the neighborhood, protect its historic resources, and develop affordable housing in the area. As of July 2005, the City of Stockton had yet to make a decision on the fate of what remains of the historic Little Manila neighborhood.

ANGELO N. ANCHETA

6 Filipino Americans, Foreigner Discrimination, and the Lines of Racial Sovereignty

IN 1903, SCHOLAR AND civil rights activist W.E.B. DuBois in *The Souls of Black Folk* declared prophetically that "the problem of the Twentieth Century is the problem of the color-line."[1] History has demonstrated DuBois's prescience, and at the start of a new century, race and color continue to be major sources of demarcation in U.S. society. Indeed, racial justice often proves as elusive today as it was in the early twentieth century.

Yet, to speak of a color line—a single boundary dividing whites and nonwhites—belies the true complexity of U.S. race relations. An inquiry into historical and contemporary discrimination against Filipino Americans demonstrates that there have been several color lines, dividing not only by race but also by national origin, language, culture, and citizenship. Anti-Filipino discrimination has created hierarchical divisions between the more powerful and less powerful, subordinating Filipino Americans, like African Americans and other minorities, to reinforce notions of racial superiority and inferiority. But anti-Filipino discrimination has also created divisions along a different set of axes, separating citizen from noncitizen, American from foreigner. Along these lines, anti-Filipino discrimination underscores notions of racial sovereignty and operates to exclude Filipino Americans from full membership in the national community.

This essay explores the various color lines that have defined discrimination against Filipino Americans. In particular, I analyze the problem of "foreigner discrimination," which encompasses forms of discrimination that have assigned to Filipinos the role of foreigners in U.S. society. As defined here, foreigner discrimination encompasses laws that have restricted the immigration and citizenship of Filipinos; anti-immigrant policies that have allocated employment and government benefits on the basis of U.S. citizenship; public and private limits on the use of Filipino languages in deference to the use of English; and individual discrimination that has subordinated Filipino Americans based on language, accent, and noncitizenship. All these manifestations of foreigner discrimination reflect a norm of racial exclusion rather than inclusion and reinforce an American national identity that does not fully incorporate the breadth and depth of Filipino American experiences.

ANTI-FILIPINO DISCRIMINATION AND FOREIGNER RACIALIZATION

A color line between whites and nonwhites can explain much of the historical discrimination against Filipinos in the United States. Racial segregation in its many forms—housing, employment, education, public accommodations, the political process—was imposed with full force against Filipinos throughout much of the twentieth century. Racial violence was a common occurrence, and the "no Filipinos allowed" banner was often seen in California and other states with large Filipino populations, enjoying the full sanction of government. As the U.S. Supreme Court noted in 1948 in *Shelley v. Kraemer,* the landmark case that invalidated racially restrictive housing covenants, Filipinos, like blacks, were among those targeted for exclusion from the ownership or occupancy of real property.[2] And even in those instances when Filipinos were not initially included in a racial prohibition—such as antimiscegenation laws prohibiting intermarriage with whites—they were quickly added.[3]

Moreover, overt discrimination against Filipino Americans as a class of non-whites has not been simply the product of a bygone age of Jim Crow segregation, long since abandoned. In litigation during the 1980s, for instance, Filipino Americans were among the plaintiffs who challenged employment and housing segregation in the Alaskan cannery industry and provided extensive evidence of blatant racial discrimination: nonwhite workers were relegated to the lowest-paying jobs, ate in separate dining facilities, and were housed in segregated quarters. Filipino Americans in particular were assigned to the "Filipino mess" and the "Flip bunkhouse" in one cannery. Indeed, as U.S. Supreme Court Justice John Paul Stevens noted in his 1989 dissenting opinion in *Wards Cove Packing Company v. Atonio,* the cannery working conditions bore "an unsettling resemblance to aspects of a plantation economy."[4]

Nevertheless, a binary model of racial discrimination that divides whites from nonwhites provides an incomplete analysis of the discrimination that Filipino Americans have encountered since the early twentieth century. A black-white model of discrimination is often invoked to explain in broad strokes the experiences of all racial and ethnic minorities in the United States; legal remedies for discrimination are in turn predicated on a black-white model that focuses on subordination based on racial difference. But a black-white model of discrimination cannot readily explain the specific history of discrimination against Filipinos in the laws of immigration and naturalized citizenship, the public and private restrictions on the use of Filipino languages, or the unequal treatment of Filipino immigrants as noncitizens. In particular, a black-white model fails to account for the discrimination against Filipino Americans who are perceived as foreigners and who, despite their length of presence in the United States, continue to fall outside accepted definitions of "American."

Why is anti-Filipino discrimination distinct from antiblack racism? Theories of racialization propose that race is not fixed biologically but is instead a dynamic category that can take on various social and political meanings.[5] Racial meanings involving Filipino Americans can thus diverge from racial meanings involving blacks. For blacks, racial difference typically implies racial inferiority, a subordinate status relative to whites based on color. But for Filipinos, as well as for Asian Americans, Latinos, and Arab Americans, racial difference can also carry separate and distinct meanings: racial difference implies that members of these groups are treated as foreign-born outsiders.[6] Through racialization, the assignment of foreigner status can transcend actual immigration or citizenship status, and all members of a racialized group can be ascribed the attributes of foreigners.

For example, popular discourse often attributes to Asian Americans the role of foreign "competitor" or "conspirator," as demonstrated by the recent racial profiling of Chinese American scientists such as Wen Ho Lee, who were presumed to be disloyal and risks to national security. A similar form of racialization occurred during the campaign finance scandals of the late 1990s, when Asian American donors were demonized as foreign operatives, but with little evidence of any connection to foreign money. In the case of Japanese Americans during World War II, race assumed the specific meaning "enemy alien," leading to the evacuation and internment of all Japanese Americans living on the West Coast, most of whom were U.S. citizens. The racialization of Latinos as unwelcome immigrants has encompassed a wide set of meanings, ranging from "cheap laborer" to "illegal alien." The immigrant designation persists even though large numbers of Latinos have resided in the United States for generations. And, as demonstrated by the extensive discrimination following the destructive acts of terrorism of 11 September 2001, Arab Americans and those mistaken for Arab are conveniently racialized as "terrorists" and enemies of the state. Racial profiling and hate violence against Arab Americans and Muslims have become commonplace in the new era of counterterrorism.

Foreigner discrimination is manifested in a variety of ways, from individual interactions to laws and institutional structures. Verbal assaults or acts of violence are tinged with nativism—"Go back to your own country" is a common refrain. Citizenship and loyalty can be questioned. The use of languages other than English becomes a source of division. Religious and cultural differences are accentuated. Foreigner discrimination is especially destructive during periods of war and military conflict because racialized foreigners may take on the characteristics of invaders and state enemies, providing license for jingoism and patriotic violence. Laws regulating immigration and the rights of immigrants can institutionalize foreigner discrimination by limiting the entry of racialized groups or by denying them the rights afforded to citizens.

Addressing foreigner discrimination also presents special challenges, not only because the dominant view of U.S. racial discrimination is black-white, but also because the basic notion of national sovereignty can prevent a more thorough and nuanced analysis of the racial implications of foreigner discrimination. If groups are racialized in ways that place them outside the national community, then the rules of sovereignty—protecting national security, controlling the integrity of the borders, regulating membership in the political community—can trump constitutional considerations such as due process and equal protection of the laws that might otherwise enter into a calculus of legal rights.

Three types of anti-Filipino discrimination help illustrate some of the problems of foreigner discrimination: (1) the laws of immigration and naturalization that have excluded Filipinos from formal entry and membership in the national community; (2) the subordination of Filipino immigrants through citizenship-based discrimination and language-based discrimination; and (3) the treatment of Filipino Americans—even those whose family roots in the United States go back several generations—as foreign-born and alien to U.S. society.

LIMITS ON IMMIGRATION AND CITIZENSHIP

Immigration Restriction
U.S. immigration policy has always been tainted by discrimination based on race and national origin. Beginning with the Chinese Exclusion Acts of the 1880s, immigration from Asian countries other than the Philippines was virtually eliminated by 1924, and restrictions based on national origin remained in place through the mid-1960s. The Philippines' status as a colony of the United States during the first part of the twentieth century postponed limitations on Filipino immigration for several years, reflecting the tension between U.S. reliance on the Philippines as a source of trade and labor on the one hand and calls for race-based exclusion on the other. Inevitably, racial considerations took hold to curtail Filipino immigration with the passage of the Philippine Independence Act of 1934, also known as the Tydings-McDuffie Act, which created mechanisms for the eventual independence of the Philippines but nearly eliminated Filipino immigration to the United States.[7]

The race-based exclusion of Filipinos through the immigration laws illustrates a familiar cycle in U.S. immigration history: immigrants are invited and welcomed as laborers during periods of economic growth, economic cycles lead to downturns in the economy, immigrants are scapegoated, and race-based calls for their exclusion and removal are the ultimate result.[8] When viewed as part of a series of measures designed to limit labor migration from Asia—the Chinese Exclusion Acts, the Gentleman's Agreement between the United States and Japan, the creation of an Asiatic Barred Zone, the national origins quotas that limited immigration from each

Asian country to fifty per year—the limits on immigration from the Philippines are hardly surprising.

However, the status of the Philippines as a colony of the United States from 1898 to 1946 adds an extra dimension that helps illustrate how foreigner discrimination can operate within federal immigration policies. The passage of the Tydings-McDuffie Act involved a literal conversion of Filipinos as members of the national community—Filipinos possessed status as noncitizen U.S. nationals from the advent of U.S. colonialism—to foreigners living outside the nation-state. After taking over control of the Philippines from Spain and quelling Filipino resistance, the United States government implemented numerous measures to Americanize the Philippines and to encourage the entry of Filipinos into the United States. Among several initiatives, a U.S.-style public school system was established in the Philippines, English was imposed as the language of instruction, and a two-house legislature patterned on the U.S. Congress was created. Filipino men became America's "little brown brothers" who were welcomed to the United States as students and as laborers in Hawai'i and on the West Coast, primarily as substitutes for Chinese and Japanese laborers who had been recently excluded from the United States.

Not unexpectedly, the growing numbers of Filipinos in California and other states on the West Coast led to calls for exclusion. The American Federation of Labor passed resolutions for the restriction or exclusion of the "third wave of Oriental immigration." In 1929, the California legislature urged Congress to limit Filipino immigration and instructed the state's Department of Industrial Relations to study and report on the "Filipino problem"; released the following year, the report chronicled the dangers to the state caused by the presence of Filipinos. Representative Richard Welch of San Francisco introduced federal legislation in 1930 that would have included Filipinos among the categories of Asians excluded from the United States. Welch claimed that U.S. labor interests were threatened by the latest "horde of nonassimilable Asiatics" and the "third invasion."[9] By attributing the inability to assimilate to Filipinos, exclusionists could apply the same arguments that had been used to limit the entry of Chinese, Japanese, and Asian Indian immigrants.

Arguments of unassimilability were particularly powerful because they carried the imprimatur of the U.S. Supreme Court. In cases such as *Chae Chan Ping v. United States (The Chinese Exclusion Case)* and *Fong Yue Ting v. United States,* the Supreme Court upheld the powers of the federal government to employ explicit racial classifications in excluding and deporting immigrants.[10] Grounding Congress's "plenary power" to regulate immigration in the powers of national sovereignty, the Supreme Court underscored the exclusion and deportation of Chinese immigrants who were "of a distinct race and religion, remaining strangers in the land, residing apart by themselves, tenaciously adhering to the customs and usages of their own country, unfamiliar with our institutions, and apparently incapable of assimilating with our people."[11] Unlike the segregationist decisions of the same era, such as *Plessy v. Ferguson,* the plenary power cases have never been overruled, and they provide ongoing constitutional support for race-based restrictions on immigration by the federal government.

Notwithstanding extensive efforts to create an Americanized Philippines, the racialization of Filipino immigrants as "nonassimilable Asiatics" prevailed and helped lead to the passage of the Tydings-McDuffie Act in 1934. The Philippines was granted commonwealth status that would lead to independence in 1946, but the conversion of Filipinos from U.S. nationals to foreign nationals for immigration purposes was immediate. Except for immigration to the then territory of Hawai'i, with its powerful agricultural interests that required Filipino labor for plantation work, the Philippines fell under the same immigration limitations that were applied to Asian countries under the 1917 and 1924 immigration acts: a quota of fifty per year. Filipino immigrants in the United States also became deportable, and legislation introduced by Representative Welch in 1935 appropriated $300,000 to subsidize the return of Filipinos who would voluntarily repatriate to the Philippines.[12] Annual quotas for the Philippines were eased in 1946—the quota doubled from fifty to one hundred Filipinos per year—but it was not until 1965 that the discriminatory national origins quotas were finally eliminated from the law.

The Immigration Act of 1965 relaxed formal laws of racial sovereignty and engendered a groundswell in Filipino immigration to the United States.[13] Eliminating quotas based on national origin, the 1965 act amended the law to equalize and expand the number of immigrant visas available for each country. Family reunification became the primary vehicle for immigration, allowing close relatives (spouses, children, parents, siblings) of U.S. citizens to immigrate, as well as a subset of relatives (spouses and unmarried children) of lawful permanent residents. Employment-based visas also became a significant method for skilled professionals to enter the United States. The revised immigration system facilitated large numbers of Filipino immigrants entering on both family-based visas and employment-based visas—many as health care professionals. As a result, the Filipino American population grew from slightly over 180,000 in 1960 to over 1.8 million in the year 2000, with approximately two-thirds of the current Filipino American population being foreign born.

Nevertheless, the current immigration laws have not been without racial consequence. Although designed to eliminate discriminatory quotas, the immigration laws limit the number of immigrant visas per country to 7 percent of the worldwide total, regardless of the size of the country's population and regardless of the qualified number of immigrants waiting for visas. With the demand for visas greatly exceeding supply, the visa system has extensive backlogs in the family-reunification categories, particularly from India, Mexico, and the Philippines. The most heavily backlogged categories are those affecting Filipino immigrants. In 2005, the category for unmarried adult children of U.S. citizens had a waiting period of over fourteen years for Filipino immigrants, compared to over four years for most of the countries of the world; the category for married children of U.S. citizens had a waiting period of nearly fifteen years for Filipino immigrants, over twice as long as most of the other countries of the world.[14] The most severe backlog has been in the brother-sister category: in 2005, Filipino siblings of U.S. citizens had a waiting period of twenty-two years, more than ten years longer than the waiting period for most other countries of the world. Attempts to relieve the backlogs through corrective legislation in Congress have repeatedly failed.

A more explicit race-based limitation on immigration can be found in the "diversity" visa program, which is a lottery system designed in theory to promote immigration from countries with low immigration flows under the family-based and employment-based system. Fifty thousand visas are available each year through the diversity lottery, but countries such as the Philippines, China, South Korea, India, Mexico, El Salvador, Colombia, and the Dominican Republic are excluded from the program because of their relatively high levels of immigration. Implicit in the exclusion of many Asian and Latin American countries from the list of those eligible for diversity visas is the assumption that there is sufficient, if not excessive, immigration from these countries. Ironically, given the long history of race-based exclusion prior to 1965, a predicate for immigration is now the overrepresentation of Filipinos and other immigrants from Asia in the immigration stream.

The current flaws in the immigration system are correctable through legislation that would reduce backlogs, adjust visa allocations relative to a country's population and the demand for visas, and allow a more evenhanded distribution of visas through a lottery system. Yet, the more recent trends in immigration policy reflect movements in the opposite direction. Immigration restrictionists, often echoing the exclusionary rhetoric of earlier eras, have called for strict limits on immigration, ranging from a moratorium on immigration to the elimination of family-reunification categories, such as the brother-sister category. The shift in recent immigration policy to border security and antiterrorism efforts following the attacks of September 11, along with increased discrimination against immigrants of color, means that there will continue to be restrictive immigration policies that will have adverse effects on Filipinos. For example, because of allegations of potential ties to terrorist networks, Filipino immigrants were targeted in the U.S. Department of Justice's Absconder Apprehension Initiative put in place in early 2002 to apprehend and deport more than 300,000 immigrants who had outstanding orders of deportation against them, of whom more than 12,000 were immigrants from the Philippines.[15] Hundreds of Filipino immigrants have been deported under the program, often tearing apart families that include spouses and children who are U.S. citizens.

Restrictions on Naturalized Citizenship

Limitations on immigration prevent entry into the United States, but limitations on citizenship can be more insidious: although welcomed to the United States—if only for the fruits of one's labor—full membership in the U.S. community is nevertheless denied. Foreigner discrimination against Filipinos in the area of citizenship has arisen in two significant areas: restrictions on naturalized citizenship based on race, and denials of naturalized citizenship arising from service in the U.S. armed forces.

Race-based restrictions on naturalized citizenship preceded restrictions on immigration and date back to the earliest days of nationhood. The naturalization law enacted in 1790 limited citizenship to "free white persons."[16] After the Civil War, the naturalization law was amended to allow naturalized citizenship for individuals of "African nativity" or "African descent," and the Fourteenth Amendment provided for birthright citizenship to all persons born in the United States. Nevertheless, Congress rejected the elimination of race-based restrictions on naturalization when applied to Asian immigrants.

Many individuals, including Filipino immigrants, attempted to challenge the racial bar on naturalization by arguing that they were "white persons" under the law, but they were rebuffed by the courts.[17] Filipinos also attempted to employ a special provision in the law applicable to U.S. nationals: section 30 of the naturalization laws was enacted in 1906 to allow residents of the U.S. territories who were left in the nether world between U.S. citizenship and alienage to obtain citizenship. In 1912, in the case of *In re Alverto,* a Filipino petitioner attempted to gain naturalized citizenship, but the court held that the racial bar in the naturalization laws trumped section 30 and that the Filipino petitioner was neither a "white person" nor of African nativity or descent.[18] In 1917, the court in *In re Rallos* elaborated on the barriers to Filipinos gaining U.S. citizenship: "A contrary interpretation would mean that Chinese, Japanese, and Malays could become citizens, if they were inhabitants of the Philippine Islands . . . and if they thereafter moved to the United States."[19] The U.S. Supreme Court later endorsed the racial bar on naturalization against Filipinos in *Toyota v. United States.* Racialized as nonwhite and unassimilable, Filipinos were ignored as "persons already owing allegiance to the United States."[20] The racial bar on naturalization was finally repealed for Filipinos in 1946 and was not repealed for all racial and ethnic groups until 1952.

A related prohibition on U.S. citizenship was the denial of naturalized citizenship to Filipino veterans of World War II. Military service in the U.S. armed forces has been a popular method to obtain U.S. citizenship, and the U.S. colonial and postcolonial presence in the Philippines encouraged the entry of Filipinos into the military, particularly the U.S. Navy. During World War II, several thousand Filipinos were called into service in the U.S. Armed Forces in the Far East (USAFFE), which represented a combined military force that comprised U.S.

Army units in the Philippines, including the Old Philippine Scouts, the Philippine Commonwealth Army, several recognized guerrilla units, and the New Philippine Scouts, a unit that after the Japanese occupation focused on military activities in the Pacific. The contributions of Filipinos to the wartime effort against the Japanese empire are renowned and proved critical to the ultimate victory in the Pacific.

In 1942, Congress passed amendments to the Nationality Act of 1940 that provided for the naturalization of individuals, including residents of its territories, for service in the U.S. military.[21] Thousands of Filipinos became eligible to naturalize under the new law, but the Japanese occupation of the Philippines curtailed naturalization efforts during most of the period from 1942 to 1945. After the Japanese occupation ended in August 1945, naturalization procedures were put in place but were revoked two months later based on concerns that widespread naturalization efforts would adversely affect the development of the soon-to-be independent country. However, naturalization authority was restored in August 1946, allowing approximately four thousand Filipino veterans to obtain citizenship before the application period terminated on 31 December 1946.

The passage of legislation in 1946 that rescinded the veterans' status of Filipinos also played a key role in limiting the availability of full citizenship rights. The First Supplemental Surplus Appropriation Rescission Act contained language which declared that the service of Filipino veterans in the Philippine Commonwealth Army "shall not be deemed active service for purposes of any law of the United States conferring rights, privilege, or benefits." A second rescission act similarly restricted the eligibility of veterans who served in the New Philippine Scouts.[22]

Because of both the nine-month gap in 1945–46 during which naturalization authority was unavailable in the Philippines and the legislation rescinding Filipino veterans' status, numerous lawsuits were filed beginning in the 1950s to challenge the denials of citizenship to Filipino veterans.[23] Despite the litigation, including unsuccessful appeals in the U.S. Supreme Court, only a small number of veterans were able to obtain citizenship through the federal courts by the late 1980s. The veterans' rights were at least partly vindicated with the passage of the Immigration Act of 1990, which authorized Filipino nationals who served on active duty during World War II to apply for citizenship, nearly fifty years after the first legislation authorizing naturalization had been enacted.[24] Approximately twenty-eight thousand Filipino veterans were naturalized under the 1990 law. Tragically, many of the veterans had died during the decades following World War II, and the limitations of the immigration system prevent Filipino veterans from reuniting with many of their family members in the Philippines, who must wait several years to enter the United States because of the severity of the visa backlogs.

Despite their attaining citizenship, many Filipino veterans have been precluded from receiving full veterans' benefits. Because of language in the 1946 rescission legislation, Filipino veterans have been ineligible for most benefits, except death benefits and benefits available for serious illness or disability. Consequently, many of the Filipino veterans residing in the United States live in poverty. Federal legislation enacted in 2003 granted limited war-related veterans' disability and burial benefits, as well as veterans' health benefits, to Filipino American veterans living in the United States, but Filipino veterans living outside the United States did not receive coverage, and pension benefits were not included in the 2003 legislation.[25] Unfortunately, the passage of time only means that more veterans will die without having the full benefits of citizenship arising from their military service during World War II.

The longtime denial of citizenship to Filipino veterans and the ongoing denial of full citizenship benefits provide insights into the relationship of foreigner discrimination to race, immigration, and citizenship. The exchange of military service for the United States for citizenship recognizes that foreigners can gain access to full membership in U.S. society, at least on some condition of reciprocity. The colonial status of the Philippines during World War II reflected an even closer relationship to the United States than that of most countries, for which there should have been fewer barriers to citizenship.

Nevertheless, the almost immediate placement of Filipino veterans outside the bounds of membership following World War II suggests that foreigner racialization played a role in their having been denied citizenship. The first limitations on veterans' naturalization came at the same time that immigration laws continued to restrict the entry of Filipinos to the United States; Filipino immigrants had already been racialized as unassimilable through the immigration restrictions in the Tydings-McDuffie Act of 1934. The naturalization of tens of thousands of Filipinos, who could easily enter the United States as citizens, would have severely compromised the national origins restrictions that were already in place under the immigration laws.[26] Notwithstanding their loyalty and service to the United States, Filipinos were still foreigners under the law. Race was not an openly stated factor in denying Filipino veterans their citizenship through the late 1980s; however, the ardent and lengthy opposition of the federal government to Filipino naturalization suggests that race, with its long history of influence in the immigration and naturalization laws, was part of the equation.

RESTRICTIONS ON IMMIGRANTS' RIGHTS

Because immigration has driven the growth of the Filipino American population in the United States—approximately two-thirds of the Filipino American population is foreign born—governmental policies that discriminate on the basis of immigration status, citizenship, or language have adverse effects on large numbers of Filipino immigrants. Foreigner discrimination based on citizenship status is especially subordinating because noncitizens are disenfranchised and lack much of the power that citizens possess to address discrimination through the political process.

Citizenship Discrimination

Historically, race and citizenship discrimination have been closely intertwined. Because of the racial bar on naturalization, discriminatory laws could be couched in language that made no mention of race but were designed to subordinate on the basis of race. For instance, several states passed "alien land laws" in the 1920s to prohibit the ownership by or transfer of land to persons "ineligible to citizenship." The clear targets of these laws were Asian immigrants, who were barred under the naturalization laws from becoming citizens. The state of Washington went so far as to amend its alien land law, which had been upheld as constitutional by the U.S. Supreme Court in 1923, to extend coverage to Filipinos, even though they were U.S. nationals at the time.[27]

The conversion of Filipinos living in America from U.S. nationals to the equivalent of aliens following the passage of the Tydings-McDuffie Act of 1934 left many immigrants vulnerable to citizenship discrimination by the federal government. For example, during the Great Depression, Filipinos living in the United States found themselves ineligible for assistance from New Deal programs such as the National Youth Administration and the Works Progress Administration. The Relief Appropriation Act of 1937 gave preference to U.S. citizens first and then to aliens who had declared their intention to become citizens. Barred from naturalized citizenship because of race, thousands of Filipinos were unable to gain access to critical governmental assistance.[28]

Court decisions and changes in the laws following World War II removed many citizenship-based restrictions, but the problem of anti-immigrant discrimination has persisted in both federal and state governmental infringements on noncitizens' rights. The linkage of race and citizenship status further compounds the problem, because citizenship discrimination largely affects immigrants who are members of racial and minority groups, which form the largest percentage of the immigrants entering since 1965. A recent example of citizenship-based employment discrimination having an adverse impact on Filipino immigrants was the citizens-only policy adopted by the federal government when it federalized the security screening at airports and vested authority for security with the Transportation Security Administration following the September 2001 terrorist attacks. At the major airports in Northern California, the majority of screeners prior to the federalization were noncitizen and Filipino, who became ineligible to continue their work as screeners.[29]

During the late 1960s and 1970s, several court cases involved challenges to citizens-only restrictions in government employment. Because the federal government possesses "plenary power" to regulate immigration, the courts have upheld federal citizens-only restrictions on government employment as consistent with the regulation of immigration and naturalization. However, state and local governments lack the federal government's power over immigration and must comply with the equal protection clause of the Constitution. The Supreme Court struck down many state classifications based on citizenship status, including restrictions on eligibility for state civil service positions, for practicing law, for becoming licensed engineers, and for becoming notaries public.[30] Nevertheless, the courts have also allowed exceptions to the general rule that state citizenship classifications are unconstitutional. If a classification involves functions that "go to the heart of representative government," then the classification may be upheld as constitutional. Under this exception, the Supreme Court has upheld citizenship restrictions in government employment for state troopers, public schoolteachers, and probation officers.[31]

Yet, a distinction between citizens and noncitizens seems unnecessary in a profession such as public school teaching. As the dissenting justices in *Ambach v. Norwick* noted, "Is it better to employ a poor citizen teacher than an excellent alien teacher? . . . The State will know how to select its teachers responsibly, wholly apart from citizenship, and can do so selectively and intelligently."[32] In any case, many Filipino immigrants, despite their skills and experience, have been unable to gain employment in the key sectors of the government because of citizenship restrictions.

A more severe form of citizenship-based discrimination has revolved around the availability of public benefits for immigrants. In 1996, the passage of the Personal Responsibility and Work Opportunity Reconciliation Act, a federal legislative package designed to reform the nation's welfare system, imposed harsh limitations on immigrants' eligibility for subsistence benefits from the government.[33] As originally enacted, the welfare-reform law discriminated against lawful permanent residents by prohibiting their receipt of basic public benefits, including food stamps and Supplemental Security Income (SSI) for the elderly, blind, and disabled. Much like the restrictions placed on Filipinos during the Depression, noncitizen restrictions on food stamps and SSI affected some of the most vulnerable individuals living in the United States. The impact was felt by thousands of low-income Filipino immigrants nationwide. Although corrective legislation eventually tempered some of the harshness of the welfare-reform law by restoring benefits to immigrants already living in the United States in 1996, the law's citizenship-discrimination provisions continue to apply to new immigrants entering the United States.

A related law passed in 1996, the Illegal Immigration Reform and Immigrant Responsibility Act, restricted the due process rights of immigrants in immigration proceedings and deprived undocumented immigrants of many rights.[34] Already forbidden from working in the United States by federal law, undocumented Filipino immigrants have been particularly vulnerable to discrimination and abuse. Many employers ignore the law and hire immigrants without authorization; employers can then exploit undocumented immigrants because they lack legal immigration status. The 1996 federal immigration law restricted the rights of undocumented immigrants by denying them government services and benefits, including access to federal grants, contracts, loans, and entitlements. The federal restrictions, grounded in the government's plenary powers over immigration, remain in effect. Although the exact number of undocumented Filipino immigrants is unknown, estimates run into the tens of thousands, and thus a large segment of the Filipino population in the United States has been affected by these restrictions.

The lines drawn between citizens and noncitizens present some of the clearest forms of foreigner discrimination. Distinctions between citizens and noncitizens in areas such as voting or holding elective office have traditionally defined full membership in the political community. However, the same distinctions in employment or the provision of subsistence benefits are more draconian than definitional. Denying welfare benefits to poor, elderly Filipino immigrants on the basis of citizenship status defines the U.S. nation-state by subordination rather than by the exercise of political rights.

Language Discrimination

In addition to facing discrimination based on citizenship status, Filipino immigrants often encounter discrimination based on language. Language can be a defining characteristic of ethnicity and national origin, and limitations on language usage can constitute illegal discrimination. Like citizenship discrimination, language discrimination reinforces the notion that Filipinos are not full members of the U.S. polity, which by both custom and law is English dominant. Indeed, the naturalization laws require evidence of English-language proficiency to obtain citizenship, with limited exceptions for elderly, long-term residents. While Filipino Americans have one of the highest rates of English fluency among predominantly immigrant populations, many Filipino immigrants possess limited English ability, and many Filipinos, even those with great fluency in English, are vulnerable to discrimination based on their accents. Foreigner discrimination can thus arise in a number of ways: limitations on the use of languages other than English, including restrictions on the availability of government services in other languages, and discrimination based on a "foreign" accent.

Attempts to limit the use of languages other than English are common during a climate of strong anti-immigrant sentiment, often appearing through state laws making English the official language of government, as well as through English-only rules in the workplace. Calls for English to be the official U.S. language date back to the eighteenth century and have arisen during periods when nativism is a powerful force in the political landscape. For instance, during the early part of the twentieth century, numerous state and local governments adopted laws that prohibited the use of languages other than English, including foreign-language instruction in public schools; later found to be unconstitutional, the laws came largely in response to anti-German sentiment that peaked during World War I. During the 1980s and 1990s, several states with large immigrant populations, including California, enacted laws making English the official language of government. Although some of the laws have been challenged in court, only the most restrictive laws, such as Arizona's law prohibiting the use of non-English languages by government workers, have been found to be illegal.[35]

The availability of language assistance in government services, including public school education, presents a potential dividing line between immigrants and the native born. Language assistance for limited-English-proficient public school students is required under federal law, and many jurisdictions are required under the federal Voting Rights Act to provide language assistance to limited-English-proficient voters. State and local governments can also provide multilingual services such as court translation, health care, and social services. English-only laws threaten these types of services and can deter many immigrants from seeking services at all. Although unsuccessful, attempts to enact federal legislation that would make English the official language of the United States and that would repeal federal requirements for language assistance have been regularly introduced in Congress. State ballot initiatives that restrict the availability of bilingual education, such as California's Proposition 227, also pose a threat to the rights of Filipino immigrant children who have limited English proficiency.

English-only rules in the workplace have become more common in recent years, primarily in response to the growing number of immigrants in the workforce. Some courts have struck down English-only policies for violating laws that prohibit national origin discrimination, but other courts have upheld English-only policies, even though they can infringe significantly on an individual's use of language. In particular, the courts have been willing to uphold limits on the use of languages other than English when the speaker is bilingual and can choose to speak in either English or another language.[36]

Upholding an English-only policy often rests on the devaluation of the non-English language. For instance, in a case litigated during the early 1990s, *Dimaranan v. Pomona Valley Hospital Medical Center*, a Filipino nurse challenged an employment policy that limited the use of Tagalog during work hours. The hospital forbade Filipino nurses to use Tagalog among themselves, even though they spoke English to other workers and to patients. The court upheld the policy as necessary to maintain conformity within the workplace. According to the court, language uniformity was required to maintain cohesion within the work unit and to allay labor-management differences, and "Tagalog was . . . merely caught in the cross-fire."[37] Reflecting a value that conformity should predominate over ethnic identity, the court's reasoning ignored the linkage between a language restriction and discrimination on the basis of national origin. In essence, the no-Tagalog policy and the court's decision reinforced the notion that Filipinos, as Tagalog speakers, were not fully welcome as participants in the workplace.

Accent discrimination similarly serves as a dividing line between those who are full participants in the workforce and those who are not. For example, in the early 1990s Filipino immigrants were removed from their positions as security guards at the federal office building in San Francisco because of "language barriers." The removal occurred even though all of the security guards spoke English fluently. Instead, the removal was based on the assumption that Filipino accents hindered communication, although there was no solid evidence to suggest problems in the guards' communications with the public. The security guards successfully challenged their removal and won a settlement against their employer and the federal government.

Yet, claims of accent discrimination can be unsuccessful because courts often rely on subjective judgments when evaluating a particular accent and the relative importance of accent in communication. In *Fragante v. City and County of Honolulu,* a federal court upheld the dismissal of a discrimination claim involving a Filipino civil service applicant who, despite having great fluency in English, spoke with an accent that the employer considered an obstacle to communication. Fragante, who ranked first out of more than seven hundred applicants on a written civil service examination, was denied the position by interviewers who found him difficult to understand. Even though the trial court had no trouble understanding Fragante's testimony during trial, the court accepted the employer's evidence, as well as expert evidence that in Hawai'i, "listeners stop listening to Filipino accents, resulting in a breakdown of communication." Despite the obvious catering to the prejudices of listeners and the discrimination against Filipino accents, the court dismissed Fragante's claim.[38] In doing so, the government and the court placed Filipino immigrants outside the norm of acceptable employees and reinforced notions of inferiority based on language and national origin.

FILIPINO AMERICANS AS PERPETUAL FOREIGNERS

A third major form of discrimination against Filipino Americans is their racialization as "perpetual foreigners." Despite the presence of Filipinos in the United States since the 1700s, Filipino Americans, whether immigrant or U.S. born, continue to be ascribed the status of foreigners who are outside the definition of "American." Racialized as foreigners, Filipino Americans are subject to both private discrimination and governmental policies that limit full participation in U.S. life because of the ascription of foreignness. Especially during times of military conflict and emergency, maintaining sovereignty and protecting national interests makes Filipino Americans particularly vulnerable to anti-immigrant and anti-foreigner discrimination.

Incidents of racial violence and harassment provide the most telling examples of the racialization of Filipinos as foreigners. For instance, in June 1997, while walking near a secluded reservoir in Southern California, a Filipino American woman was attacked by a group of teenage boys who threw rocks at her and shouted, "Go back to Japan, bitch." In November 1997, a Filipino American study group at George Washington University in Washington, D.C., received a message stating: "I hate black people, and after looking at your page, I want to kill you people as well. Why don't you [go] back to China or wherever you're from, because this great country doesn't need people like you who turn out such a great big pile of crap.... Every time I'm cleaning my shotgun, I'll be thinking of you. Hope that death is quick."[39]

In August 1999, Joseph Ileto, a Filipino American postal worker, was gunned down in Chatsworth, California, by a white supremacist who earlier in the day had riddled a Jewish community center with bullets and wounded three small children. Ileto's killer admitted that he had targeted Ileto because he was a "chink or spic." Such targeting of course conveys more than a statement of racial designation; it suggests an ascription of foreignness. The ultimate irony is that at the time he was killed, Ileto was a U.S. citizen and was a wearing a clear symbol of membership in U.S. society—a U.S. Postal Service uniform.[40]

Less violent forms of foreigner discrimination can occur through daily encounters at the workplace. For example, under the 1986 Immigration Reform and Control Act, all employers are required to verify the identity and the authorization to work of all new employees. In essence, employment verification is an extension of immigration enforcement designed to prevent the hiring of undocumented immigrants, with employers functioning as private border patrol agents to ensure that only U.S. citizens and authorized noncitizens are legally employed. Yet, discrimination based not only citizenship but also on race and national origin has become a significant problem because of the verification requirements. A study by the General Accounting Office found widespread patterns of discrimination against Asian Americans and Latinos arising out of these requirements. Using a national survey of employers, the GAO study found that nearly one of every five employers committed unlawful discrimination based on citizenship or national origin, with even higher percentages in areas such as California, Texas, and New York City with large minority populations.[41] A private survey conducted in San Francisco found similar results: one-half of the employers felt that it was riskier to hire people who spoke limited English and that approximately 40 percent of the employers found it riskier to hire Asians or Latinos.[42] Filipino Americans, regardless of actual citizenship, can thus encounter significant discrimination when the laws mandate differential treatment of citizens and noncitizens, and of documented and undocumented workers.

Governmental policies explicitly based on foreigner discrimination have often extended beyond the range of individuals targeted for differential treatment. The internment of Japanese Americans during World War II provides the most salient example. Assuming that the federal government was justified in investigating and addressing genuine threats to national security during the war, the relocation and internment of all Japanese Americans living on the West Coast went far beyond what was actually needed. The vast majority of internees were U.S. citizens, and the remainder were permanent residents barred from naturalization because of race; there was no evidence to suggest that significant numbers were disloyal or posed a threat to national security. Yet, once they had been racialized as "enemy aliens," all individuals of Japanese ancestry, regardless of citizenship or of loyalties, were incarcerated. Because the constitutionality of the government's policies was upheld and never reversed by the courts, the same threat against civil rights looms during periods of war or military conflict, when one racial or ethnic group may be identified for differential treatment. Notwithstanding the long colonial and postcolonial relationship between the United States and the Philippines, group-based discrimination can still be applied against Filipino Americans. During a period when many members of racial, ethnic, and religious minority groups—including Filipinos of Islamic faith—may be racialized as terrorists or enemies of the state, Filipino Americans are no less at risk.

Addressing foreigner discrimination should require, at minimum, differentiating accurately between those individuals who are supposed to be affected by policies—such as noncitizens who lack authorization to work in the United States—and those who are not. More fundamentally, however, basic policies must be revisited to understand their effects on Filipino Americans and other groups who are racialized as foreigners. Policies that require verification of citizenship will have direct effects on the subordination of noncitizens, but they will almost always have effects on citizens as well.

One method of addressing foreigner discrimination would be to recognize in the civil rights laws that citizenship discrimination should be illegal. Antidiscrimination protections for noncitizens are poorly developed in the law, and some forms of discrimination, such as restrictions on government employment, are legally mandated. Minimizing governmental discrimination against noncitizens and expanding the civil rights laws to include citizenship discrimination are important starting points in addressing foreigner discrimination. In addition, the treatment of citizens who are *perceived* as foreigners or noncitizens should constitute illegal discrimination based on race or national origin.

That race can take on meanings of foreignness for groups such as Filipino Americans implies that policies must be examined for a broader array of potential harms. And some policies, such as the employment-verification requirements of the Immigration Reform and Control Act, which are poorly enforced, poorly implemented, and cause discrimination in and of themselves, should simply be abandoned.

CONCLUSION

Color lines have a long history in U.S. society, and Filipino Americans continue to encounter discrimination based on race, national origin, citizenship, and language. Despite governmental attempts to rectify the effects of exclusionary immigration laws, segregation, and overt discrimination, racial sovereignty still persists as a dividing line for Filipino Americans and other groups racialized as foreigners. Changes in law and public policy can shift and undermine the lines of racial sovereignty, but the challenge, particularly during a period of heightened defense of national security, is much greater. The challenge lies in developing and strengthening a core set of values that both accommodate and celebrate differences in race and ethnicity, in citizenship, and in language. The basic meaning of "American" must be broadened and redefined, and Filipino Americans must be part of that new and expansive definition.

III.

RECONFIGURING THE SCOPE OF FILIPINO POLITICS

Antonio T. Tiongson, Jr.

7 On the Politics of (Filipino) Youth Culture

Interview with Theodore S. Gonzalves

On the Politics of Culture

Tony Tiongson: Could you please introduce yourself and talk about your university affiliation, research interests, and interests outside of academia?

Theo Gonzalves: My name is Theo Gonzalves. My research interests concern Filipino American performing arts and Asian American culture and history. I am also interested in expressive forms of culture and how they inform Asian and American history. I'm particularly interested in performance as an exciting site for thinking about identities, how histories are compressed in performances, the kind of burden that these performances take up in the absence and presence of social movements. I am also very much interested in what these performances tell us about how Asian Americans relate to their parents' generation. We'll find that culture isn't necessarily handed down from one generation to another but is a series of discontinuities and breaks and slippages and interesting turns— lessons that aren't learned well but seem to get repeated over and over again, anxieties that surface in artwork or visual work, poetry, literature, dance, theater, and comedy—all things that haunt us for generations. A lot of it has to do with challenging not only dominant U.S. culture but also Asian America itself—our own relationship to our elders, the generations that went before us.

TT: One of the things we are trying to do with the project is to map the broader implications of Filipino politics. We are particularly interested in looking at culture as a site not just for the consolidation of power but also for the contestation of power. First of all, how do you conceive of "culture"? Also, I wonder if you could talk about the complexities and contradictions of interpreting culture, why culture is difficult to read.

TG: One of the reasons why culture can be difficult to read is because so much of what the mass media does is aimed at the most common denominator. Commercial culture or the mass media requires passivity. It requires subjects to be accepting and to be asleep. Neferti Tadiar put it this way at a recent talk she gave. She spoke of two senses of culture. One is that culture is now the organizing principle of the world economy, to which I add that such a principle disciplines subjects to be passive, to be asleep. When we think of this sense of "culture," we should tune in to questions like, How can culture discipline subjects as compliant actors in a world economy, to respond to market forces in a way that you would want them to? The other aspect of culture would be to see it as a resource that comes from the ground up. This is a notion of culture that is ethnographically informed, one that relies on improvisation and recombinations of symbols and myths, and sensibilities at the most local level. Culture is all that we take for granted—things that we eat, the gods that we worship, how we speak, and the kinds of accents that we use.

TT: It's also important to note that the notion of cultural industries fashioning passive consumer subjects is not an absolute, total process.

TG: No, it never is. You read Antonio Gramsci a certain way and you realize that hegemony is still hard work. People are arguing at the very top of corporate boards and within war rooms as to how to actually maintain certain amounts of order. It's never seamless. It's never unified. It's never completely successful. If it were, then we would not be having this kind of conversation. We would remain silent. We would be afraid to speak out. We would be afraid to identify things that we find are important. Culture, in the other sense we are talking about—in the liberatory sense, the democratic sense that we are talking about—opposes that. Culture never precludes resistance. Sometimes it becomes the grounds for resistance.

It's more important not to deny a sense of gravity that's there, that there are people working hard every day, in terms of how to market food and how to create appetites for subjects as young as two years old. Billions of dollars are spent on crafting flavors and desires and tastes and needs at the earliest ages to create brand loyalty for the rest of your life and foster an addiction to high-caloric fast food, music, fashion, culture, and just about everything else we consume. No, it doesn't preclude resistance, because otherwise, we wouldn't have people trying in different times and different places and ways to reconnect their lives and what they feel is important outside those schemes, outside those industries. Some people like to swim within the mainstreams of culture, but there are others who choose to swim deeper or outside of that altogether.

TT: That actually leads me to my next question, and that is the significance of popular cultural forms and practices to marginalized groups like Filipinos. I'm particularly interested in the kinds of possibilities it opens up or affords.

TG: Filipino youth culture, like many other youth cultures, has the potential to challenge parents' worldviews. For students of social movements, it is important to think about the relationships of youth culture to politics but also to keep in mind that some popular cultural forms are not always political, meaning that they don't always change the way in which resources are allocated. They can provide a challenge to certain values and discourse—kind of interrupt the sense of what's comfortable. It depends on what the targets are, but they don't necessarily have to be self-conscious. Youth culture, especially for many Filipino Americans, has a possibility to define a sense of values over and against their parents. This is not necessarily before attacking the dominant culture, but youth culture is always about marking generationally the "where and when" you enter into history. It answers that kind of question. You say to your parents: "This is not my war. Those aren't my jobs. These aren't my dreams. These are our possibilities." And when youth begin to speak that way, they are not only challenging the dominant mainstream order; they are also making the challenge at the level of the kitchen table. I find these kinds of generational tensions in moments inhabited by the zoot suiters, the music of Joe Bataan, and the buried history of Chinese American performers in the 1940s in Forbidden City in San Francisco, just to name a few. They're all interesting performers and performing cultures that seem to challenge dominant notions of race and sexuality. But in truth, one of the first challenges that they issue before they issue it to the world is to their parents, challenging conventional ways to access an immigrant's dream. So we find folks like Joe Bataan who are important to Puerto Rican and black kids in Spanish Harlem. The salsa they are listening to coming out of Joe is more percussive. For some, it sounded like marching music, music for the streets. It speaks to their percussive environments. And when he talks about his life being an ordinary life (with tunes like "Afrofilipino/Ordinary Guy"), he's saying, "I don't drive around in fancy cars. I don't know anyone of wealth or fame." Ordinary people understood that, ordinary people trying to make sense of their dilapidated living conditions in the cities. So they were able to fashion a political critique but using Joe's music. What it meant for them, though, was different from what it meant to their parents. It wasn't their parents' salsa music. It wasn't ballroom-dancing music. It wasn't middle-class Friday-night music. This was music that was to be played out in the streets wherever possible. And it was louder. It was more aggressive. It was fusing soul from African America and turning it into something different.

We can find some parallels to some of the zoot suiters. These are kids that are not necessarily following the middle-class expectations that their parents had. There's a great scene in *Zoot Suit,* the play by Luis Valdez, where the kids are getting ready to get out for an evening and they have their zoot suits, they are primping and getting ready, they call themselves Chicanos. The parents take issue with that. They say, "Why do you call yourselves that? We are Mexicans." There is a clash of values that's emerging at the site of fashion, at the site of music, at the very site of naming oneself. They wanted to call themselves "Chicano" which was different from the parents. There's not a value judgment there. There also was not necessarily even a political content. Not yet. Not until someone like Luis Valdez and his contemporaries look backward into that history and then find political content in that. At the time, they're looking for a social space that's comfortable and outside of the racialized violence of 1940s L.A. or Chicago or New York or Boston. So youth cultures allow us to think about generational tensions.

Looking at youth cultures also allows us to think about how culture can anticipate politics. What seems to be oppositional culture in the 1940s would be recovered and would become so important for folks in the 1960s. Filipino Americans would find themselves similarly in one of those kinds of areas—in taxi-dance halls, in gambling houses, and as musicians, as well as zoot suiters. There are not that many well-publicized examples, but that's been the role of social historians, to get at those kinds of stories.

TT: Culture, therefore, illuminates our understanding of Filipino history.

TG: Yeah, absolutely. For the kind of cultures that I am looking at—twentieth-century Filipino American cultures—we have to look at the site of culture, because so much of Filipino American history has been a history of defeat. A failed revolution identifies a paradigm for many Filipinos and Filipino Americans. It's as if everything else becomes then a recovery of the nation, of a failed revolution, failed constitution or republic. It seems that's the catalyst for attempts to recover a sense of what the nation should be or could be, and our places in it. For Filipino Americans, because there aren't those kinds of hooks on a mountain to think about, those landmark achievements to think about, culture becomes absolutely crucial. Where else are we going to find the political outside of defeat, in the absence of social and political victories? How do Filipino Americans continue to think about their sense of Filipino identity? Where does it come from? And because there aren't those kinds of well-publicized or well-documented notions of Filipinos that have actively contested the dominant in their contemporary lives, culture becomes a way to help fill in our knowledge.

Studying cultures, specifically the expressive forms of cultures that I am studying, allows us to look at different kinds of objects to study when Filipinos are omitted from historical records or even when they are included in historical records, because there's either an omission or a distortion. If Filipino Americans fail to be authors of their own histories in a traditional sense of what a text is, then it places a special burden on culture to represent a sense of what that is. A yearning for historical knowledge or continuity doesn't stop just because the texts aren't there. Cultural expressions take up that burden. These are explained in performances. Histories are carried forward by music and dance. So we have to look to different objects of study. We have to look at these different things that can inform us of what actually transpired. But they're not necessarily just texts that can be pulled off the shelf and looked at further and examined for their veracity. They don't necessarily answer the questions that are being asked, meaning that there's not always political content in expressive forms of culture. There are often contradictory notions of political identities, which is fine because there aren't any identities that are without contradictions. But when we look at objects of expressive forms of culture, we have to do more than merely celebrate culture for being there. We can't just celebrate what we find. We also have to deal with the contradictions.

TT: So we therefore can't conclude that expressive forms are inherently progressive.

TG: We know that just because something is popular doesn't mean that it's right. It means that it may not have been studied in a certain way. It means that we take on the mantle of social historians, who look for evidence of the past outside the great minds and the great books. We can turn to culture and performance to see history and culture from the ground up. But we don't necessarily assume that what we find has the political content to answer what we're looking for. Otherwise, we trivialize what we end up finding and uncritically celebrate cultural forms. And that's a mistake. That's a mistake because it feeds into a very comfortable notion of what culture is, and it allows us to stop because we have a goal. We have a very specific and undertheorized goal, which is merely to find something that represents us in a so-called positive way. That's not necessarily what a student of Filipino American studies should be aiming for. We're trying to dispense with that. Instead, we are trying to find tools in analyzing the present and also trying to make sense of what happened in the past, but not necessarily validate what we find.

FILIPINO YOUTH CULTURE: PCNs AND MURALS

TT: I want to talk about your own work. Let's first talk about Pilipino Cultural Nights. What attracted you to PCNs? What kinds of questions and issues did it raise for you?

TG: I was first involved with PCN when I was working on my master's degree in political science at San Francisco State University. I participated in a PCN because I found a sense of comradeship with other students. The first year that I participated, I attended a lot of rehearsals, like so many other students. In many ways, it felt like a nice substitute for politics, because it was a way to think of collective action and feel a sense of collective purpose that we were all in the same room for the same thing. I guess in the absence of a political movement or a moment, it feels like the closest thing possible, the next best thing. It's like attending a rock concert. You're there for a collective purpose. There's an energy and spirit behind it. There's a sense that even though you're all crammed into one place, you could be freed by the music and experience something at a very visceral and sometimes transcendent level. Culture has a lot to do with that. It allows us to be able to think that way. The PCN was such an interesting experience because it relies on hundreds of folks to make it happen. It requires a lot of time. You celebrate the labor of that. You celebrate the friendship of that.

By my second year in the program, I had already seen at least a couple dozen PCNs just as a visitor or as a guest of others. But this following year, the entire CSU [California State University] system was experiencing budget cutbacks, and student fees were going up at San Francisco State. It would mean that many more students would not be able to come back to campus, because they couldn't afford it. It would force the question: Why are we continuing to perform these shows if we are losing the people in our own organization? What is it that we're actually here for? We began to question the purpose of what we do and the purpose of these shows. It revealed something about culture that I didn't like at the time, which was that we were participating in forms of culture that would go on year to year unquestioned. It's like putting on a prom. You don't necessarily think about changing the theme of it. Everyone thinks it's the most special prom ever because it is happening to you. But it is predictable. It has its own logic of its own. So we began asking these questions and it led us to really think about what we put on stage.

Initially, it allowed us to think just in terms of representation. Representationally, what goes on in the PCN is very predictable. There are other questions concerning not just relevance but politics. Do we really want to see ourselves in that way? Is there more to us than what we put on stage as we've done it? It forces us also to consider our own sense of creativity. What I liked about the process is exactly that. Instead of culture being rather a mechanical labor of fixing widgets and fastening bolts in the same places they've been fastened before, we had to think about culture as we've experienced it. We attempted to document and create a sense of what we wanted to see ourselves.

The traditional model of the PCNs deals with the presentation of various suites of Philippine folk dance accompanied by live or recorded music interspersed with a script that deals specifically with Filipino American experiences. The presentation of the folk dance and music don't necessarily have anything to do with the script, but that's not really a major consideration. That genre of performance had been going on for about twenty years and had become rather predictable. What we wanted to do was to play with the sense of that structure, and instead of collapsing all of that energy into one evening, we decided to deal with three or four different evenings. One evening showcased Filipinos in hip-hop. It was a night where we invited MCs, DJs, break-dance crews, and graf artists to take over a large hall and have at it. We had some doors painted that shouldn't have been painted. But it was where a whole aspect of Filipino youth culture was, and it created space for it to take place within a cultural night that really doesn't exist except in the PCN. Another evening dealt with spoken word, literature, poetry, and jazz music. And another dealt with films that our own group members shot or edited or acted in.

The idea was to be rather interdisciplinary in what we meant by culture and make it more relevant, to put us in charge of creating rather than just reproducing it. So in that sense it became more of a process and more informed and more exciting because we were asking ourselves what is really relevant to us. And we found out a lot of things were. Usually, the space to ask those kinds of questions is reserved for the skit or the play. But the problem is that it had become so clumsy and mechanical that usually you have to focus on one story or you insert a bunch of story lines where it becomes diluted and rather hackneyed. You have homophobia, or religious intolerance, pregnancies, generational fights. Sometimes they can all take place in one script. It just didn't feel like the format that we were using was terribly democratic or relevant—in other words, the PCN had become undemocratic, in that no one was actually responsible for creating or addressing contemporary forms of Filipino American culture. It was merely handed down. So when that happens, it's like you might as well not have a voice. "Just tell me where to line up and I'll perform the dances." There is no question of how is it relevant to us and how can we choose to make these performances our own. Those are democratic kinds of questions.

So that's how I entered this area of thinking about culture. When I thought about it a little more, this topic of PCNs touched on a lot of areas, in that it dealt with mass organization and it dealt with a cohort of young folks that have attended colleges and universities in California since the 1980s, the children of the post-1965 generation. So it's interesting for a lot of those kinds of reasons. It's interesting also because it tries to narrate history where most of the students themselves don't have direct access to Filipino or Filipino American histories. So they end up teaching each other these histories for a little while. At first blush, you might think that there is a heavy political comment or progressive messages in it. I always tried to resist forcing that onto the material because it's simply not the case. Instead, it has become a very safe space and a very predictable space for understanding Filipino and Filipino American culture.

What's also interesting when we study the PCN is that it represents a notion of history and culture that is fatalistic; for a lot of young Filipino Americans, it's as if it happens on this night or it doesn't happen at all. One way to get at that is to ask the question, "Why are these cultural nights so long—why are they six hours on some campuses?" You think about other forms of entertainment, nothing lasts for four hours—maybe German opera. But what in postmodern

American culture could last for four hours and demand that kind of time? Hardly anything, really. There are a lot of incredibly well-paid professionals whose jobs rest on the idea that the public's attention doesn't last beyond the length of television commercials and campaign spots that are timed to the second. Four hours is an incredible amount of time.

There's more going on than simply entertainment. It is an engagement with history. It is an engagement with Filipino culture. But like I said, it's a specific and unique form through which Filipino Americans are attempting to do it either because of the generational silence of their parents, or because of dominant culture's distortion or omission. It's not necessarily one or the other. Many of the students find that their parents speak about their history. But we have to balance certain things. There is a lot of both, meaning there's the dominant distortion or omission in mainstream media, in textbooks, and in curricula, but also, at the home level, there's a reticence or almost a shame that perhaps Filipino culture is not even needed in U.S. society, which might be the reason why many parents believe that they shouldn't have to teach their children the languages or the foods. The silence concerning culture creates this hunger. You can find a sense of that hunger from not being able to see it within the dominant culture or just being in the home. But the reason PCNs are so long is because so many of us insist on the comprehensive nature of the presentation. It must include a number of dance suites. It must include these elements, and if it doesn't, it's not an accurate portrayal of history.

TT: Would you then say that what we're seeing is a politics of authenticity and nostalgia operating? If so, why do you think this kind of politics has so much currency not just for Filipinos but for other diasporic communities as well?

TG: Oh, absolutely, yeah. But when you insist that history and cultural forms must be represented authentically, then leaving anything out or augmenting it in creative ways means that you've done an injustice to it, that you've actually sacrificed that sense of authenticity. So we have to have it six hours. That's the reason cultural nights tend to last so long: if it's not presented on that night, it won't ever be presented. It means there's no room to tell other stories later on or other venues outside of this. If it doesn't happen here, then it doesn't happen.

TT: You've also done work on murals. Could you talk a little bit about the meanings and uses of murals in Filipino communities, how they are implicated, for example, in the projects of nation building and community formation?

TG: Murals have been important for Filipino American communities. The three that I looked at—one in San Jose, one in San Francisco, and another in Los Angeles—were all built with the help of nonprofit organizations, including

Precita Eyes Mural Arts in San Francisco and Social and Public Art Resource Center in L.A. All are nonprofit organizations who work with community artists, and they're part of community-based efforts to convey a sense of history. And the notion is simple. It is to develop visual literacy and to deepen historical knowledge through visual literacy.

TT: How does the engagement of history in mural productions differ from the engagement of history in PCNs?

TG: Well, they're different in terms of their actual construction. Murals usually don't rely on hundreds of people to mount. They rely on a community to be able to see them, and they reflect to a community a sense of who it could be and what it has been. They reflect the biases and the prejudices and the inclinations and sensibilities of the mural makers and also of the nonprofit organizations that work on behalf of these communities. But just in terms of the kind of human labor required, they're very different. Murals are static representations of the community that work more like mirrors. They reflect the communities that they are situated in. Also, murals are different from PCNs in that they have more of a sense of durability, whereas PCNs are fleeting, as are all performances. The domain of the performances is merely the night or the day of the performance, and so it's assembled, then dispersed. The murals are similar in that there's a lot of energy accumulated to create and assemble one. But once the artists are gone, its presence is still felt.

FILIPINO PARTICIPATION IN HIP-HOP AND OTHER CULTURAL FORMS

TT: Let's move on to hip-hop. We've seen Filipinos along with other groups gravitate to what is generally considered a black cultural form. So this affinity to hip-hop is not unique among Filipinos. What do you make of the participation of Filipinos in hip-hop?

TG: It's consistent with how Filipinos have participated in other popular cultural forms, whether it's Latin jazz or Latin music in the sixties and seventies or hip-hop today. In many ways, Latin American music was also a very popular medium that many Filipino Americans and Filipinos found themselves getting into. I guess there's a couple ways to look at this. One is the notion that hip-hop is an authentically black cultural form, which I think can be quarreled with for a minute. This is not to say that some of its greatest innovators were not African Americans. But if we were to historically situate hip-hop, that is, where and when it enters U.S. culture, we can always think about Puerto Rican break dancers, Greek graf writers like Taki 183, and African American and

Jamaican DJs. We could think about hip-hop being a multiracial/multiethnic space. We can think about how it was racialized as an African American space by its innovators and by transnational capital later. But that's the way I want to emphasize hip-hop, in the same way I emphasize jazz music. Jazz music can be seen as authentically a black cultural space, and that's probably what Winton Marsalis would want us to believe—that there's an unbroken line of African Americans from Louis Armstrong to musicians like Marsalis. But I would also emphasize the multiracial character of popular cultural forms like jazz, because New Orleans is not just in the Deep South of African America, it is also at the cusp of the Caribbean and also part of Latin America culturally, with a Haitian, French, Jamaican, African, and even a Filipino presence in southern Louisiana in the eighteenth century. So I have to think about the notion that hip-hop culture being an authentically black cultural form is, in its present form, the language of transnational capital. Hip-hop is also the language of Sprite, KFC, and Coca-Cola. So to the extent it is authentic, we have to think about its historical roots and think of how actually it spoke multiracially to a group of people. In that regard, Filipinos aren't necessarily participating in an authentically black cultural form. They are participating in what becomes popular American music, as they have, say, in the earlier part of the twentieth century with Mardi Gras parades in the thirties, zoot-suiters in the forties, as members of Latin jazz and rock combos of the sixties and seventies. These instances illustrate the ways Filipino Americans have been part of popular music in many different guises.

TT: So the affinity with hip-hop extends to other forms of music as well.

TG: Even if we were to go back just a few years to a very different San Francisco of the anti-Marcos era, there were not only bands like the San Francisco–based Dakila that was onto a Latin-rock stream but many other bands that had Filipinos in them, like Malo and Mundo and many others that went into Latin jazz. It was just so common for Filipino Americans to be part of the Latin jazz or Latin soul scene. So in that regard I don't think it's necessarily all that different from Filipinos gravitating toward hip-hop. I think there are connections between aggrieved communities throughout the twentieth century, Africans and Asians sharing social spaces and workplaces. So you would find a sharing of those recreational and expressive forms of culture as well. But I don't necessarily see anything that's especially unique about the experience of Filipinos in hip-hop, because so much of that is reflected in Latin jazz and Latin rock just a generation before. And even before that, we see Filipinos coming from the Philippines who already have a notion of what tango and mambo are. That's over a century's worth of music, and dance, and song styles that are shared between Latin America and the Philippines and Filipino Americans. But it's not talked about that way. I think maybe because its just the urgency of what hip-hop has become for so many people, because it would speak to a kind of political rage or a political articulation, especially in '89 with Public Enemy and their popularization in Spike Lee's *Do The Right Thing*. I think if you look through the long history of the twentieth century, you'll find very deep connections between Filipinos and Latin American cultural forms from the beginning of the twentieth century to the present. Actually, a lot of that has to do with the introduction of European modernity to the Philippines in the sixteenth century. In that regard, it wouldn't be uncommon to find Filipinos participating in Western musics, because they've been doing so since the sixteenth century. It's nothing necessarily new.

I think too much might be made of the Filipino connection to African Americans. I mean, we also find Filipinos participating in very vibrant cultural forms such as the blues and jazz. So that's not necessarily unique to me. It's not even necessarily terribly interesting. I mean, if I were trying to make the point that Filipinos and African Americans share an affinity because they're structurally similar as racial minorities in the United States, that might be relevant. But I don't necessarily think that music is the best way to make the point, because you can travel to Los Angeles and find Filipinos participating in hip-hop, which has absolutely nothing to do with politics. Car clubs and hip-hop dances have been the lingua franca of the youth since the eighties. But if we're attempting to find the political content, or make a statement about the shared social experiences of Filipinos and African Americans, sure we can. It's just that hip-hop ensnares middle-class white kids that have actually popularized the music to the rest of the world. I mean, there isn't the international popularity of hip-hop without middle-class white youth. In that regard, I'm not interested in making the topic of Filipino Americans in hip-hop a fetish, because it seems that we are trying to find something that's unique as a set of linkages and I don't necessarily find it.

INVOLVEMENT IN PERFORMANCE GROUPS

TT: Talk a little bit about your involvement in Filipino performance groups and what attracted you to this medium—theater performance arts—and also talk about what makes this medium different from other media, like film. What kinds of things does it open up and allow you to do, for example, that film and other kinds of media do not?

TG: Bindlestiff Studio is a forty-four-seat black box performance-arts space in San Francisco's South of Market area that has been home to a lot of Filipino communities since the beginning of the twentieth century. The theater was founded in 1989 by Chrystene Ells, who helped to fashion the space with a number of actors and performers and turned it into a space for avant-garde theater that drew from traditions of Grand Guignol and commedia dell'arte. Ells worked with a consortium of artists based at the theater. A few Filipino American artists began to work with her in the late '90s. She was able then to recruit other Filipino performers to mount their own shows. In 1998, Allan Manalo became artistic director of the theater, and he began to fashion it as a performance-arts base devoted to promoting original Filipino American performing arts work. So that meant work for a theater group called Tongue in a Mood. It would later mean the inclusion of another theater group that had been in existence for eleven years, TnT, Theatro Ng Tanan. And it was a great place, because a performing arts base means that artists actually have the ability to build skills in their craft. It means you have ability to sit and rehearse. And because the space was run by a group of us, it meant that we didn't have to charge a lot in order to mount our own productions. It would mean that most of the shows would be just about breaking even, but for Tongue in a Mood, it would mean a performing arts group would get a chance to play with sketch comedy, with live music, and would help to develop and give a theater audience something they had not necessarily seen before, which was a strong dose of irreverent comedy. It tackles subjects that seemed to be taboo. Tongue in a Mood was able to build an audience along three different lines. One was college-age Filipinos who attended local colleges and universities who were taking Asian American or Filipino American studies classes. We found Filipinos that were postcollege age but young professionals who also dug theater and found something new to say outside of movies and other traditional fare. And then we also found an audience among other performing artists in the mainstream San Francisco community— other folks who were also involved with theater or shadow puppetry or other music. It was an interesting base of patrons. I always think of Bindlestiff in relation to the Sony Metreon, because it's about two or three blocks up the road. Sony Metreon is this adult-entertainment complex where adults can mostly just watch movies, get something to eat, buy expensive gadgets, and spend a lot of money for parking. The Metreon is a hulking giant tribute to mainstream sensibilities and corporate-controlled culture.

So while there might be Filipinos that are interested in getting into film to be on the Fox Network or any of the major networks, the artistic sensibilities of the folks at the theater have been rather to promote original—and when possible, experimental—works; to be unapologetic about their comedy, their music, their theater, or their choreography; and to pay attention to notions of history without making politics a fetish or propagandizing their art in that way. So in that sense, it has been a particularly great way for performing artists to express themselves. We found a large music scene of Filipinos outside of hip-hop communities who play punk music, alternative forms of music, pop music, R&B, soul, and even the band that I play in. So we found other ways to express Filipino America again at the visceral level, at the bodily level that demanded our presence but which also sometimes stood outside our own traditional notions of how we understood performance, which was the PCN. So I think for the thousands of students who have come to know what a theater experience is like through the PCN, coming to one of our shows would be a surprise that would find either a punk-rock band that's singing in either Tagalog or English, or a comedy troupe like Tongue in the Mood that would focus on sexuality or the coming apocalypse.

So we were able to put all those anxieties onstage and to do so without apology. We weren't slaves to a profit-driven industry or to the tradition that would force us to promote only so-called positive works or positive images of what it means to be Filipino. For me, it has been an incredible place, because even though I've performed in a theater group, I never stopped thinking about what actually all these things could mean. It would mean that Filipino America wouldn't necessarily be defined. I mean, we wouldn't find the limits of Filipino America. Instead, we would find some possibilities that we have not even thought about before. And that's a more interesting place to inhabit, to deal with the possibilities of culture rather than its limits.

DEAN ITSUJI SARANILLIO

8   Colonial Amnesia

Rethinking Filipino "American" Settler
Empowerment in the U.S. Colony of Hawai'i

> A history that serves as a guide to the people in perceiving present reality is
> itself a liberating factor, for when the present is illumined by a
> comprehension of the past, it is that much easier for the people to grasp the
> direction of their development and identify the forces that impede real
> progress.
>
> —Renato Constantino, *The Philippines: A Past Revisited*

> There has been deliberate, intentional, purposeful miseducation and
> disinformation by the government, by the schools, and by the
> communications media to hide the truth of this [colonial] exploitation, and to
> promote the fairy tale that Hawai'i is a democracy, that everyone has equal
> opportunity, and that it's a paradise with racial harmony.
>
> —Kekuni Blaisdell, *Autobiography of Protest in Hawai'i*

AS A RESULT OF the countereducation afforded Hawai'i residents by the
Native Hawaiian sovereignty movement, Hawai'i's history of conquest by the
United States has resurfaced, exposing numerous contradictions and questions
for those who claim Hawai'i as their home. Previous studies of race relations
and popular ways of imagining Native Hawaiians have employed a domestic "civil
rights" framework, framing Native Hawaiians as an ethnic "minority group" within
Hawai'i's multicultural state competing for their fair share of the American pie.[1]
On the other hand, the body of work produced by many Native scholars and Native sovereignty supporters uses a broader discourse of "indigenous human rights"
that recognizes Native Hawaiians as a "peoples" who have a genealogical continuity with Hawai'i distinct from that of other racial or ethnic groups.[2] This latter
framework situates Hawai'i within an international political arena, calling for a
reconceptualizing of Native Hawaiians as a colonized indigenous people with
specific human rights that have been violated by the imperialist United States of
America.

As the Native Hawaiian sovereignty movement reminds Hawai'i of a history
of colonialism, how can Filipino communities in Hawai'i use these challenges to

rethink our own past, present, and imagined futures? How do our beliefs, actions, and investments in the U.S. system collide with the aims of the Native Hawaiian sovereignty movement? What are the continuities between Filipino struggles in Hawai'i and the various anti-imperialist movements in the Philippines? How can we link these movements to the Native Hawaiian movement for self-determination? In this essay I show how the U.S. colonization of Hawai'i conceals itself, maneuvering historically oppressed groups against indigenous peoples. Specifically, I examine the apparent contradictions and implications of a Filipino settler identification with the United States in a U.S. colony. I situate this contradiction within the context of colonial miseducation, to show how this identification is the product of a history of U.S. colonialism in both the Philippines and Hawai'i. As a fourth-generation settler of Filipino and Japanese descent from Hawai'i, I would like to add a different point of reference, one that is in dialogue not with the U.S. settler state but instead with the indigenous peoples under colonial domination. As Vicente Diaz, Native Pacific cultural studies scholar, stated to Filipinos and Chamorros in the U.S. colony of Guam: "If the history of relations between Chamorros and Filipinos is one of a shared struggle within colonial and neocolonial realities, then it is we who should be orchestrating the history, not allowing it to play us."[3]

For Filipinos in the United States, marginalization and subordination seem to be requisite for U.S. citizenship. The newspapers, books, articles, and journals that focus on racism against Filipinos in Hawai'i have pointed out the inequities and systemic structures of racism engrained in Hawai'i's society.[4] Ethnic studies scholar Jonathan Okamura's analysis of socioeconomic data from the 1990 U.S. Census reveals that Hawai'i's unique ethnic/racial stratification of power consists generally of whites, Japanese, and Chinese holding dominant positions in the state, and Filipino Americans, Samoans, and Native Hawaiians comprising the lower levels of ethnic/racial stratification.[5] Compared to more dominant groups, Filipinos in Hawai'i lack social, economic, and political power, yet we often seek empowerment as "Americans" within a U.S. settler state. While Filipino communities in Hawai'i must continue to resist various inequalities, we must also be aware of the colonial structures engrained in U.S. nationalism which render invisible the U.S. violation of Native Hawaiians' human rights to self-determination.

By shifting our historical perspective from Hawai'i as the fiftieth state of the United States to a Native-centered history in which Hawai'i is a colony under U.S. domination, terms that at one time seemed commonsensical now ring hollow and look perversely constructed as rhetoric that functions to obscure the colonial domination of Native Hawaiians. As Native Hawaiian nationalist and Hawaiian studies scholar Haunani-Kay Trask points out, words such as "immigrant" and "local" contribute to dominant ideologies that paint Hawai'i as a multicultural utopia, eliding the colonization of Native Hawaiians and the collaboration of non-Natives with this subjugation.[6] Thus Trask has introduced the term "settler" to describe the non-Native community. The usefulness of the term, for me, is that it shatters U.S. paradigms by forcing non-Natives to question our participation in sustaining U.S. colonialism while making important political distinctions between Natives and non-Natives. I do not see the term as derogatory or, as some critics suggest, as pitting Natives against settlers. Instead, I appreciate the term because it exposes how Native and settler interests are often in opposition and consequently presents non-Natives with a clear choice, as Trask points out: "Either they must justify their continued benefit from Hawaiian subjugation, thus serving as support for that subjugation, or they must repudiate U.S. hegemony and work with the Hawaiian nationalist movement."[7] Because the United States invaded Hawai'i, Filipinos, like other settlers who immigrated to Hawai'i, live in a colonized nation where the indigenous peoples do not possess their human right to self-determination, and because of this Filipinos are settlers. The word "settler" is a means to an end. The goal is not to disagree over semantics or to engage in name calling, but rather for settlers to have a firm understanding of our participation in sustaining U.S. colonialism and then to support Native Hawaiians in achieving self-determination and decolonization of Hawai'i.

The concept of settler colonialism also disrupts notions that minorities who are racially oppressed are incapable of simultaneously participating in the colonial oppression of Native Hawaiians. Because Filipinos in Hawai'i live in a colony, our U.S. citizenship and desire for equality within a U.S. political system are crucial components of a complex hegemonic colonial structure that must be carefully questioned. For instance, although the term "Filipino American" combats the racist notion that only haole are Americans, it also asserts a U.S. nationality within a U.S. colony. For those committed to social justice, a U.S. identification is deeply problematic, because it is a colonial identity. I use the term "Filipino settler" in this essay not to reproach Filipinos but instead to challenge us to think critically of our position in the U.S. colony of Hawai'i.

COLONIAL MISEDUCATION IN THE PHILIPPINES

Filipino migration to the United States is due in large part to the U.S. colonization of the Philippines. As ethnic studies scholar Yen Le Espiritu states: "U.S.-bound Filipino migration takes place within the context of the (neo)colonial association between the Philippines and the United States. The glorification of the United States through the colonial educational system; the historically specific recruitment of Filipino nationals to serve in the U.S. armed forces as health practitioners and as low-wage laborers; and the differentials in wage and job opportunities between the two countries: all provide pressure to migrate to the United States."[8]

As Espiritu points out, the Filipino communities in the United States are founded on and shaped by the colonial relationship between the United States and the

Philippines. The historical recruitment of Filipino laborers is often coupled with romanticized colonial images of the United States as a land of opportunity, peddled in the Philippines by the colonial educational system, the media, and relatives and friends in or returning from the United States. Espiritu, however, also makes clear that Filipinos who migrate to the United States "are neither passive victims nor homogenous 'pools of migrant labor' responding mechanically and uniformly to the same set of structural forces. Instead, they are active participants in the process of migration who vary by gender, generation, class, and culture."[9] As "active participants" in the migration process, Filipinos have settled in the colony of Hawai'i, imagining it an escape from the imperial violence in the Philippines. Filipinos and many other groups are fed illusions that Hawai'i, because it is portrayed as "America," offers escape from the poverty caused by U.S. imperialism. Yet, as many Native Hawaiians have argued, Hawai'i is not America. Hawai'i is under colonial occupation by the United States, and Native Hawaiians, engaged in a struggle for decolonization, suffer the consequences of oppressed settler groups who have a vested interest in the American dream. Yet many Filipinos in Hawai'i have also argued that the promise of the "American dream" has proven false.

One example of how U.S. colonialism conceals itself appears in Virgilio Menor Felipe's biography *Hawai'i: A Pilipino Dream,* which tells the story of an aging *sakada,* or plantation laborer, named Bonipasyo, who migrated from Laoag, Ilocos Norte, in 1925 to work on the sugar plantations in Hawai'i.[10] Weaving the narratives of Lilo Bonipasyo's life in the Philippines and Hawai'i, Felipe's book situates it within these historical contexts. In the Philippines, Bonipasyo questions the colonial violence of the United States:

> We heard from elders that many barrios were destroyed by cannons of the Amerikanos. This was to hunt the Katipuneros and to scare the civilians from helping them. Many civilians were killed because they were not on guard. They were not hiding—only working to farm a living. And this is what I can't understand and I believe it is the same with a lot of Pilipinos today—why were Amerikanos hunting down our Katipuneros who were already fighting for our independence? Someone has been lying on this. All I know is that we Pilipinos do not come to America with guns and armies. We come to work in America.[11]

Bonipasyo is describing the little-known yet devastating Philippine-American War (1899–1902), in which approximately a million Filipinos died as a result of the U.S. campaign to colonize the islands. Comparing what the elders told him of U.S. soldiers killing innocent civilians and fighting against the Katipuneros while portraying themselves as "liberating" the Philippines from the Spaniards, he sees the United States as a colonizing nation.[12] His words, however, also reveal two things about Bonipasyo's understanding of his migration to Hawai'i. First, he describes Hawai'i as "America" when he states that "we Pilipinos . . . come to work in America," which indicates the power of colonialism to equate the two, eclipsing the related struggles against U.S. colonization of Filipinos and Native Hawaiians. Second, he says that Filipino sakadas traveled to Hawai'i for economic reasons, with no intent of subordinating another colonized group. Yet the colonial system in Hawai'i often maneuvers Filipino settlers to align themselves with the U.S. colonial state, leading them to unintentionally support colonialism in Hawai'i.

One of the results of colonial miseducation is to erase the connections between the anti-imperialist struggles of Filipinos and Native Hawaiians. Felipe notes in his introduction:

> Sometime while going around the island is when I began taping our talk stories. When we were past Kaneohe town by the Heeia Boat Harbor, we could see the numerous picket signs protesting to save their farming community from urban development. As I read them off loudly, "Keep the Country Country!" "Hawaiian Lands in Hawaiian Hands!" "Stop Imperialism!" and "U.S. Military, Get Out!" Lilo began to remember the first days when he arrived in Hawai'i.
>
> "Wen I came hea in Hawaii, you cannot took like dat, you know," Lilo said. And I asked, "What do you mean, Lilo?" "Da oldtimers told us when we had meeting dat making oonyoon, union, was against da law. Da govahment can arrest you or shoot you. As wot dey said. In Kauai, dey said plenty people get shot and killed," Lilo said.[13]

The picket signs protested urban and military development on the windward side of the island of O'ahu. In this moment where we might expect Bonipasyo to speak about the connection between the struggles of Native Hawaiians and those of him and his family against the Spanish and U.S. imperialists in the Philippines, Bonipasyo instead speaks about his experiences with the labor union and the violence Filipinos suffered during the 1924 Hanapepe strike, in which sixteen Filipino strikers and four police officers lost their lives. While Bonipasyo is able to make the connection between the sugar planters' oppression of the Filipino laborers and Native Hawaiians' colonial oppression, he is unable to see that the aims of Native Hawaiians, unlike those of Filipino strikers, is to reclaim their land and nation, similar to aims of the Katipuneros in the Philippine Revolution.

As Melinda Tria Kerkvliet explains, the 1924 labor strike used U.S. patriotic narratives to gain Filipino workers' rights.

> On July 27 [1924] about 1,000 Filipinos took part in a parade through the streets of Hilo. The parade started from the strike headquarters. At the head of the parade were strikers carrying a poster of Abraham Lincoln and a large American flag.... Why Lincoln and the American flag? The strikers, by displaying the American flag, probably wanted to reaffirm their recognition not only of the United States' authority

over Hawai'i but also their avowal of American values, including justice and a fair deal for everyone.[14]

Kerkvliet's analysis indicates that Filipino protests against labor exploitation also participated in recognizing the authority of the United States over Hawai'i. Although resistant Filipino laborers suffered blacklisting, imprisonment, beatings, deportation, and even death, the use of U.S. symbols such as Lincoln and the U.S. flag had ideological significance in providing support and legitimacy to U.S. colonization.

As I have pointed out, it is the concealment of U.S. colonialism in Hawai'i that leads to these deep contradictions. Dean Alegado, a scholar of Filipinos in Hawai'i, explains that the early Filipino labor leaders such as Pablo Manlapit, Cecil Basan, Epifanio Taok, and Antonio Fagel were "militant labor reformists and ardent nationalists" who "passionately supported the demands of their countrymen in the Philippines for 'immediate, absolute and complete independence' from the U.S." Alegado also writes about the leading Filipino community newspaper in Hawai'i during the 1940s and 1950s, the *Ti Mangyuna*, which reported on international events that highlighted the anticolonial liberation struggles in Asia, Africa, and Latin America and the civil rights struggles of African Americans on the U.S. continent.[15]

Colonial miseducation in the Philippines and Hawai'i thus led to a contradiction: Filipinos who took a strong stance against the colonization of the Philippines and other places unintentionally supported the colonial authority of the United States over Hawai'i. Although Filipinos in Hawai'i then may have been unaware of Native Hawaiian resistance to colonization, Filipino settlers today know that the Native Hawaiian sovereignty movement seeks self-determination. Because it is easier to see the blindness of the past than of the present, we can learn from and build on the anticolonial struggles of these sakadas.

COLONIAL MISEDUCATION IN HAWAI'I

> Spurred by parents who had no intentions to return to the Philippines, the children all considered themselves natives of the land where they were born—there was nothing else to be but American. . . . The primary drive, for the time-being was to speak English, learn about America, practice American morality and espouse American values.
>
> —Joshua Agsalud

> Today, modern Hawai'i, like its colonial parent the United States, is a settler society. Our Native people and territories have been overrun by non-Natives, including Asians. Calling themselves "local," the children of Asian settlers greatly outnumber us. They claim Hawai'i as their own, denying indigenous

history, their long collaboration in our continued dispossession, and the
benefits therefrom.
—Haunani-Kay Trask

Joshua Agsalud, former cabinet member and chief of staff under governors George
Ariyoshi and John Waihe'e and a Department of Education superintendent, and
Haunani-Kay Trask, a Native Hawaiian nationalist, express differing visions of
Hawai'i and its relationship to the United States, and of the Americanization or
U.S. colonial process.[16] Trask points out the current status of Hawai'i and Native
Hawaiians as colonized by the United States and cogently states that Asian settler
groups in Hawai'i collaborate with and benefit from that U.S. colonial project.
Agsalud's statement, written twenty years prior to Trask's 2000 article, is an example of Trask's contention, but Agsalud further explains that when he was growing
up on the sugar plantations in the late 1940s and 1950s, there was no other known
option for a national identity afforded to Filipinos besides being American. Stating
that his family never expected to return to the Philippines, Agsalud explains that he
was educated by the assimilationist philosophy of the colonial education system in
Hawai'i to "speak English, learn about America, practice American morality and
espouse American values." In this section, I use Agsalud's paper not to critique it
but to provide a historical context for further understanding the colonial influences
that shaped a Filipino national identification with the United States. Since the writing of Agsalud's 1981 paper, Hawaiian activists have worked to make Hawai'i's
history of colonialism far more visible.

Agsalud describes his experiences as a second-generation Filipino growing up
on the sugar plantation in Waipahu and speaks specifically to the state apparatuses
that shaped his views about "America" in the 1940s and 1950s:

> All the influences which shaped my views on the Americanization process were
> natural outcomes of the plantation experience. They were congruent to the scenario
> that was evolving. These influences—family, church, school and the plantation it-
> self, along with a major world event taking place at that time, World War II; the
> views that were shaped, and the process, were all American. They were not con-
> flicts among the variables, one pulling or pushing against the other—they all seemed
> to flow in the same direction, a direction which was inevitable under the circum-
> stances . . . Americanization.[17]

Agsalud states that the Americanization of Hawai'i was often viewed as "inevitable," a natural process toward "modernity." By portraying everything good,
civilized, and modern as a product of the U.S. presence in Hawai'i, the project of
Americanization declared to its colonized Native subjects and diverse settler populations that their participation in building and maintaining a U.S. system would
be in the best interests of every hardworking American. It offered an avenue of

success but elided the fact that the pavement ran over a stolen Hawaiian nation. In the 1940s and 1950s, Hawai'i experienced fast and tremendous changes as a result of specific events; the U.S. fervor attached to each of these—the bombing of Pearl Harbor, World War II, labor strikes, martial law, statehood, the Democratic Party's capture of the state, the cold war—underpinned an ideology that justified U.S. colonial control of Hawai'i. The U.S. system rewards its citizenry for being colonialist yet masks this colonization as U.S. exceptionalism. U.S. exceptionalism denies that the United States participates in colonialism or empire building and instead argues righteously that it brings U.S.-fashioned civilization and democracy even to peoples who oppose them.

As a result of the massive immigration of Asian laborers to Hawai'i's colonial sugar plantations and the racist imagining of people of color as biologically and culturally inferior, the U.S. educational system in Hawai'i acculturated both Natives and settlers of color to becoming American. Agsalud explains that though "the family and church contributed immensely to the Americanization process, unequivocally, it was the educational system which influenced the process more than any other variable." Further, "the schools were almost perfect in molding my views on being a good, successful American. As an educator, I have always subscribed to the philosophy that the public schools serve as tools for the national purpose. While some may question the effectiveness of the educational system today in meeting this goal, I am fully convinced that the schools of my time met this aim. The skills and attitudes that I developed have indeed made me a confident American."

This education system was intimately tied to the sugar plantations, as Agsalud points out: "Even the schools were dominated by the plantation influence; plantation managers were consulted regarding faculty appointments, especially the principalship."[18]

Agsalud describes himself as a "confident American" representing his American identity as fully formed and unquestionable. I suggest that Agsalud's description of himself as a "confident American" constitutes a strategy: to use a hyper-American discourse to disprove a white supremacist construction of Filipinos as incapable of becoming fully "American" and colonial stereotypes of Filipinos as backward, ignorant, and unassimilable. Through this Agsalud finds a way to assert his humanity and civility in a racist and colonialist society. But because Agsalud was a state official who held high-powered positions and who had vested interests in the U.S. system, he and his success should not be taken as representative of the experience of Filipino settlers of his generation. Although I have no intention of faulting Agsalud for such an antiracist strategy, especially in that historical moment, antiracist projects that celebrate an American nationality must be rethought, for the grim reality is that U.S. citizenship and "success" as a good citizen relied upon the U.S. "success" of colonizing indigenous peoples.

PHILIPPINE INDEPENDENCE DAY

> An American establishment usually considers ["minority newspapers"] to be
> in opposition simply because they appear in languages other than English or
> represent ethnic cultures. Their dual function, however, is peculiarly
> American: fostering assimilation into the new society while helping to
> preserve ethnic identity.
>
> —Helen Geracimos Chapin

As a journalist and former president of both the United Filipino Council of Hawai'i
and Filipino Coalition for Solidarity, the late Zachary Labez was a well-respected
community organizer and also one of the first Filipinos to publicly support Native
Hawaiian sovereignty in the community newspapers.[19] In a March 1996 issue of
the *Hawaii Filipino Chronicle*, Labez asked Filipinos in Hawai'i to support and
question their role in the Native Hawaiian sovereignty movement. In an interview
with Native Hawaiian nationalist Pōka Laenui, Labez writes that though "most
people are apprehensive if not outrightly against the separation from the United
States, . . . every citizen in Hawaii today could have a stake in the new nation, giving
the native Hawaiians special privileges that are due to them while still remaining
true to the aloha spirit for all in a multi-ethnic society."[20] Though I here point to
the limitations of his writings on the Philippine Independence Day celebrations, I
wish to acknowledge first that Labez was a key voice asking Filipinos to support
Native Hawaiians. His writings offered a critical voice that would influence other
Filipinos, including me, to support Native Hawaiian sovereignty. The problem in
his writings is not that Labez did not support Native Hawaiian self-determination,
but rather his failure to recognize the centrality of the U.S. colonization of Hawai'i
when interpreting the major events narrated in Filipino "American" settler history.

In June 2001, the *Fil-Am Courier,* a Filipino community newspaper with a
circulation of fifty thousand in Hawai'i, celebrated the 103rd anniversary of the
anticolonial Philippine Independence Movement with a three-part series of articles
designed, as Labez wrote in the series foreword, to "re-visit the past in order to
understand where we *Pinoys* are at now." Labez's articles, specially prepared for
the Talakayan Community Forum, part of Hawai'i's Kalayaan Celebration on 17
May 2001, in Honolulu (Kalayaan is Tagalog for "freedom"), contextualize the
Filipino community's history of oppression and resistance in both the Philippines
and Hawai'i. Their primary objective is to combat Filipino marginalization by developing a strategy for empowerment within U.S. society. Labez states: "Here in
the United States, we Filipino Americans find ourselves reflecting on the historical milestones perennially reminding us of how inextricably linked both countries are—our ancestral homeland we call *Pilipinas* and our adopted homeland of
America."[21] While alluding to the fact that Filipinos' "ancestral homeland" and
the United States are linked by a history of colonialism, the "adopted homeland,"

Hawai'i, is erased from this discussion. The statement equates Hawai'i with the United States, not acknowledging the current status of Hawai'i as a U.S. colony or the fact that in 1898 both Hawai'i and the Philippines were colonized. The contradiction of the Kalayaan celebration of anticolonial Philippine independence was that it took place in a colony of the United States where Filipinos were participating in the perpetuation of U.S. colonial patriotism. By obscuring Hawai'i's history of colonialism within the narrative of Filipino settler history and celebrating an American identity in a U.S. colony, the two groups' historical and contemporary resistance to colonialism is bound yet concealed.

Labez's first article, "*Pinoys* in Paradise: From the Sugar Plantations to the State Capitol," opens: "The first 15 Filipino pioneers ventured to the fabled land of Hawai'i on December 20, 1906." By dating Filipino settler history in Hawai'i to the 1906 entry of Filipino laborers, we are unable to contextualize our presence within a larger history of crimes committed earlier against indigenous peoples. Some have argued that Filipinos are free from complicity because they did not arrive until after Hawaiians had been dispossessed of their land and government. However, to focus only on the labor exploitation of Filipinos on the sugar plantations is to obscure the connection of Filipino labor oppression to the colonial dispossession of Native Hawaiians. While the overtly racist sugar plantations were exploiting Filipinos, among them my family, Filipino laborers, who were also U.S. colonial subjects, were maneuvered hegemonically within the colonial machine of the sugar plantations. Between 1906 and 1935 approximately 120,000 Filipinos traveled to Hawai'i, and while almost half went back to the Philippines or on to California, our presence in Hawai'i was critical to building and maintaining the sugar plantations and thus the colonial system. As Bonipasyo recounts in *Hawai'i: A Pilipino Dream*: "With my bare hands I helped build Hawai'i. I plowed lands for the canefields with mules, I cut cane, I *hapaiko*, carried cane and watered sugarcane."[22]

In the second June 2001 article, "*Pinoys* in America: From Philippine Sovereignty to Empowerment in America," Labez writes:

> Long before "empowerment" became a buzzword in political, economic and academic coteries of American society, Pinoys already understood its significance in the quest for dignity, acceptance and equal opportunity. Our story was, after all, a story of continuing struggle for self-determination, from the fight for political sovereignty after over 300 years of absolute rule by our Spanish colonial masters in the Philippines to the quest for a fair share of the proverbial pie in [the] "Land of Immigrants."

Labez refers to two ideas relevant to my arguments here: "empowerment" and the problems that arise when Filipinos seek empowerment without addressing colonialism, and the colonial ideology attached to "Land of Immigrants."

Filipinos have long asserted their human right to self-determination by opposing the colonial domination of the Philippines by Spain, Japan, and the United States.

The primary difference in Hawai'i is that Filipino settlers are not the colonized people, since it is not our land, resources, and government that are under occupation. Yet we live within a colonial system, and in our attempts to become "American" we align ourselves with the colonial state. "Empowerment," or our quest for our "share of the proverbial pie," becomes oppressive when the political and economic system relies on denying Native Hawaiians their right to self-determination. I am not saying that we Filipinos in Hawai'i should not resist our oppression but rather that our framework for understanding Hawai'i's political and economic system and consequent actions needs to contend with issues of colonialism.

"Land of immigrants" is an imperialist term that in three words erases fifteen hundred years of precontact Hawaiian history, Hawaiians' rights as indigenous peoples, and their claims to sovereignty. The use of the term exposes a U.S. narrative that constructs a phantasmic land with no indigenous people, vacant land where immigrants have settled to construct a "modern" democratic society. Often implicit in such a narrative is the argument that indigenous peoples also are immigrants, that Native Hawaiians immigrated to Hawai'i some fifteen hundred years ago. This reclassification of Native peoples as "immigrants" attempts to justify conquest. The use of the term "land of immigrants" reenforces a U.S. ideology that erases indigenous peoples from history and clears the way for foreign settlement.

Labez's third *Fil-Am Courier* article in June 2001, "Filipino Americans: Empowered Citizens in the Making?" challenges Filipinos in Hawai'i to realize our full political potential by organizing and becoming involved in politics: "Population growth augurs hope for greater empowerment of the Filipino community, specifically in the political area. Given the increasing visibility of the Fil-Am community, the dynamic economic opportunities in this market, and, most importantly, the rapid growth of its population. It is just a matter of time that full empowerment will be achieved."

Filipinos currently comprise 18.4 percent of the settler community, and an estimated four thousand settle in Hawai'i every year, making Filipinos the fastest-growing ethnic group in the islands. Because Filipinos in Hawai'i remain divided by generational, linguistic, and regional affiliations, solidarity is a crucial component to successful organizing, yet an important question we must ask of ourselves is whether our political leaders will advocate protest or accommodation to a U.S. colonial nation-state. One example of a Filipino settler leader who has not advocated protest but rather accommodation to the political system that colonizes Hawaiians is former governor Benjamin Cayetano.

Whose Side Are We On?

The Honolulu Academy of Arts held an exhibition entitled "*Nā Maka Hou*: New Visions," from 13 May until 17 June 2001, displaying more than one hundred works of art by fifty-eight artists, an overview of the artistic expression of Native

FIGURE 8.1. *Benocide*, by Kēwaikaliko.
Source: Courtesy of the artist.

Hawaiians in a variety of media. A piece by artist Kēwaikaliko, *Benocide*, explicitly addresses the violent effects of colonialism, specifically the collaboration of Filipino settler and former governor Benjamin Cayetano (1994–2002) with the legal assaults on Native Hawaiian entitlements.[23]

Kēwaikaliko uses art as a weapon to convey a Hawai'i that often goes unseen. Central to *Benocide* is a loaded illustration of a lynched Native Hawaiian man and his executioner, Cayetano (see Figure 8.1). The powerfully built Native man is being lynched on a tree with leaves made of money; Death, smoking crystal methamphetamine or "ice," is figured as its trunk. A haoleman in a swastika-covered aloha shirt patriotically waves the State of Hawai'i (former Kingdom of Hawai'i) flag in the face of the lynched Native. Next to him is what I perceive to be a Native figured as a *pua'a* or pig in Western-style clothing. A pua'a with tricksterlike qualities, perhaps a colluding Native, appears to be fondling Conklin's rear. Depicted in black and gray, and comprising the ground beneath this mob, are Natives who appear in all manner of suffering. The black and gray envelop the green mountain that overlooks the urban sprawl of Waikīkī. On the horizon is a nuclear mushroom cloud rising into the sky, a direct reference to nuclear testing in the Pacific and more generally to the U.S. military's devastating impact in Hawai'i and the Pacific. A note from the artist accompanied this aptly named piece: "This artwork was created in October 2000. It was completed in a week and has been getting both positive and negative feedback. Grandma hates it."

There are numerous issues interwoven in Kēwaikaliko's artwork, but I wish to focus on Cayetano's collaboration in the lawsuits that have sought to dismantle Native entitlements. At the 1978 State of Hawai'i Constitutional Convention, the Office of Hawaiian Affairs (OHA) was formed to oversee the trust assets of Native Hawaiians designated in the Admissions Act of 1959. The Admissions Act transferred an estimated 1.8 million acres of ceded lands—lands stolen by the United States at the time of annexation—from the U.S. federal government to the state to be administered in a trust-ward relationship, with "the betterment of the conditions of Native Hawaiians" listed as one of the five responsibilities of the "ceded public lands trust." In 1980 a Native Hawaiian–only vote was established to elect nine trustees who would administer OHA assets.

On 23 February 2000 the U.S. Supreme Court in *Rice v. Cayetano* opened all Native Hawaiian entitlements to legal assault. The Court struck down the 1980 voting scheme, ruling that the elections were "race based" and consequently discriminatory on the grounds of the Fifteenth Amendment. In spite of the more than 150 federal laws passed by Congress acknowledging Native Hawaiians alongside American Indians as beneficiaries of federal programs for indigenous peoples, the Court ruled that Native Hawaiians are not a federally recognized Indian tribe.[24] On 3 October 2000 a settler resident of Hawai'i, Patrick Barrett, filed a complaint in the Hawai'i federal district court alleging that Article XII of the Hawai'i State Constitution violated the Equal Protection Clause of the U.S. Constitution insofar as it created the Hawaiian Homes Commission and the Office of Hawaiian Affairs, and protected Native Hawaiian gathering rights. Barrett's lawsuit followed John Carroll's similar lawsuit, which also alleged that the creation of OHA was illegal on equal protection grounds. These lawsuits were eventually thrown out of court because the plaintiffs had never applied for any Native Hawaiian entitlement program. Kēwaikaliko's *Benocide*, completed in October 2000, is a response to these lawsuits; the haole caricature represents haole settlers like Rice, Barrett, and Carroll who use the court system to legally terminate an indigenous category.

While Cayetano is physically hanging the Native, he does not gaze at the hanging Hawaiian, but rather looks to the haole for recognition of his act.[25] This is a subtle but apt illustration of the performative role that Cayetano as a Filipino American must play in order to maintain his political position. Japanese educators and activists Ida Yoshinaga and Eiko Kosasa exposed the chain of command in the state where soon after the U.S. Supreme Court ruled in favor of the plaintiff in the *Rice v. Cayetano* case, Hawai'i's U.S. senator Daniel Inouye issued a statement to both the Office of Hawaiian Affairs (OHA) and Cayetano requesting the removal of all OHA trustees. Inouye instructed in his letter: "I believe that the Governor has authority under a separate State of Hawaii statute to appoint interim trustees so that the important work of the Office of Hawaiian Affairs need not be interrupted."[26] Cayetano, under Senator Inouye's instructions, called for the nine trustees to step down voluntarily or risk OHA's termination, and then appointed his own trustees to office. As Yoshinaga and Kosasa point out: "The intended result of Inouye's statement was to facilitate the control of OHA by the state and away from the electoral process."[27] In *Benocide*, the pua'a and Cayetano choose not to look at the lynching but instead both look to Conklin as they work within the constraints of the system struggling for subordinate supremacy. In other words, the imposing but vulnerable position of a minority within political positions of colonial power coincides with the role of affirming the colonial order that makes their position possible.

Providing historical depth to the scene, Kēwaikaliko places at Governor Cayetano's feet the bearded and bloodied skull of Sanford B. Dole, the first territorial governor of Hawai'i and a colonial official intimately involved in the 1893 overthrow and 1898 annexation of Hawai'i to the United States. Cayetano is positioned over Dole's remains and appears to have Dole's blood on his hands. The settler contest between representative figures Dole and Cayetano frame the art piece. In what Haunani-Kay Trask describes as an "intra-settler struggle for hegemony," the victor holds the noose.[28] Cayetano stands where Dole once stood, exercising political power which is only made possible by maintaining a U.S. colonial order.

By holding the noose and looking to the haole, Governor Cayetano represents the collusion of the State of Hawai'i with the legal assaults. Since the appearance of the legal challenges, the State of Hawai'i has been in the peculiar position of having to defend Native entitlements from lawsuits while being negligent in administering these same entitlements. In *Benocide*, Cayetano lynches the Native on a tree with leaves made of money. In 1991 the Hawai'i Advisory Committee to the United States Commission on Civil Rights published a report entitled *Broken Trust* stating that both the Territory and State of Hawai'i had been negligent for seventy-three years in fulfilling their fiduciary duties as trustees of the Ceded Public Lands

Trust. As a result of the report the State of Hawai'i and OHA throughout much of the 1990s were tied up in court attempting to resolve back payments the State of Hawai'i owed OHA.[29] On 12 September 2001, the Hawai'i Supreme Court ruled that Act 304 conflicted with the 1998 Forgiveness Act passed by Congress, which prohibited further payment of airport revenues for claims related to ceded lands, and was therefore invalid. The high court, however, reaffirmed OHA's right to benefit from the ceded-lands trust. Based on the ruling, Governor Cayetano ordered state departments to stop payments to OHA. He instead offered to settle the issue of repayment in 1999 with a global settlement of $251 million and 360,000 acres of ceded lands, but OHA declined.[30]

Kēwaikaliko's *Benocide* forces the viewer to see the often uncomfortable and harsh realities of colonialism in Hawai'i while asking one to bear witness to the contemporary situation of Hawaiians. I would lastly like to point out that the artwork frames the viewer as a spectator to the lynching. In much the same way that lynchings in the United States were viewed publicly and necessitated general public support or at least silent complicity, we view the lynching as it happens, from the same perspective as the other spectators, which implicates the viewer in the symbolic lynching of Hawaiians. Framing the viewer in this way, the artwork poses a difficult question: what are you going to do about this? As Hawaiian scholar Manulani Aluli Meyer asserts: "We speak to you in shapes, colors, and metaphors. We view angles distinctly; we prioritize contours differently; we have different politics based on our experience of rape, pillage and transformation. We are speaking in the language of imagery and you are learning more about the passion and priorities of a people. The time demands it of all of us. And I believe we are ready to listen."[31]

Benocide offers a vision of Hawai'i that reveals the current consequences of the blinding ideologies underpinning the current legal assaults against Native Hawaiian trusts and assets. Hawaiian artwork such as Kēwaikaliko's demystifies the illusions of Americanism, revealing the current violent effects of the legal challenges and the continued U.S. settler colonization of Hawai'i.

FILIPINA SETTLER ACTIVISM AGAINST U.S. MILITARY EXPANSION

In 2002, as a result of 9/11 and U.S. president George W. Bush's reactionary global war on terrorism, an arrangement ensued that illustrates the unequal relationship between the constrained Philippines and the imperialist United States. Philippine president Gloria Macapagal-Arroyo invoked the Visiting Forces Agreement and the Mutual Defense Treaty to invite U.S. troops to help suppress the so-called terrorist group Abu Sayyaf, a Muslim group that may have had ties to Al Qaeda. With the Philippine government's collaboration in exchange for much-needed U.S. aid, the Philippines received, as President Arroyo stated, "over $4-billion and counting" from U.S. government and private firms. President Arroyo said in a 20 November 2001 meeting with President Bush in the Oval Office that Bush repeatedly asked her what the Armed Forces of the Philippines needed to eradicate Abu Sayyaf. President Arroyo added: "What's important is that we're getting military and economic assistance that will help us in the fight against terrorism and help us in our battle against poverty."[32]

After two joint U.S.-Philippine military operations failed—Balikatan '02-1 and Balikatan '03-1 (*balikatan* in Tagalog means "shoulder to shoulder"), the United States attempted to train U.S. soldiers for a third joint U.S.-Philippine military operation to hunt down the so-called terrorist group. Native Hawaiian groups protested to stop the military from carrying out the training in the Waiâhole-Waikâne valley on the windward side of the island of O'ahu, chosen for its similarities to the rainforests in Mindanao.[33]

The history behind the protest was this. During World War II, the U.S. Army had used Waikâne and Waiâhole valleys for military training, as did the Marines in 1953. The Kamaka family, who has ancestral links to the valley, was granted a settlement in a disputed land-title case and farmed that land from 1976 to 1983.[34] The Marines, however, had failed to clean the land before vacating it in 1976; because the land was contaminated with unexploded ordnance, the Marines condemned it and the Kamaka family lost their land.

Linking the presence of the U.S. military in the Philippines and in Hawai'i, an informal collective of ten Filipinas released a statement in March 2003 entitled "Filipinos Stand in Solidarity with Native Hawaiians in Opposing United States Military Expansion"—Grace Alvaro Caligtan, Darlene Rodrigues, Melisa S. L. Casumbal, Catherine Betts, Grace Duenas, Gigi Miranda, Cindy Ramirez, Sonya Zabala, Tamara Freedman, and Maile Labasan:

> As Filipino co-habitants of Oahu, we strongly oppose the U.S. military's proposal to expand its training sites to include Waikane, Kualoa, Hakipuu, and Kaaawa, or any other sites in the Hawaiian archipelago. We demand that the US military take full responsibility for the human displacement and environmental damage caused by its usage of Hawaiian lands. We fully support the Kamaka family's struggle to hold the US military accountable for its failure to properly clean up their land. We join with Kanaka Maoli groups in calling for a return of control of all land in use by the US military to its rightful ancestral stewards and descendants.

Through a politics of diaspora that locates itself within the specificities of the history and anticolonial struggles of both Mindanao and Hawai'i, these Filipina activists stated their opposition in detailed and concrete terms. For instance, the activists voice support for the nationalist struggles in Mindanao, stating that the Balikatan operations "destabilized the fragile and ongoing process of peace talks" and resulted in the death of innocent civilians in Zamboanga and Basilan. They argued that the joint U.S.-Philippine military operations were in "violation of the terms of the Mutual Defense Treaty and the Visiting Forces Agreement," since the earlier joint operations had "not achieved their purported goal of ridding the Philippines of Abu Sayyaf." Stating that the military has created devastating environmental pollution in the Pacific and that "native Hawaiians and other indigenous peoples and nations have shouldered the brunt of military build-up," the statement asserts that the "colonization of the Philippines and Hawaii are intimately tied together."[35]

Given that Filipinos are a diaspora who, as Jonathan Okamura argues, maintain "cultural, social and economic linkages" with the Philippines, the statement of these activists helps us realize that U.S. imperialism in the form of U.S. militarism in the Philippines is part of the same imperialist global forces colonizing Native Hawaiians.[36] The activism of these ten Filipina settler activists illustrates the positive role Filipinos in Hawai'i can play in supporting the anti-imperialist struggles of Native Hawaiians and of Filipinos in the Philippines—as Filipino settlers in Hawai'i, we are historically bound by these struggles against U.S. imperialism.

Particularly significant is the combination of strength and humility in the politics of the Filipina activists. By calling for a return of all land by the U.S. military to its "rightful ancestral stewards and descendants," they locate themselves in Hawai'i in a way that respects Native Hawaiians' right as indigenous peoples to be self-determining. For Filipinos in Hawai'i to support Native Hawaiians in their struggle for self-determination, it is important that we be supporters and not leaders in this movement.[37] Here, the role of ally is not to make decisions for Native Hawaiians but to speak out against colonialism while challenging others in our communities to do the same. Members of our communities have a variety of resources, skills, and talents to offer, and the movement for self-determination occurs on numerous fronts. Identifying our own spheres of influence—including family, friends, institutions, or organizations—can be a critical way to begin to consider how we might together interrupt the cycle of colonialism.[38]

As a result of protests in Manila and elsewhere in the Philippines, the United States was not allowed to land troops in the islands. In 2003, government officials in the Philippines were able to stop the joint U.S.-Philippine military operations by enforcing the Philippine constitution's stipulation that foreign troops cannot engage in combat against Philippine citizens on Philippine soil. Although the Philippines continues to conduct joint U.S.-Philippine exercises also termed "Balikatan" in the Philippines while receiving military aid from the United States to fight the "war on terrorism," this effort to stop U.S. troops from engaging in combat against "Filipino" citizens was an important victory in resisting U.S. imperialism.

CONCLUSION

The Philippines and its more than seven thousand islands, with diverse languages, customs, and epistemologies, had no conception of a Philippines or a Filipino people before colonization appeared, along with anticolonial resistance. In 1521, Ferdinand Magellan, like Christopher Columbus three decades earlier in the Americas, named many of the indigenous peoples of the Islands "*indios*," a name that stuck for more than 350 years in the Philippines. The term was eventually dropped in the late nineteenth century when a "Filipino" national consciousness began to take shape and a large number of Native peoples who referred to themselves as "Filipinos" united to resist the domination of Spanish colonizers. Philippine historian Reynaldo Ileto, in an analysis of the Philippine revolutionary Andres Bonifacio's poem "Pag-ibig sa Tinubuang Bayan" (literally, love for the country of one's roots), explains that the poet sought to "release the people's energies in the right direction" by evoking memory to dissolve *utang na loób* (feelings of indebtedness) toward Spain and to foster utang na loób toward the anticolonial movement: "To have compassion and *utang na loób* for the mother country means participating in the act of freeing her, and by this one becomes 'Filipino.'"[39] According to Bonifacio, identifying as "Filipino" meant committing oneself to resisting colonial oppression.

The Filipino settler communities possess a fierce history of resistance to colonization and can become powerful supporters of the Native Hawaiian movement for decolonization. Racism against Filipinos in Hawai'i is a problem; I encountered it in numerous forms growing up there. While these issues hurt, anger, and hinder us, as long as Native Hawaiians remain colonized, empowerment through the colonial system means that we stand on the backs of indigenous peoples. My hope is that we instead combat the discrimination and marginalization that Filipinos in Hawai'i face while also working toward a new consciousness that supports the Native Hawaiian struggle for self-determination. To adopt an ideology of U.S. empowerment while remaining aware of the colonial structures that exist is to state that colonialism is justified as long as we are not the colonized. To remain silent or neutral is to support the status quo; if we opt for such escapism, we turn our backs on the people to whom we are most indebted. In Hawai'i, utang na loób belongs to Native Hawaiians, not to the U.S. government, because we live in a stolen Hawaiian nation and it is Native Hawaiian land, culture, and people that are being subjugated.

IV.

RESIGNIFYING "FILIPINO AMERICAN"

DYLAN RODRÍGUEZ

9 "A Million Deaths?"

Genocide and the "Filipino American" Condition of Possibility

CULTURAL ESTRANGEMENT

More than a century after its genesis in the crucible of war and competing colonial hegemonies, the historical condition—in fact, the very possibility—of a "Filipino American" relation remains a vexing question. The process of creating and reproducing this relation has encompassed the discursive-material labors of mythmaking (the production of popular knowledge, a sense of shared history, the ideological stuff of the "common"), institution building (schools, churches, economies), and formal nationhood (the "Philippines," the "United States"). Each of these presumptively progressive endeavors, in turn, suggests a teleology of definitive outcome, a social and political state of mirroring in which the post-1898 incarnation of the Philippines and Filipina/o spurs a contingent debut into modernity, a forced birthing into the American gift of liberal democracy through what President William McKinley infamously and oxymoronically named a "benevolent colonialism." Karnow insists on a narrative of parenthood and mirroring in his notoriously entitled liberal apologia for U.S. empire in the Philippines, *In Our Image*. Waxing nostalgic in the wake of the People Power movement and Corazon Aquino's subsequent rise to the Philippine presidency in 1986, Karnow writes:

> Most Americans may have forgotten, perhaps never even knew, that the Philippines had been a U.S. possession; for those who remembered, Cory [Aquino] symbolized anew that *special relationship*. During its half-century of colonial tutelage, America had endowed the Filipinos with universal education, a common language, public hygiene, roads, bridges and, above all, republican institutions. Americans and Filipinos had fought and died side by side at Bataan and Corregidor and perished together on the ghastly Death March. The United States was still in the Philippines, the site of its two largest overseas bases, and more than a million Filipinos lived in America. By backing Marcos, even as an expedient, the United States had betrayed its protégés and its own principles, but, as if by miracle, Cory Aquino had redeemed her nation—and redeemed America as well. [emphasis mine][1]

Karnow's pro-imperial text offers a convenient shorthand rendition of the Philippines-U.S entanglement, the very relation in question: it is as if the aforementioned labors producing that relation—complex, contradictory, and irreconcilable though they may be—have finally (perhaps inevitably?) *converged* in the production of a discrete, polished commodity, that which many academics (from Philippines studies to Filipino studies to Filipino American studies), entrepreneurs (from community businesses to global corporations), ruling institutions (local and national governments, the World Bank and World Trade Organization, etc.), and military officials reproduce as the intersection of the United States and the Philippines in a shared—if conflicted—history of national formation.

Fred Cordova, venerable "pioneer" and self-appointed guardian of Filipino American history, thus looks to the watershed of World War II for the seminal moment of union and nationalist solidarity between Filipino Americans, the United States, and the feminized homeland in need of vindication and rescue. For Cordova, it is the historical spectacle of Pinoys waging an "American" war—crucially, under the sanction of a suddenly solicitous U.S. military ("'Remember Bataan!' That slogan was echoed throughout every Filipino American community in the U.S. . . . as Pinoy men, women, and children geared up for the long war effort.")[2]— that constitutes the time of redemption for Filipino American history. Resonating Karnow, Cordova writes:

> Even at its earliest stages, World War Two was very real for Filipino Americans, especially Philippine-born immigrants. They had lost their "homeland," symbolic of their American-indoctrinated belief in freedom and democracy. Filipino Americans had just witnessed the fall of the Philippines. . . .
>
> As the war progressed, the racial climate towards persons of Filipino ancestry changed dramatically in the U.S. The Philippines—despite its devastation and the atrocities inflicted on wounded soldiers and innocent civilians—became America's staunchest ally in the Pacific war. Brown men from the Philippines were no longer called "Little Brown Monkeys" in America. *Overnight, they gained some respect as "Little Brown Brothers."* [emphasis mine][3]

The emergence of Filipino American studies as an academic field begs the very line of critical inquiry that its self-naming disavows: at the nexus of the intersection and sometime conflation of the "Filipino" and the "American" sits an unnamable violence that deeply troubles the very formation of the field itself. For current workers in Filipino American studies, the very rubric of the field ("Filipino" "American") naturalizes an *essential* relation of death. Under the umbrella of the "Filipino American," linguistic, religious, ethnic, class, gender, and other differences frequently lose historical specificity, as well as their inherent capacity for antagonistic contradiction, effectively disappearing through incessant rhetorics of unity. A benevolent, noncontradictory conception of "diversity" passes for complexity, and some have simply insisted on reinscribing a fetish of existential agency (one can *choose* to be Filipino American, implying that one can also choose not to be). While a comprehensive literature review of the field is beyond my intent, some examples from a recent anthology should suffice:

I have taken the liberty of defining *Filipino American* in the most inclusive sense. We are immigrants-now-citizens, American born, immigrant spouses awaiting eligibility for green cards, mixed-heritage Filipinos, students or workers on visa, *tago ng tago* (undocumented), and transnationals moving between the Philippines and the United States. Thus, *Filipino American* is a state of mind rather than of legality or geography. Under the same roof, family members hold different meanings for and attachments to being Filipino American.[4]

Whether planful or accidental, centuries of invasion and visitation by traders, seafarers, missionaries, warfarers, and colonists guaranteed that Filipinos across the archipelago would fuse multiple ethnic influences and physical features. Across families, the family portrait defies neatly delineated boundaries; *Filipinos belong to no race and belong to all.* [emphasis mine][5]

For the purposes of this chapter, Filipino American ethnic identity is assumed to be the product of our historical and cultural backgrounds and the process of negotiating and constructing a life in the United States.[6]

Such language is the contingent institutionalization of a collective identity that, in its very discursive form, implicates a historical relation of violence and domination. The currency of a "Filipino American" identity, history, community, and politic is at once the reification of a deeply troubled contact point between Frantz Fanon's paradigmatic "native" and "settler," while also a rhetorical valorization of a postconquest rapprochement between the U.S. nation and its undifferentiated Philippine subjects.

Fanon's seminal critique of the "native intellectual" resonates the historic dislocation of postcolonial Pinay/oy intellectuals from their collective, presumptively secure housing in the former colony. Disrupting contemporary pluralist and liberal multiculturalist paradigms of U.S. professional intellectualism (wherein, for example, descriptive categories of "race," "gender," and "sexuality" displace relations of power and domination—for example, racism, white supremacy, patriarchy, heteronormativity), Fanon elaborates on the qualitative conditions of domination and disruption that ruin possibility for authentic dialogue within the historical dialectic of conquest. In this analysis, the very idea of the "Filipino American" intellectual—to this point, a coherent and *presumed* intellectual subject—collapses on the possibility of its own internal disarticulation, the potentially rupturing antagonism between the "Filipino" and the "American." Fanon resonates the current state of cultural estrangement in Filipino American studies when he writes: "When we consider the efforts made to carry out the cultural estrangement so characteristic of the colonial epoch, we realize that nothing has been left to chance and that the total result looked for by colonial domination was indeed to convince the natives that colonialism came to lighten their darkness. The effect consciously sought by colonialism was to drive into the natives' heads the idea that if the settlers were to leave, they would at once fall back into barbarism, degradation, and bestiality."[7]

Fanon's longer discussion of cultural estrangement in the chapter from *The Wretched of the Earth* entitled "On National Culture" captures in shorthand an antagonistic historical tension that echoes through the field of Filipino American studies. One side of this tension involves a creeping sense of absolute cultural and historical loss—the accompanying structured legacy of the genocidal U.S. conquest. The other side of this tension is reflected in anxious assurances of authentic collective (academic and intellectual) identity: at times essentialist, though more frequently a flexible, dynamic, and straightforwardly antiessentialist (yet no less insistent) claim to Filipino American-ness that works through the logic of an existing social formation and cultural hegemony. Fanon's concern with the native intellectual is most clearly founded in his desire for a decisive departure from colonialism's cultural logic: "The efforts of the native to rehabilitate himself and to escape from the claws of colonialism are logically inscribed from the same point of view as that of colonialism."[8]

While use of the term "Filipino American" in and outside the field of Filipino American studies incorporates several dimensions of civic life—citizenship, location, national allegiance, and most importantly, a fundamental (though not necessarily exclusive) identification with "America"—I am interested in rearticulating this term as a point of contact and departure: that is, to consider "Filipino American" as the signifier of an originary relation of death and killing, the ongoing inscription of a genocidal condition of possibility for the Filipina/o's sustained presence in (and proximity to) the United States. While most scholars and researchers acknowledge the mass-scale killing and sophisticated campaigns of cultural extermination and displacement waged by the United States during (and after) the so-called Philippine-American War (1899–1905, depending on the author), few have explored the implications of this death and destruction as constitutive and productive elements of the Filipino-American (Philippine-U.S.) relation.

This essay offers a schematic reinscription of Filipino American and Filipino studies through a working, critical theory of the intersections—material, ideological, historical, and political—between (1) the United States' production of a particular relation to the Philippines and Filipinas/os through changing modalities of political, military, and economic domination (direct relations of force) and/or hegemony (structured consent under the threat of force);[9] and (2) the premises of this ongoing, dynamic relation in the nexus of genocide.

"Genocide"

A pause is appropriate and necessary here, an opportunity to consider the generalized refusal, and sometime moral objection, to the descriptive and theoretical use of the term "genocide" in current popular cultural and academic discourses. Beyond references to the liquidation of indigenous peoples in the Americas and the industrialized elimination of Jews, "homosexuals," racialized minorities, disabled people, and others under Hitler's German National Socialism, few incidents of (ethnically/racially) targeted, mass-scale physical and cultural extermination have obtained the status of authentic human holocaust. It is one of modernity's constitutive contradictions that the proliferation and evolution of technologies of killing is irrevocably tied to the varieties of social formation produced and reproduced by "modernization" itself.[10] In fact, the paradigmatic frontier question—civilization or barbarism?—has always and immediately required the marshalling of a vigorous popular might, an eager and often ritualized willingness to carry out the necessary and inevitable, if unfortunate and bloody, human sacrifice at the figurative altars of modernity (e.g., nationhood, bourgeois liberal democracy, capital).

The question of how genocide simultaneously manifests as a military and *social* logic of and for modernity is critical and overdue for producers of critical, progressive, and radical knowledges and pedagogies. This anthology presents one such opportunity for reflection on the historical and institutional location of Filipino/Filipino American studies, at the convergence of modernity's telos and its hallowed sanctuary in the U.S. academy. How might this emergent field of research, teaching, and activism take its point of departure in a historic encounter wherein the toll in human lives—the vast majority of whom would have fallen under the categorical designation of Filipina/o "civilians" rather than *ladrones* (bandits), guerillas, or *insurrecto* soldiers—was undeniably astronomical yet is forever beyond the historical record (estimates of indigenous Filipinas/os killed during the four-year U.S.-Philippine struggle range from two hundred thousand to two million)?

> An American congressman who visited the Philippines, and who preferred to remain anonymous, spoke frankly.... "You never hear of any disturbances in Northern Luzon...because there isn't anybody there to rebel.... The good Lord in heaven only knows the number of Filipinos that were put under ground. Our soldiers took no prisoners, they kept no records; they simply swept the country and wherever and whenever they could get hold of a Filipino they killed him."[11]

What are the political-intellectual implications of the historic and geographic progression of U.S. white supremacy and its genocidal logic, initiated in the territories of indigenous peoples throughout North America, sustained in the transatlantic holocaust and chattel enslavement of Africans, and momentarily culminating in the razing conquest of the newfound Philippine archipelago?

> In short, [soldiers and veterans] wanted to wage "Injun warfare." A Kansas veteran stated it more directly: "The country won't be pacified until the niggers are killed off

like the Indians." Howard McFarlane agreed: It was necessary "to blow every nigger into a nigger heaven." Adapting an old frontier adage, another veteran explained that "the only good Filipino is a dead one. Take no prisoners; lead is cheaper than rice."[12]

Such declarations of commitment to racialized slaughter are supplemented by the U.S. government's own official records (including a wealth of congressional testimony by veterans of the Indian and Philippine wars)[13] which construct a history of the Philippine-U.S. encounter that defies conventional definitions of "war." Contesting this reification of military conflict requires a more substantive theoretical engagement with the history of genocide discourse.

The United Nations' adoption of a resolution on the "prevention and punishment" of genocide in 1948 is defined by the very acts it fails to implicate. Polish legal scholar Raphaël Lemkin's original formulation of the document was comprehensive in scope and contained the outlines for effective enforcement of its content. His draft "specified that acts or policies aimed at 'preventing the preservation or development' of 'racial, national, linguistic, religious or political groups' should be considered genocidal, along with a range of 'preparatory' acts, including 'all forms of propaganda tending by their systematic and hateful character to provoke genocide, or tending to make it appear as a necessary, legitimate, or excusable act.'"[14] The prevailing superpowers of the time, however, conspired to strip the document of its definitional scope and legal context. In an interesting moment of cold-war collaboration, the United States and the U.S.S.R. forced Lemkin out of the approval process, eliminated the provision regarding the wholesale destruction of "political groups," got rid of provisions for a permanent international tribunal (instead allowing each state "to utilize its own juridical apparatus in determining whether it, its officials, or its subjects were to be considered guilty of genocidal conduct"), and deleted the full second article of Lemkin's original draft.

Critically, it was this second article that spoke to the question of cultural genocide: "In the original draft, Article II had specified as genocidal the 'destruction of the specific character of a persecuted "group" by forced transfer of children, forced exile, prohibition of the use of the national language, destruction of books, documents, monuments, and objects of historical, artistic or religious value.'"[15] The elimination of this provision was central to the eventual ratification of the watered-down genocide convention, particularly as it alleviated for the United States the burden of confronting its own history of mass-based killing and cultural destruction within its continental and transpacific frontiers. The eventual text of the UN convention allowed for little more than symbolic moral gesturing:

Article 2. In the present Convention, genocide means any of the following acts committed with intent to destroy, in whole or in part, a national, ethnical, racial or religious group, as such:

(a) Killing members of the group;

(b) Causing serious bodily or mental harm to members of the group;

(c) Deliberately inflicting on the group conditions of life calculated to bring about its physical destruction in whole or in part;

(d) Imposing measures intended to prevent births within the group;

(e) Forcibly transferring children of the group to another group.

In addition to excluding political groups and social-economic classes from the realm of target populations, the convention makes "no distinction between violence intended to annihilate a group and nonlethal attacks on members of a group."[16] This lack of specificity is only compounded by the fact that the resolution has never had any practical effect.

While most scholars, activists, and state officials have foregone critique of the UN Genocide Convention in exchange for acknowledging its significance as a landmark in human rights discourse, Chalk and Jonassohn's analytical 1990 study suggests the resolution's entanglement in the internal politicking of the UN's member countries and in broader contestations over global hegemony, including implicit and explicit assertions by individual nation-states of the militarized right to kill. In this sense, the ratified document has actually institutionalized a profound juridical contradiction—that between a radically implicating conception of mass-based human extermination, on the one hand, and a pragmatic provision of de facto amnesty to states that have carried out the largest-scale forms of wholesale categorical killing, on the other.

> Although the UN condemnation of genocide has undoubted symbolic value, it has never had any practical effect. There are several reasons for this. In negotiating the convention the member countries wanted to make sure that it applied only to the losers of World War II. . . . Another reason for its ineffectiveness is the nature of the United Nations itself. It is composed of sovereign member countries who are interested in using it as a political platform, but who are strongly opposed to the establishment of international judiciary and policing powers that would override their own sovereign powers. Since the perpetrators of genocidal killings are almost always sovereign states, it seems unlikely that the UN member countries would act against one of their own—and they have not yet done so, in spite of the fact that there have been no lack of opportunities.[17]

The contested history of the UN convention indicates the difficulty of arriving at a widely accepted theoretical, much less juridical, definition of genocide. While this essay does not suggest a closed definition of the term, it offers an intervention on the existing scholarly discourse around genocide by attempting a conceptual departure from conventional accounts of the "Philippine-American War." In this sense, Ward

Churchill's "functional definition" of genocide and his proposed revision of Article II prove most appropriate:

> Although it may or may not involve killing, per se, genocide is a denial of the right of existence of entire human groups, as homicide is the denial of the right to live of individual human beings. . . .
>
> Article II.
>
> In the present Convention, genocide means the destruction, entirely or in part, of any racial, ethnic, national, religious, cultural, linguistic, political, economic, gender, or other human group, however such groups may be defined by the perpetrator.[18]

Churchill's revision goes on to note three primary forms of genocide: the physical, biological, and cultural. Crucial for this essay is his elaborated notion of cultural genocide, a practice that I will argue was essential to the U.S. conquest of the Philippines. Churchill defines this form of categorical killing, following the line of Lemkin's original draft, as

> the destruction of the specific character of the targeted group(s) through destruction or expropriation of its means of economic perpetuation; prohibition or curtailment of its language; suppression of its religious, social or political practices; . . . destruction or denial of use and access to objects of sacred or sociocultural significance; forced dislocation, expulsion or dispersal of its members; forced transfer or removal of its children, or any other means.[19]

The remainder of this essay works through this dynamic conception of genocide, resonating the conventional notions of direct physical killing, though heavily implicating a contextualized understanding of genocide's cultural dimensions. I am especially interested in how cultural genocide has articulated through the violent progression of U.S. white modernity through and beyond its initial contact with the Philippines. This articulation, I argue, is at the unspoken nexus of Filipino American studies as an emergent institutional and discursive field.

(Dis)Locations

It is now necessary to rethink the field of Filipino American studies through its contested institutional location.

Housed in the university (as well as in other ideological/schooling institutions), Pinay/oy professional intellectuals and academics sustain the legacies of cultural displacement and disappearance as a matter of course. Few institutions of either state or civil society can claim as central a role to the trajectory of social formation as schools of higher education, shaping as they contest and transform the cultural hegemony of the United States over the rest of the world while directly facilitating relations of (militarized) force and unmediated domination over underdeveloped nations and historically oppressed communities, including the Philippines. The systemic role of the academy in training workers, soldiers, managers, owners, and rulers is inescapable—this is the institutional condition of Filipino American studies, the constraint and subversion of its socially transformative possibilities. As students, teachers, and scholars of this emerging field, our collective position and location situates us within the agendas of neoliberalism and global capital, even as some of us attempt critical engagement with or radical resistance to state and corporate violence.

The contemporary university's reproduction, in part through the pedagogical and intellectual labor of Filipina/o subjects, is more than a novel contradiction of the "postcolonial" moment, however. In fact, the uneven and ambivalent incorporation of one-time colonial and imperial subjects into the institutions and increasingly nuanced pedagogical modalities of U.S. empire might be understood as the logical and productive outcome of "modernization's" movements through historical time, in particular modernity's manifest gravity on the Philippine schools and universities erected in the idealized image of the American (-izing) education. Barbara Gaerlan, excavating this primary site for modernity's production and pretense, speaks to the entanglement of language, discourse, and education in the 1908 establishment of the University of the Philippines. Her analysis further suggests that an expansive conception of genocide—especially its articulations through cultural aggression and conquest—is necessary for understanding the constitutive logic of the U.S.-Philippine relation: "The University has been very successful in training Filipinos to pursue *modernity*. One hundred years after its introduction, the notion that modernization best occurs through English language education remains a powerful concept in the Philippines. The 'controlling domains' of language—the arenas of political, social, and economic power—continue to be pivotal locations where English is the gatekeeper."[20]

While the struggle to shut down Subic Bay naval base and Clark airfield—long crucial strategic outposts for cold war–era U.S. imperialism and neocolonialism in the Pacific region—has obtained significant attention among progressive activists and scholars in recent years (most often framed by arguments that military justifications for the base's continued operation were obsolete, and less frequently by radical critiques of U.S. global militarism), there has been little discussion of the symbiosis between the century-long U.S. occupation of and militarized hegemony over the Philippines, and the somewhat more valorized institutional legacies of the U.S. conquest and subsequent colonization (such as the University of the Philippines). While the uneven history of "collaboration" between the Filipino petit bourgeoisie and *comprador* classes and the U.S. settler state does constitute a field of critical inquiry within Filipino American studies, the lines of inquiry remain generally divorced from the 1899–1902 moment. In this sense, the era of U.S. mass killing and ecological devastation in the archipelago is constructed as an episode in the long history of Filipino/American, Philippines/U.S. relations. Yet, to take seriously that the genesis of these relations historically inscribes through the genocidal (westward and transpacific) movement of white modernity is to break with the conventions of historical periodization. The violence of this encounter with U.S. modernity intersects as it shapes time, subjectivity, and the collective life of the social.

Kleinman provides a useful schema for conceptualizing violence as an active historical force, a constitutive aspect of the social, through which institutions and infrastructures are (partially though fundamentally) shaped.

> Rather than view violence, then, simply as a set of discrete events, . . . the perspective I am advancing seeks to unearth those entrenched processes of ordering the social world and making (or realizing) culture that themselves are forms of violence: violence that is multiple, mundane, and perhaps all the more fundamental because it is the hidden or secret violence out of which images of people are shaped, experiences of groups are coerced, and agency itself is engendered. Because the cultural prefiguring and normative social workings of violence shape its consequences as forms of suffering and means of coping, such violence must also be at work in the institutions that authorize response and in the ordinary practices of engagement. *Policies and programs participate in the very violence they seek to respond to and control.* [emphasis mine][21]

Herein lies the entanglement of Filipino American studies with the generative legacy of an epochal, genocidal contact with the United States. In seeking to constitute a historical subject that reconciles the killer with the killed, the field fabricates a peculiar and powerful "Filipino American" sentimentality—a structure of affect and historical sense that forces the essential violence of the Filipino-American relation into silence and invisibility for the sake of coherence—the existential necessity for an identity otherwise permanently fragmented by a structure of irreconcilability. This sentimentality cuts across institutionalized discourses and textual forms—from academic works to popular cultural forms, there is a relative consistency in form and content, a vigorous assertion of Filipino American subjectivity that insists on the primacy of (U.S.) location and residence, a reification of (U.S.) nationhood, and the presumptive entitlements of (an admittedly ambivalent) membership in things American. A one-year survey of editorials from the *Philippine News,* the most widely circulated Filipino American publication in the United States, offers an organic glimpse at this production of sentimentality.

One series of editorials entitled "When Being Filipino Is a Plus" provides an appropriate marker for the political trajectory of this discourse. The author, Ludy Astraquillo Ongkeko, opens the concluding installment of the series by contending that, "owing to the burgeoning Filipino population in the United States, there has been a need to reflect on what has been described as the 'Filipino image' it [*sic*] stems from Filipino identity, its uniqueness and its own way of defining the pride of being Filipino." What follows in the body of the editorial text clearly outlines the investments that constitute this conception of collective identity.

> Many a time, I'm certain observers like us have been seen [*sic*] that the very persons who initially refused to have anything to do with being a Filipino take back their former stand because there are occasions when being Filipino is an advantage.
>
> The advantage of being one can be seen in the outcome of affirmative action when one can sail on being a Filipino because being so means that he/she belongs to the minority; and being so means an advantage because in the past, those slots meant only for the minority had to be filled up.
>
> (Since Proposition 209's passage in California, there might be an erosion of the pluses of affirmative action, but it is hoped that the legal system would take care that this policy be kept alive.) Although identity might be directed to the façade rather than the niche-constructing self, *it is still a decided advantage to be Filipino these days* ... because many doors are open to qualified members of the minority. [emphasis mine][22]

Complementing Ongkeko's bold inventory of advantages accruing to the Filipino American "minority," the newspaper's editor-in-chief, Alex A. Esclamado, offers a grand historical and existential vision for the "next generation" of youth. Esclamado's self-published transcript of a 1997 speech at the Filipino Intercollegiate Networking Dialogue in Stony Brook, New York, posits a direct appeal to notions of inherent biological racial superiority:

> My friends, we have a big task to transfer to you, and that is the future. The future is yours. The community has grown. Now is the time to empower you.
>
> The world is yours.
>
> You are a superior race. You are.
>
> Why not?[23]

Such vulgar and frequently bizarre formulations of identity reflect something worse than a repression of memory—this is the eclectic, organic production of a collective lifeworld immersed in sentimentality, the discursive institutionalization of a gaping silence that is in excess of trauma or revisionist denial. E. San Juan, Jr.'s materialist elaboration of a "foundational" condition in colonialism and subjugation provides a critical departure from the metaphysical obscurantism of these somewhat more popular liberal pluralist conceptions of Filipino American studies and identity.

> It is now axiomatic to hold that identity is constituted by the total ensemble of social relations articulated in any given historic formation. Premised on that principle, I offer the following theses: The chief distinction of Filipinos from other Asians residing in the United States is that their country of origin was the object of violent colonization and unmitigated subjugation by U.S. monopoly capital. It is this foundational circumstance, not the settling of Filipino fugitives in Louisiana or

anywhere else, that establishes the limit and potential of the Filipino life world here.[24]

While San Juan's critique has broad and potentially transformative paradigmatic implications for scholarship and research in Filipino American studies, here I am more concerned with its implications for the contested subjectivity of Pinay/oy intellectuals. Colonization and its historically genocidal logic suggests a radical departure from conventional notions of the subject, and fundamentally alters the political constraints through which the "native intellectual" produces knowledge.

Hegemonic Filipino American discourse inscribes a certain fantasy: the disappearance of mass-scale death, a decisive movement beyond an originary violence and toward an idealized metaphysical reconciliation between native and settler. This is a contrived peace overshadowed by its historical condition of possibility in genocide, and generative of an altogether different (though nonetheless profound) structure of violence. Following Kleinman's critique, the very grammar of things "Filipino American" collaborates in the social logic of a genocidal colonialism (and its descendants in underdevelopment, imperialism, and neoliberalism). Refracting Gaerlan's cognitive mapping of the University of the Philippines' institutional and intellectual formation, Fanon renders the image of one paradigmatic colonial subject, the linguistically assimilated native intellectual.

> To speak means to be in a position to use a certain syntax, to grasp the morphology of this or that language, but it means above all to assume a culture, to support the weight of a civilization.
>
> A man who has a language consequently possesses the world expressed and implied by that language. What we are getting at becomes plain: Mastery of language affords remarkable power.[25]

The legacy of physical extermination and cultural-ecological devastation entails far more than the formal inception of an oppressive and exploitive colonial regime: in the case of the United States' relation to the Philippines and Filipinas/os, one also finds the birth of a modernist racial pedagogy, wherein the native becomes the preeminent embodiment of progress and its unstoppable historical telos. For Fanon, colonial educated native intellectuals (the prominent subject of Fanon's political critique and anticolonial polemic in *The Wretched of the Earth*) work in a field of cultural death, advancing the mission of white modernity through a dialectical process of "adoption" and "renouncement."

> Every colonized people—in other words, every people in whose soul an inferiority complex has been created by the death and burial of its local cultural originality— finds itself face to face with the language of the civilizing nation; that is, with the culture of the mother country. The colonized is elevated above his jungle status in

proportion to his adoption of the mother country's cultural standards. He becomes whiter as he renounces his blackness, his jungle.[26]

Proximity to blackness and the jungle become primary signifiers of backwardness, premodernity, the dead past. The epochal killing of the initial contact, having allegedly and decisively ceased, is now replaced with the relative benevolence of liberal state institutions and a state-sanctioned cosmopolitan civil society, the grammar of modernity having sustained a logic of cultural displacement. Humanistic progressivism—the lifeblood of cultural conquest—restores the supremacy of modernity's presumptive white subject in magnanimous fashion, inviting the native's selective and always partial membership. David Theo Goldberg writes in *Racist Culture*:

> The spirit of modernity is to be found most centrally in its commitment to continuous progress: to material, moral, physical, and political improvement and to the promotion and development of civilization.
>
> Basic to modernity's self-conception, then, is a notion ... of a Subject that is abstract and atomistic, general and universal, divorced from the contingencies of historicity as it is from the particularities of social and political relations and identities.
>
> Enter race. It pretends to universality in undertaking to draw otherwise disparate social subjects together into a cohesive unit in terms of which common interests are either found or fabricated; ... race offers itself as a category capable of providing a semblance of social cohesion, of historical particularity, of *given* meanings and motivations to agents otherwise mechanically conceived as conduits for market forces and moral laws.... It is an identity that proves capable of being stretched across time and space, that itself assumes transforming specificity and legitimacy by taking on as its own the connotations of prevailing scientific and social discourses.[27]

Perhaps the nexus of what I have been calling the "Filipino-American relation" is the convergence between the physical extermination of an object native people and colonialism's contingent production and incorporation of native intellectuals as subjects of modernity and agents of modernization.

In turn, cultural displacement—long understood by indigenous peoples worldwide as the quintessential form of genocidal conquest—manifests in the formal structure, grammar, and institutional location of Filipino American studies. The field, in its ritualized subsumption of epochal death in exchange for a troubled historical rapprochement and a declarative U.S. patriotism, thus becomes a complex bearer of the legacy of mass extermination. Here it is the very gesture of American belonging, simultaneously a sentimental and theoretical move, that constructs the transpacific "return" of the native intellectual, interpellated by the colonizer's syntax and personifying modernity's fatal dialectic of civilization and genocide.

"Zones of Death"

Whether the site of modernity's presumptive progress is civilization, barbarism ("the jungle," in Fanon's vivid rendition), or deeply conflicted, liminal sites of contact (in the segregated and militarized post/colonial city, for example), the pedagogical mission of modernity, advancing in and through the collective whiteness of colonizers and the violent displacements of their transplanted institutions, is persistent and clear. As the trite popular saying goes, "Knowledge is power"—and in the context of genocide, the production of truth simultaneously authorizes mass-scale killing while inscribing the historical death of cultures and communities as the precondition for a backward people's authentic freedom.

Discussing a set of master texts that blueprinted the subsequent U.S. colonization of the Philippine Islands, E. San Juan, Jr. writes that,

> together with other institutional apparatuses, these texts of legitimation constructed the object of knowledge and exercised mastery over it. They were in turn authorized by a whole panoply of regulations (economic, political, cultural), at once hortatory and conciliating, governing the relations between the United States as a colonizing sovereignty and the subjugated inhabitants of the territory once administered by the Bureau of Indian Affairs. What is more insidious is that this archive has also profoundly conditioned the configuration of people-to-people relations in everyday life, sanctioning patterns of deliberation and decision-making that reproduced stereotypes and "common sense."[28]

These archival, truth-making texts performed their ideological work in and through the fabricated calm in the wake of what General Jacob Smith called the "howling wilderness" of the U.S. military campaign against anticolonial guerrillas, soldiers, and ordinary civilians alike. San Juan's appropriately blithe reflection on the convenient transition from the institutional proctoring of the Bureau of Indian Affairs to the direct control of U.S. military, governmental, and subgovernmental apparatuses only emphasizes the fundamental role of imperialist academic circles in the discursive production of the conquest and (in San Juan's terms) popular subjugation of the Philippines. These "texts of legitimation" accomplished far more than the facilitation of U.S. imperialism's "real" work (i.e., the gritty materiality of military domination, the valorous erection of "democratic institutions" in the U.S. image). Discourse, rhetoric, and knowledge production did not simply grease the gears of a genocidal machine—rather, these texts accomplished the crucial work of rendering genocide the necessary work of a civilizing conquest, providing a sober academic refraction of the mass-based killing that the U.S. government had organized during (and since) the war against the Philippine anticolonial resistance. It is this refracted rendering—an artful portrayal that literally creates a social and historical reality by selectively inventing, altering, exaggerating, and erasing its constitutive facets—in which Filipino American studies finds itself implicated.

The analytical gap that erases genocide as the condition of the "Filipino American" manifests the easy categorical distinction between physical killing and cultural death. It is as if the logic of a genocidal conquest and colonization were exclusive to the realm of the biological, satisfied simply with the end of the native's functioning body and somehow less invested in the disruption or cessation of indigenous cultural institutions and their unfamiliar modes of social organization.

The genesis of a Filipino-American relation in the 1898 moment is, most of all, constituted by its white supremacist articulation in provincially focused U.S. campaigns of mass slaughter and geographically organized "scorched-earth" destruction of farms, villages, and local ecologies. Preceding the era of industrialized warfare and weapons of instant mass destruction, it is worth emphasizing, the U.S. slaughter was utterly labor intensive, requiring extraordinary physical expenditures and strategic improvisation in the struggle to exterminate guerrillas and civilians, and to exert tentative military control over the countryside.

The stunning euphemisms of U.S. historian Brian McAllister Linn betray the substance of his own admiring gaze at the U.S. Army's practices during the "Philippine War": "Indeed, the key to the Army's success was its lack of adherence to rigid doctrines or theories and the willingness of its officers to experiment with novel pacification schemes.... In the Philippines there were no helicopters or radio communications to insure that each subordinate followed his instructions to the letter.... This lack of official control aided pacification. It not only forced individual officers to be responsible for the pacification of their areas, but also prevented interference from their superiors."[29]

"Pacification" here becomes an all-encompassing signifier for the condition that remains outside the historical record. Linn's professed adherence to "official" U.S. Army documents appropriately constructs a history of warfare that reifies indigenous actors, valorizes the complexities and contradictions of the U.S. conquest, and renders a narrative of "fascination" with military conquest at the limits of Manifest Destiny and American modernity.[30]

"A final lesson for students of guerrilla warfare," Linn suggests, "is the necessity of achieving a decisive military victory over guerrilla forces. Although benevolent policies such as education, self-government, and social reforms may win over the populace and demonstrate an alternative to the revolutionaries, they cannot succeed until military superiority is achieved.... As long as the guerrillas could rely on civilian support, whether inspired by patriotic motives or fear, pacification was impossible."[31]

Beyond the alleged military requirements of large-scale killing in this euphemistically termed U.S. "war" against a scandalous, treacherous, and generally criminal (hence apolitical) guerrilla resistance, it was the irrepressible compulsion of modernity—its "racist culture" of deadly, manifest whiteness[32]—to fantasize (and wage) genocide for life's sake. (What kind of life? Whose lives? Life where?) The 1902 congressional testimony of Brigadier General Robert P. Hughes is instructive here:

> *Sen. Rawlins:* In burning towns, what would you do? Would the entire town be destroyed by fire or would only offending portions of the town be burned?
> *Gen. Hughes:* I do not know that we ever had a case of burning what you would call a town in this country, but probably a barrio or a sitio....
> *Sen. Rawlins:* What did I understand you to say would be the consequences of that?
> *Gen. Hughes:* They usually burned the village.
> *Sen. Rawlins:* All of the houses in the village?
> *Gen. Hughes:* Yes; every one of them.
> *Sen. Rawlins:* What would become of the inhabitants?
> *Gen. Hughes:* That was their lookout.
> *Sen. Rawlins:* If these shacks were of no consequence what was the utility of their destruction?
> *Gen. Hughes:* The destruction was as a punishment. They permitted these people [guerrillas] to come in there and conceal themselves and they gave no sign....
> *Sen. Rawlins:* The punishment in that case would fall, not upon the men, who could go elsewhere, but mainly upon the women and little children.
> *Gen. Hughes:* The women and children are part of the family, and where you wish to inflict a punishment you can punish the man probably worse in that way than in any other.
> *Sen. Rawlins:* But is that within the ordinary rules of civilized warfare? Of course you could exterminate the family, which would be still worse punishment.
> *Gen. Hughes:* These people are not civilized.[33]

The indigenous population of the Philippines, to resonate several aforementioned quotations from military personnel, was not simply being compared or reduced to "Indians" and "niggers" through a transplanted racial analogy, readily available to the presumptively white U.S. nationalism of statesmen, generals, commanding officers, and rank-and-file soldiers. In this state of contrived war, where the distinctively U.S. rendition of modernity's aggressive movement through place and time entailed the production of (racialized) enemy/others, "Indians" and "niggers" constituted categories of death. This was the bottom line of U.S. modernity, that its path toward the good society required the categorical death of categorical others.

"Categorical death" suggests a leap beyond the realm of the biological, a modality of nonexistence that begs for more than corpses and mass graves, a process of mass killing that demands extraordinary endings, outside the realms of physical destruction waged by the U.S. military's turn-of-the-century "dum-dum" bullets and slaughter strategies. Filipinos embodied the continuity of conquest en masse, a Pacific native population that both occupied and exceeded the discourses of "Indians" and "niggers," while sharing the essential distinction of living for extermination and selective, coercive assimilation into a white (American) modernity—the very crystallization of categorical life.[34] "As early as April 1899, General Shafter gave grisly portent to the future conduct of the war: 'It may be necessary to kill half the Filipinos in order that the remaining half of the population may be advanced to a higher plane of life than their present semi-barbarous state affords.'"[35]

The notion of a "zone of death" constitutes an appropriate allegory for the relation that provides theoretical and structural coherence for Filipino American studies amidst its anxious discourses of membership, entitlement, and belonging. Taking the terroristic campaign in Batangas province as a defining incident, the fundamentally coerced nature of this coherence becomes clearer:

> In the "zone of death" outside the camp "dead line," "all rendered themselves liable," according to Bell. All property was destroyed, all houses put to the torch and the country was made a "desert waste . . . of death and desolation." According to statistics compiled by U.S. government officials, by the time Bell was finished at least 100,000 people had been killed or had died in Batangas alone as a direct result of the scorched-earth policies, and the enormous dent in the population of the province (which was reduced by a third) is reflected in the census figures.[36]

At the temporal and historical limit of the Filipino-American relation remains the desolation of the dead line. This is the manifest and allegorical border of "pacification," the condition of possibility for the production of the very discursive field under examination. The impossibility of simply grasping, negotiating, or reconciling with the dead line—as it delineates categorical death for those who wander, approach, or cross—thus forms the underside of Filipino American studies' institutional (and ritualized) logic of progress, especially as underwritten by notions of participation and historical presence within the U.S. social formation. In this sense, incoherence is the field's unspoken, undertheorized, though constitutive center.

Attention to the impact of a white supremacist genocide in the archipelago—including and beyond its formal military aspects—requires a rupturing from the problematic of U.S. imperial benevolence and democratically inspired altruism that is frequently reified in Filipino American studies. There is, after all, a historical subject that dies, breaks, disappears, and emerges in and through this genocidal encounter with the United States. Here we find a potentially radical point of departure for Filipino American studies, a critical rupturing from its relative normalization of identity, relation, and place (here an imagined Filipino America) that is permanently troubled by the power of modernity's civilizing conquest.

ANTONIO T. TIONGSON, JR.

10 Reflections on the Trajectory of Filipino/a American Studies

Interview with Rick Bonus

TONY TIONGSON: What constitutes Filipino American studies? Is it just a matter of scholarship focusing on Filipinos conducted primarily by Filipino scholars?

RICK BONUS: This question pokes at me every time I offer a course on Filipino American history and culture or give a crash course on it for a workshop or miniconference. Of course, each scholar will have a different take on it, but I'm positive we will probably also come up with several common points when given a chance to compare thoughts. Many of us have been in conversation with each other anyway informally and in conferences, and a lot of us, I'm sure, read each other's work from time to time. I attended a conference once in Berkeley on Filipino studies and one important thing that came out of many discussions is that we can imagine Filipino American studies as having no center or set parameters established by individual scholars or small exclusive groups. Rather, we can think and "do" Filipino American studies from many different nodes that are bound together by a common interest in a specific group of people but not necessarily beholden to each other, as if one cannot do something without somebody else's permission. I think it was Vince Rafael who said this, and I support his idea.

Filipino American studies, like its objects of study, constitutes a heterogeneity of ideas and scholars themselves who employ a variety of disciplines, and artists and humanists as well. Its nodes don't have to be occupied solely by people who consider themselves Filipino or Filipina. I think we learn much from "others" such as Ronald Takaki, Lisa Lowe, Yen Le Espiritu, Stuart Creighton Miller, Daniel Shirmer, Stephen Shalom, and more, as much as we learn from ourselves who get counted as Filipina or Filipino. Scholars from our communities get to see things that others don't, and scholars from outside our communities get to see things that we may not see ourselves. I believe this is the best way to think about and understand the tricky relationships between identity and scholarship. Nobody owns Filipino American studies, and if one claims so, we ought to be suspicious. I have a strong sense that because Filipino American studies is understudied and so few of us from this category do it, some of us worry when others pick up the task. I think worrying is not bad per se, but beyond worrying, we must be open to engaging with other scholars in ways that are productive for the field. This task of undoing ourselves from the restrictive and exclusionary boundaries of "authentic identity politics" is one that is not too easy to do, but we can also use it as material itself for theorizing about identity and representation in general; who can speak for whom? for example.

TT: Why is it important to have an institutional space?

RB: Of course it is important to have an institutional space or spaces for Filipino American studies because it needs to be nurtured and sustained. I'm assuming that you're referring to academic institutional space here, so if that's what you mean, I strongly think that it deserves a space because it is a legitimate and serious field of scholarly inquiry. And even if one says that such a field is heterogeneous, multiply defined, and relationally constructed—that is, it intersects with other fields and constructs—it still necessitates some form of intellectual coherence, it needs to exist within some form of framework to bring together a kind of working vision for it, and it has to have a kind of supportive infrastructure to keep it going. Or else, it's very easy to have it fall apart or just remain scattered in different places. Historically, for many who do Filipino American studies, we can think of the more established Asian American studies as an institutional space that has provided us quite a bit of nurturing. Of course, we also have particular disciplines like English, literature, history, the social sciences, and so forth, that offer spaces, although very limited, for doing Filipino American studies.

TT: Could you specify the standard assumptions, categories, and analytical frames within Filipino American studies? Within Asian American studies, for example, Gary Okihiro points out that the tendency is to conceive of "Asian Americans" in narrow terms—as male, heterosexual, and working class. In addition, the thrust has been to locate analysis within the confines of the United States and to conceptualize Asian American history and subjectivity in terms of immigration and settlement. Do you see a similar logic or set of tendencies operating within Filipino American studies?

RB: Because Filipino American studies in large part was originally integral to and, to a good extent, later grew out of the formation of Asian American studies as an institutional structure, I do see a similar logic and set of tendencies if you put them side by side. To this day, almost all Filipino American studies in academia is subsumed under Asian American studies. The rest is done under the rubric of a particular discipline or set of disciplines within a multidisciplinary program such as American studies or American ethnic studies. Even so, Filipino American studies in these places, I think, draws from the scholarship produced in Asian American studies especially, because the expectation is to at least have a conversation with it. Most importantly, many of us who are engaged in Filipino American studies either studied with or are heavily influenced by Asian Americanists. I concur with Gary Okihiro. We see certain patterns operating, specific emphases being privileged, and dominant assumptions and frameworks being stressed. Of course, most of the work that's being done is quite United States–centric, many of them focus on historical and contemporary patterns of immigration and settlement, and a significant number "presume" the heterosexuality of their subjects of study. But I don't think this is so much a function of being gripped by standards as it is about building a corpus of scholarship that has to start from somewhere and eventually move beyond. Because there are so few of us doing Filipino American studies right now, it is inappropriate to assume that we're stuck in this logic. There's little scholarship in the first place, but it is growing, and so much more exciting and innovative work is going to come up soon.

TT: Do you see a shift taking place in terms of the principal paradigms and discourses informing the study of Filipinos?

RB: I see many shifts taking place in scholarship on Filipino Americans and, on the basis of what I know from people who teach Filipino American studies, I see a good variety of alternative pedagogical trajectories being offered as well in terms of course work. I think that the most important shift that's taking place right now involves a reorientation of the historical rendition of Filipino American experience from one that is strongly based on immigration and settlement to another that connects Filipino presence in the United States with the larger histories of imperialism, colonization, global capitalism, racialization, and gendered labor, and their attendant contemporary manifestations. This is not altogether new. The bulk of E. San Juan, Jr.'s work on Filipino American studies, including the scholarship of Oscar Campomanes and, to a certain extent, Renato Constantino, the edited volumes of Maria Root and Enrique dela Cruz, the personal histories of Carlos Bulosan and Philip Vera Cruz—all have raised fundamental claims, whether implicitly or explicitly, regarding the inappropriateness of applying the immigrant narrative to the study of Filipino Americans. It's definitely inaccurate to lump early twentieth-century Filipinos in the United States into the immigrant model, because of their colonized status. If one assumes that immigrants come in out of choice, then many Filipinos cannot be considered under this term because they were actively recruited or even forcibly ejected out of their homelands as a consequence of capitalist encroachment, militarization, and colonial education. San Juan has a famous line that says the story of Filipino American immigration begins not at the moment of arrival in the United States but prior to that and long before departure from the Philippines. The shift is taking place now because many of these works are getting more accessible and taught in graduate school and in undergraduate courses, but Filipino Americanists have already been working within and through these frameworks for many years, and not only from the purviews of history, but also in the ways contemporary community efforts brush up against these histories. Soon, we will encounter the published works of several emerging scholars who will come from these perspectives. Augusto Espiritu, Kimberly Alidio, Linda N. E. Maram, Dylan Rodríguez, Nerissa Balce-Cortes, and Eric Reyes are but a few.

Another shift that's taking place at the moment involves the growing breadth of Filipino American studies that moves beyond the United States as the principal locus of identity and community formation. Again, this is not something that's totally new. Campomanes wrote a seminal essay on Filipino American literature that collectively resists the United States as the terminal point of being and becoming Filipino American. San Juan, in almost all of his writings on Filipino Americans, takes a global perspective on the interlocking histories and contemporary trajectories of capitalism, racism, and sexism. Martin Manalansan's work on Filipino gay men is always situated within and beyond the borders of both the United States and the Philippines. And Rhacel Salazar Parrenas's book *Servants of Globalization* is about Filipina labor across several locations. We can definitely say that the movement of Filipino and Filipina labor on a worldwide scale that was begun at least a century ago, that was a fundamental component of the U.S. global or imperial project, and that is increasing rapidly in this century, is a condition that has preoccupied our scholars.

Lastly, I want to mention a most important and critical shift that's taking place not so much yet in Filipino American scholarship, but one that's been brewing for quite some time already in classrooms, conference sites, forums, and so forth. This shift involves Filipino American studies and its relationship to Asian American studies in terms of identity, community, and political alliance from one that appeared to be solid in an institutional sense to another that is materializing as a set of complex and difficult conversations. I find it tricky to narrate such a history here because I only started to become active in Asian American studies in 1992 and we're still waiting for someone to do a more thorough discussion of this relationship that goes all the way back beyond 1992 to the founding moments of Filipino American studies. It is a relationship that's been fraught with questions regarding how Filipino Americans became "Asian Americans" and whether or not that identification will persist, especially in the aftermath of the Michigan and Hawai'i conferences of the Association for Asian American studies. In the Michigan conference in 1994, for example, many Filipino American scholars raised questions about the association awarding a book to an author who allegedly perpetuates Filipino stereotypical representations in her work. And this happened again in 1998, surprisingly and in a very messy way. Hawai'i was indeed a defining and climactic moment, as many would like to imagine it, because many Filipino American scholars' relationship with the institutional formation of Asian American studies became more vexed and, to some, unbearable. Even though many of the discussions focused on a particular book that was being given recognition, this event raised very important larger and uneasy questions about the presence or, for some, absence of adequate Filipino voices in the association and in Asian American studies in particular.

This is as much a question of identity as it is a question of power. Many Filipino Americans here in Seattle, for example, resist being identified as Asian Americans not only because they realize how "different" we are from Asians in many ways, but also they know that Filipino Americans turn into a minority when included within the larger group of Asian Americans. In other words, they don't see the benefits of being part of this larger group. As a matter of fact, they see themselves losing out because their histories are marginalized and their power is minimized. And because many of them have stronger identifications with other groups, they have chosen to be called African Americans, Native Americans ("Indipinos," as Fred Cordova would report), Chicanos/as, or most especially, Pacific Islander Americans. I think this stance is getting stronger from ground level, and I'm sure that many of us who teach Filipino American studies are being nudged by this with more frequency now. Some institutional data-gathering procedures have already recognized this call by either disaggregating the Asian American count to have a separate count for Filipino Americans or by removing the Filipino American count from the Asian American category altogether to have Filipino Americans be listed separately. It is a condition that we need to address with caution and sensitivity. I try to explain to my students that Filipino American studies scholars recognize this unique dilemma: we need Asian American studies because it provides us with the necessary institutional framework and resources, but at the same time, we have trouble identifying with the category like you do. Some scholars, including myself, have suggested that for the time being, we need to consider ourselves "included, but under protest." It is indeed a condition that is unsettling both for Filipino American studies and for Asian American studies, but it is also one that has precipitated provocative discussions about the processes of identification themselves, offered different ways of asking, picking subjects and objects of study, using traditional frameworks, and theorizing, and one that continues to connect scholarship with questions of power.

TT: I wonder if you could talk about the dearth of Filipino Americanists in places you would expect to see them—in ethnic studies and Asian American studies departments across the country.

RB: It is annoying and definitely worrisome. Do we have someone at U.C. Berkeley? University of Colorado? Oregon? Harvard? USC? But it's not puzzling. There are still only a few of us, and I think many of these departments, unfortunately, still follow that "one [Filipino Americanist] faculty is enough" rule. San Francisco State is an exception, of course. So in places like ethnic studies departments where there's a Filipino Americanist, you could expect that that's the only person there, all alone. We're still fighting for legitimacy and value in many places, and many of these places, I assume, use our presumed limited numbers to not even attempt to hire. The good thing, though, is that those of us who do Filipino American studies can be found in other departments besides ethnic studies or Asian American studies. I know many of them who chose to do this, and I can imagine that they're also there by circumstance.

TT: What are the broad social and theoretical relevance of the study of Filipinos? In other words, what analytic possibilities does a critical study of Filipinos open up?

RB: The study of Filipinos and Filipinas tells us a wide variety of stories to theorize about so many important issues and conversations that are immensely significant to fields such as ethnic studies, American studies, women's studies, area studies, and the disciplines. I know I'm speaking from an interested position here, being a Filipino Americanist myself, but looking at the scholarship and pedagogy that have been produced so far, I think that it is a field that attracts scrutiny precisely because it draws attention to questions such as those that involve identity, situated knowledges, relevance, and interested positions. I make a claim in all of the courses on Filipino American studies that I teach that Filipino American studies should be read and taught not for Filipinos and Filipinas alone, but it should be for everyone. It is about American empire, about wars and colonization, about popular culture and representation, about global capitalism and the recruitment of particularized labor, the processes and consequences of racialization, the productions and use of gendered and sexualized subjects, the formations of collectives and solidarities, the building and maintenance of communities of resistance—all using the complexities and specificities of Filipino/Filipina experience as both products and productive of uneven relationships of power.

You see, especially with regard to Filipino American studies, these themes help us move us away from the usual "search for milk and honey" analyses of migration history that are quite limited in their descriptive emphases anyway. They assist us in rethinking the study of Filipinos and Filipinas from a view that is so bent on resettlement and assimilation, or even on victimhood and hopelessness, to one that considers people as proactive agents who do creative ways of making sense of their lives, and one that regards domination and oppression as nonmonolithic and impermanent. Of course, the study of Filipinas and Filipinos is also informed to a great extent by the works of and by other groups: Malcolm X, Gandhi, the Magon brothers, Russell Means, Lili'uokalani, among others. It is absolutely imperative that we don't study ourselves in isolation; that would be inaccurate and bad scholarship anyway. We can draw parallels and significant insights with one another within and beyond and in relation to our categories. Work through these with the uniqueness of Filipino and Filipina colonization and subjecthood and you'll get a kind of analytical force that is much more nuanced, sophisticated, and sensitive to larger stories.

TT: How do Filipinos as "objects" of study disrupt the disciplinary boundaries of Asian American, Philippine, and American studies? How would you characterize the relationship between Filipino American studies and Asian American studies?

RB: I already addressed part of this before, but maybe I ought to clarify that it is not so much a disruption of the boundaries of Asian American studies solely, as it is a disruption of the boundaries of any kind of category, be it Philippine or American studies, or even Filipino American studies. There is an unsettling of the boundaries of Asian American studies mostly because that's where Filipino Americans have been classified. That's where we're most prominent and, I guess, that's the chosen primary site of initial and sustained intervention for those who are in academic work. It is a strained relationship, but I'd characterize it more as an ongoing conversation. I'm a member of the board at AAAS [Association of Asian American Studies]; so was Martin Manalansan for a time, Dorothy Cordova before us, and others. So, it's not like we have turned our backs completely. I know others have already done so, but from my end, I think we have more allies there than in other places for now, and I believe there are more and more people in the association who recognize, understand, and respect our unique relationship with the category.

Philippine studies is a site that I am not that thoroughly familiar with, but I suspect that with the increasing awareness of the politics of Filipinoness outside the Philippines, there's a lot of rethinking about what that category "Philippines" implies, at the very least. I venture a similar notion with Asian studies. American studies is a much wider arena and one that has undergone more radical changes lately, specifically when one looks at the transformations within the American Studies Association, where we see more and more people like us participating more actively and investing in positions of power. We have a few Filipino Americanists in American studies programs too; people like Cathy Pet-Choy and Theo Gonzalves. American studies is a much wider arena, but the intervention work that is needed there is very important because scholars come from many disciplines and are bound to have the question of the "Americas" and "Americans" at the top of their research agendas. I think Filipinos and Filipinas as objects of study in this field have crucial and convincing responses.

Well, there is one arena that you missed which I think deserves attention, and that is the category of Filipino American. It's quite easy to miss but it's critical to my earlier point about being suspicious of any categorization, basically because categorization assumes and, to a good mainstream sense, requires homogeneity and some form of consensus. I write about this in my book as well, regarding this running joke about being called Ilokano and not Filipino. I think it's still provocative to raise this issue every now and then to remind us about our heterogeneity in many different respects, from province of origin to migration generation to U.S. regional affiliation, profession, and so forth, as well as to call our attention to questions and practices of power, including the oftentimes unmentioned hegemony of Tagalogs. And this is not to suggest that we should do away with categories, because they do have some use. It is to call our attention to the creation, processes, and consequences of categorization and to constantly ask ourselves what we lose and what we gain out of it.

TT: Even as you acknowledge its limited utility, do you also find the category "Filipino American" problematic? Do you find the terms "Filipino" and "American" incommensurate?

RB: Yes, it is problematic, as I alluded to earlier, but let me clarify that I recognize its limitations in certain contexts, not its limited utility. There are many ways we can understand the term, and there are enormous possibilities for continuing to reconfigure the term. So I argue that it doesn't mean that the category shouldn't exist or we should do away with it. Rather, it must be seen as a work in progress, always taking into account the ways in which it originated, how it is practiced now, what is being missed out on, and the constant transformations—demographic, political, intellectual, among others—it is and will be experiencing.

There has been much talk and work lately about the shifting terrains of intellectual and cultural work in Asian American studies, for example, that nudge us to think about many changes in our populations, from the increasing number of non-U.S.-born "Americans" to the proliferation of transnational populations, as well as the limitations of the "national biases," as Chandan Reddy says, that are inherent in the traditional organization of Asian American studies scholarship and pedagogy. Such a demographic transformation will not be appropriately and adequately dealt with if we continue to limit ourselves to an American-centric framework or to a model that privileges only and merely continuity and stability. But, given these ruptures in our fields of study, I don't think we have to be immobilized or that we should just give up. These ought to be occasions for us to rethink our models, keep the work alive, and continue to make our work situated, interesting, and relevant.

Now, as far as incommensurability is concerned, that is a question we can grapple with as long as we are in this business, so maybe the best way we can deal with it is to keep the question alive and the responses open-ended. Incommensurable for whom? we can ask. For many Filipino Americans I talk with outside the university, and as I argue in my book, they do aspire to and currently work on coming to terms with both categories at the same time. They want to be called Filipino as much as they want to be called American, on their own terms, because they believe they are both. Incommensurate terms in view of what? Historical relations and perspectives? As a political or intellectual project? As terms for building and maintaining identity and community? We need to be specific about our deployment of such a description. We need to take seriously how we're talking about incommensurability and for what reasons. In many ways, I don't see the two terms existing on separate fields, even though they are unequal to each other and they exist on a playing field that is not level, and once you combine them, we have to recognize that such an inequality gets reinforced all the more. In fact, the hierarchies get to be more prominent. They obviously are not commensurate to each other in this case because of how they are marked in relation to each other, with the term "Filipino" getting the negative—secondary—brunt of the equation. Again, this doesn't mean we have to insist on commensurability as a project, nor should we keep the two terms always apart from each other. Rather, we should be sensitive to each term's and each combination's inflections and elaborations.

TT: Finally, could you discuss the relationship between Filipino American studies and Filipino communities? Does this division even make sense to you? So for example, instead of conceiving of "community" as a formation "out there," do you consider universities and colleges as community sites?

RB: I get annoyed when questions like this come up, and so does my friend Martin, whose definition of "community" always includes the university community. This arbitrary division between and across communities is an invention of dominant culture that we don't need to accept, although we are forced to deal with it oftentimes in settings that unquestionably insist on such divisions, both from the university side and the public "community" side. Filipino American studies was not an invention of dominant culture. It came from the people. But the fact is that now, in some places, it is a part of the institutions—communities themselves too—that it is trying to transform or, on occasion, dismantle. This conversation about communities, I think, mostly comes up when people are accused of forgetting this history or neglecting to reflect on the realities of institutionalization and the work of transformation. That is how I make sense of these divisions.

But we should also remember that those of us in academia are routinely faced with challenges coming from all angles about what we do or even down to the point of what we *intend* to do and how we are developing our battle plans. Oftentimes, it's outrageously tiring and difficult work, and it doesn't get easier when we are misunderstood or unrecognized. Plus, the university is a space that can seduce scholars to tone down or take a different track for the price of some very appealing rewards. On the other hand, some of those who are not in academia unfortunately dismiss us very quickly and myopically, losing track of the fact that scholars like ourselves operate in and through several communities within and outside the campus. I think it's time for us to simply try to speak of and serve communities in the plural, or in situation-specific as well as relational tenors and instances, instead of privileging only one understanding of "the community."

11 Do You Mis(recognize) Me

*Filipina Americans in Popular Music and the
Problem of Invisibility*

In the summer of 1997, a crowd of several hundred, mostly young and mostly Filipino American, packed onto an expanse of dry grass before an outdoor stage at the Santa Clara Fairgrounds in San Jose. The audience had grown slowly during the hot and windless Saturday afternoon for Summer Fest '97, a "veritable Filipinopalooza" (noted the local music press in a front-page feature) that celebrated the arrival of Filipino Americans in popular music (Jam). The almost two-dozen performances of fashion, comedy, martial arts, hip-hop breaking, and different genres of popular music were more than enough—Kai, the R&B group that would taste its own stardom the following summer, performed one boy-man short, and Shortkut of the Invisibl Skratch Piklz and KYLD-FM's Rich Laxamana supplied their turntable skills—but what the masses had gathered for was the headliner and closing act, Jocelyn Enriquez. The dance-music artist had briefly left a nationwide tour to grace an event that celebrated, as well, her growing celebrity and that of a handful of other Filipino American music artists. What had started in the 1980s with mobile DJs in Filipino American neighborhoods, a scene compared by some to the early days of hip-hop in New York City (Cook), flourished. Filipino American DJs were soon winning DJ showcases and mixing at clubs and local radio stations (Wang). Some of these mobile DJ crews would become "turntablists" and move on to dominate international hip-hop DJ competitions and collaborate with some of the biggest-selling rap artists of the day. Others founded indie record labels that by the early 1990s were producing *Billboard*-charted hits by more than a dozen Filipino American solo artists and groups, including their most spectacular, Jocelyn Enriquez.

That summer evening on the stage, four male dancers—black, white, Latino, and Filipino—surrounded Enriquez in visible acknowledgment of her crossing the racial boundaries that define Latin freestyle, house, and R&B and claiming these genres as a Filipina American. I watched Enriquez from the center of the third row; to my immediate left were three teenage Filipina Americans. They had arrived mid-afternoon and watched the various acts with alert but casual interest. But once Jocelyn took the stage, rapture overtook them: it wasn't possible for anything human to scream louder. The girls' total identification—eyes wide open and fixed on Enriquez, hands clasped at their throats—was astonishing. They had waited to experience live and surrounded by hundreds like them, if only for an hour, what until then had been private listening before suburban bedroom radios, a quick dance on a high-school gym floor, or a garage-party get-together: Enriquez's intimate confessions of love promised forever, then abandoned in the next track, with the loss forgotten momentarily amidst thumping shouts of joy about family and dancing. Perhaps after the show, hundreds of Filipino Americans would return to their car CD players or bedroom boom boxes and engage the repeat function to reimagine the physical thrill of her voice, the audience's communal roars of adoration.

These moments of identification before Filipino American music artists and amidst overwhelmingly Filipino American audiences would be replicated dozens of times across the country that summer: at various stops on Enriquez's "Dance across America" tour; at DJ battles in the San Francisco Bay Area and New York City; at Filipina Fiestas—annual talent showcases held around Philippine Independence Day. The slew of Filipino American events and the provisional communities in the form of concert audiences during the summer of 1997 were unprecedented. And that summer, for most Filipino Americans the catalyst for community was the Northern Cali–born-and-bred Enriquez. She may have been welcomed as *kababayan* (countrywoman) on her tour of the Philippines later that summer, but the *india* Enriquez could never have emerged as a pop star in a country where popular culture idolizes anemic, light-skinned, thin-nosed mestizas. Jocelyn was absolutely Pinay.

But accompanying the mass adulation were the doubts and *tsismis* (gossip) that seem to plague any Filipino American who gains a bit of public visibility. Amidst her popularity with young Filipino Americans, Enriquez contended with skepticism over her racial authenticity and loyalty. She was accused of passing herself off first as Latina, then as black to attract listeners who would not accept someone identified as Asian American performing Latin freestyle, house, or R&B. She never denied her Filipina American identity or her loyalty to Filipino American communities; but her dark complexion, angular features, and Spanish surname allowed her visual representation to be maneuvered between prescribed Latina and black images that define dance-music genres.

But if one's perspective of the controversy shifts from her culpability to the social and musical contexts wherein racial interpretation occurs, invoked are larger problems of identity and community that Enriquez shares with all Filipino Americans. Filipino American identity is characterized by a sense of metaphorical invisibility: though the second-largest Asian American group, Filipino Americans are not represented in mainstream culture as often as other even smaller and more recently arrived Asian American groups. Indeed, the fact of Filipino Americans' status as the second-largest Asian American group is usually received with surprise and skepticism (Roley, "Filipinos"). This invisibility may be attributed to their categorization as Asian American and their experience of racial ambiguity upon not conforming to others' perceptual expectations of Asian Americans. Enriquez herself has compared her not being recognized as Asian to being lost: "Because you know, being Filipino, we get lost. People don't really know what Filipinos are. If you're Asian, you're either going to be Chinese or Japanese" (Amirrezvani).

My test case for a theory of Filipino American invisibility is the debate over Jocelyn Enriquez's racial representation and her fidelity to Filipino American identity and community. I narrate Jocelyn Enriquez's emergence as one of the 1990s' most popular music artists and the most successful Filipino American or Asian American solo artist to date. Though Enriquez's story is one of racial negotiation through musical genre and visual representation, by now it should be clear that I do not join a misguided chorus of "J'accuse." I intend to chronicle and account for a condition of racial ambiguity familiar to Filipino Americans, who are seen as everything and anything but Filipino, whose sense of ethnicity (despite a zeal verging on overcompensation for anything and everything Filipino) remains weak as others fail to reciprocate how they see themselves. To accuse Enriquez of ethnic treason assumes there exists some essential Filipino American representation, when in fact a Filipino American racial discourse does not exist. The absence of such discourse, in turn, sets the conditions of the racial subjects' transparency to others. It signals the constructed and fictive nature of race and—insofar as an unproblematized notion of Asian American panethnicity and others' ideological investments in its durability reinforces the fiction—the manner in which this fiction presents itself as unbending reality. In a less obvious but no less perplexing manner, there waits the potential for any Pinay or Pinoy to pass, just as Jocelyn was absorbed into others' racial vision.

THIS IS THE BIG LOVE: JOCELYN ENRIQUEZ AND THE RACIAL AMBIGUITY OF A PINAY DIVA

Jocelyn Enriquez was born in San Francisco to immigrants from the Pangisinan province of the Philippines and grew up in various Filipino American communities in the San Francisco Bay Area. She was a member of the San Francisco Girls Choir and a vocalist for her parents' cover band, the Nite Owls. In 1993, while an undergraduate at San Francisco State University and a member of Pinay Divas (now known as Pinay), Enriquez was recorded covering Jaya's "If You Leave Me Now" at a family gathering. The tape was seen by freestyle-dance producer Glenn Gutierrez. Gutierrez, who claims mixed white, Latino, and Asian ancestry, had played keyboard for Stevie B, the most popular freestyle artist of the 1980s. With Dadgel Atabay—a Filipino American high-school classmate who would go on to claim two gold records and later start his own label, Velocity Records—Gutierrez produced Jaya's "If You Leave Me Now." In the early 1990s Gutierrez left Stevie B and joined Classified Records, a fledgling Filipino American–owned-and-operated independent label based in the San Francisco Bay Area. Seeing much promise in Enriquez's musicianship, beauty, and charisma, Classified signed her as one of its first artists. Her first single, "I've Been Thinking About You," made the *Billboard* 100. Enriquez's debut album, *Lovely*, a freestyle tour-de-force, revived the moribund freestyle scene and heralded the arrival of "new school" freestyle. Freestyle fans of various backgrounds claimed the album as theirs: the lyrics to "Make This Last Forever"—"Tell me, tell me where it all began. / We didn't know how far / or where we were going / Somehow, we never stopped knowing that / Love, would keep us together this time"—were interpreted as a retrospective homage to old-school freestyle and a declaration of the genre's resilience. Musically, the song acknowledges its diverse influences: in the bridge, a sequence of different music genres moves from a piano montuno to turntable scratching to an ultraheavy electronic bass drum; the sequence's components represent, respectively, new-school freestyle's influences of Latin music, the mix DJ, and South Bronx–born old-school freestyle. *Lovely* won its producers, Gutierrez and Mario L. Agustin, Jr., the 1994 Best Producers of the Year Award from the dance-music trade publication *Dance Music Authority*. And to mark Enriquez's arrival as the new-school freestyle diva, the group 1 A.M. recorded a love letter to "Ms. Lovely" called "Jocelyn" (1 A.M.).

Despite the critical success of *Lovely*, the album started a controversy among Enriquez's Filipino American listeners. Understanding this crisis requires knowing a little bit about the musical and social background of freestyle. Called alternately "eighties disco," "Latin hip-hop," and "Latin freestyle," freestyle developed as a dance-music genre that had splintered from MC-oriented rap when, according to Raquel Z. Rivera, "the growing African Americanization of hip-hop during the 1980s" alienated Puertoriqueños among hip-hop's racially diverse audience (89). In addition to its popularity with Puertoriqueños and Chicanos, freestyle is claimed as an anthem of ethnicity by, on the East Coast, Italian and Greek Americans and, in California, Filipino Americans. With an electro sound attributed to Afrika Bambaataa and the Soul Sonic Force's 1982 song "Planet Rock" (Rivera, 88), and Afro-Cuban rhythms and syncopated percussion introduced the following year by Shannon's "Let the Music Play," old-school freestyle and its electronic drums, ethereal synthesizer riffs, and Latin percussion behind a vocalist's melodic line defined popular dance music until the late eighties. It was revived in the mid-nineties as a "new school" of freestyle, distinguished from its predecessor by thick synthesizer layers, faster tempos, and the influence of house music.

As the previously mentioned "top 15" freestyle chart established, new-school freestyle has many Filipino American participants. But whether Pinays and Pinoys on the freestyle charts or even the Filipino American listeners who identify with them are recognized as Filipino is another issue. Freestyle's image remains

FIGURE 11.1. Jocelyn Enriquez/"Lovely"
(CLS-2010-2)/Classified Records 1994
Source: Courtesy of Planet Hype
Records.

overwhelmingly Latino, encouraging the first rumors regarding Enriquez's identity. Enriquez's visual representation on the cover of *Lovely* pushed these rumors further (Figure 11.1). It emphasizes the brown tones of Enriquez's skin and is angled from above as if to obscure her face. Someone not attuned to Filipino American freestyle artists could conclude that with a Spanish last name, the artist must be Latina. Furthermore, the single of "I've Been Thinking About You" included a Spanish version of the song. According to Enriquez in an interview, a prominent San Francisco–based Chicano DJ who first spun the song on the radio had encouraged her to record it (Llamas, 19). Classified Records executives later defended "No Hago Mas que Pensar en Ti" as a business decision based on the predominantly Spanish-speaking freestyle market (Consul).

But Filipino Americans, as descendants of former colonial subjects of Spain, received the Spanish version of "I've Been Thinking About You" as more than an appeal to freestyle's Latino audience. In the Philippines during Spanish colonization, the colonial administrators and Catholic friars prevented native Filipinos from learning Spanish in order to keep their linguistically diverse colonial subjects divided. Even toward the middle of the nineteenh century, when a sizable mestizo middle-class had access to Philippine and European universities, no more than 5 percent of the Philippine population understood Spanish. Present-day Filipinos continue to associate Spanish with the elite, disdaining those who favor Spanish over an indigenous Filipino language as attempting to be something other than Filipino. The accusation of ethnic shame thus fell upon Enriquez, to her surprise: asked in an interview about the rumor that she was passing as Latina to woo freestyle dance's predominantly Latino audience, Enriquez was stunned (Ubalde, "Jocelyn

Enriquez," 3, 5; Friar, "Making a Place," C3; Meno, 29). Interestingly, during this same period several black R&B artists recorded Spanish versions of songs sung originally in English in order to expand their listener base to Spanish-language radio in the United States, Mexico, and Latin America. But where black popular music artists need not worry about being identified as anything but black in a cultural context where the terms of racial difference are aligned with blackness, a Filipina American artist singing in Spanish within a Latino musical genre encounters both Filipino antagonisms of race and social class from the Philippines' history of Spanish imperialism and Filipino American anxieties about being perceived as Latino.

To promote her debut album, Enriquez performed throughout California, Texas, and Florida, regions where freestyle's popularity never abated. She performed as well at Filipino cultural events such as the annual Fiesta Islands celebration sponsored by the Philippine Consulate in San Francisco and at collegiate Filipino American events throughout California. When she accepted the 1996 San Francisco Bay Area Music Award (BAMMIE) for best dance-music artist, Enriquez thanked the Filipino American community. Filipino media in the San Francisco Bay Area reciprocated her gratitude: the San Francisco magazine *Filipinas* featured her on the cover of the July 1994 issue with another Filipina pop music artist, and again on the September 1998 cover.

Meanwhile, Classified Records became admired in dance-music circles as a producer of well-crafted freestyle, house, alternative, and hip-hop music by its diverse roster of music artists. But of all its artists, Enriquez was the only one whose music sold, and Classified nearly went bankrupt. During the production of Enriquez's second album, Classified entered a joint-affiliate agreement with the New York City label Tommy Boy. Established in the early 1980s and known mostly for hip-hop, Tommy Boy featured a dance-music subdivision, Timber! which produced many successful freestyle and house artists and a twelve-volume freestyle compilation series. Tommy Boy, while technically an independent label, had major label distribution through Warner Brothers, making it an attractive business partner for the much smaller and financially unstable Classified. Under the joint agreement, Tommy Boy would determine the marketing and distribution of albums while Classified controlled musical production. The second album, *Jocelyn,* was produced mostly by Glenn Gutierrez. A crossover album intended to introduce Enriquez to mainstream popular music listeners, it is one-third freestyle, one-third pop-oriented dance/club, and one-third ballads with a *kundiman*. Classified had released the freestyle song "Do You Miss Me" as its first single. Tommy Boy rereleased "Do You Miss Me"; but in deference to the dominance of house music on the U.S. dance scene during the 1990s, Tommy Boy chose as its second single release what ultimately became the dance/club anthem of 1997 and the seventh-best-selling maxi-single of 1997, "A Little Bit of Ecstasy." Both songs were lauded by the music industry: at the Winter Music Conference, the dance-music industry convention held annually in Miami, Enriquez won the award for best freestyle single in 1997 for "Do You Miss Me" and in 1998 for "A Little Bit of Ecstasy."

But though "A Little Bit of Ecstasy" was recognized as freestyle, it had been adapted to mid-nineties dance radio, which was most influenced by house. Characterized by steady drum and base lines under thick, pulsating synthesized chords, house had emerged in Chicago dance clubs and spread to East Coast cites to become regarded as the primary inheritor of disco's legacy. Racially, it is associated with an East Coast, urban black aesthetic. So on the public talk pages of the Classified Records Web site, Enriquez would be criticized for abandoning a Latino form for an African American one. And under Tommy Boy's influence, Enriquez's visual representation would be pushed in a direction that correlated with her move toward African American music. The photograph gracing the cover of the maxi-single "A Little Bit of Ecstasy" comes from the song's music video (Figure 11.2). Through clothing associated with urban African American culture, braids black and blonde, skin darkened through colortiming, dark eye shadow, and a "fierce" look which sharpens and rectangulates her countenance, Enriquez could be misrecognized as black were she presented in an African American musical context. Likewise, the song features Enriquez scat singing while another female voice echoes her in a call-and-response pattern seen as characteristic of black music. In response to the song and her visual representation, Enriquez was accused of trying to pass as black, as she had been accused of trying to pass as Latina on her previous album. Enriquez defended her representation in the "A Little Bit of Ecstasy" music video and single covers as her portraying an Indonesian princess (Friar, "Making a

Figure 11.2. Jocelyn Enriquez/ "A Little Bit of Ecstasy" (CLS-0190-2)/ Classified Records 1997
Source: Courtesy of Planet Hype Records.

Place," C3). While this may be true, such an attempt to represent herself as another Asian nationality fails, since the American and Filipino American recognition that Enriquez "looks Indonesian" relies on their preconception of things Indonesian, a knowledge that most Americans (Asian American or not) do not possess.

The controversy over Enriquez's representation in promotions of "A Little Bit of Ecstasy," however, was not as intense as the previous one over "I've Been Thinking About You." After the accusations came to her attention, Enriquez became more diligent in her outreach to Filipino Americans. During the 1997 Dance across America national tour in support of *Jocelyn*, Enriquez took time off from the tour to perform at San Francisco's Fiesta Islands celebration as well as the San Jose Summer Fest. The CD maxi-singles to "Do You Miss Me" and "A Little Bit of Ecstasy" close with one-liners or speeches by a heavily accented *manong* character named Mr. Bolisario. In the acknowledgments section of *Jocelyn*, Enriquez thanks profusely the Filipino American community and dedicates the album to them. To erase any doubts regarding Enriquez's identity, integrity, and racial loyalty, *Jocelyn* includes a Tagalog kundiman, "Kailanman." Accordingly, the cover photo of *Jocelyn* represents an "Asian" Jocelyn: her skin tone is yellow; her long, layered hair creates an oval frame around her face; and her eye shadow extends toward her temples to emphasize her eyes' almond shape (Figure 11.3).

Accepting images where Enriquez "looks Asian" as the closest approximation to a Filipina American representation is tempting. Though often reluctant to call themselves Asian American, Filipino Americans accept that they are racially Asian and would approve of Enriquez's arrival at what might be seen as the correct strategy of Filipina racial representation. Yet to place the weight of racial representation

FIGURE 11.3. Jocelyn Enriquez/"Jocelyn"
(CLS-3049-2)/Classified Records 1997
Source: Courtesy of Planet Hype
Records.

FIGURE 11.4. Jocelyn Enriquez/"Do
You Miss Me: The Remixes"
(CLS-186-2)/Classified Records 1996
Source: Courtesy of Planet Hype
Records.

upon the individual Pinay is to evade acknowledging that a Filipina American in an everyday situation—not a Pinay before a photographer, a fashion stylist, a hair stylist, a make-up artist, a lighting coordinator, an art, design, and editing director, a producer, a project manager, and a troop of record-label executives—may still be misrecognized as something other than Filipina. Consider the cover of the Tommy Boy single release of "Do You Miss Me" (Figure 11.4). Except for an inversion of the photo still (the moles on the right side of Enriquez's face are actually on her left), this is one of the most unmediated of all of Enriquez's promotional photos. But position this photo among those of Latino freestyle artists, such as in the insert to the Tommy Boy compilation album *Freestyle, Volume 10,* and look again (Figure 11.5). Placed in a Latino context, Enriquez can be misrecognized as Latina. The markers we believed would alert us to a Pinay's presence fail.[1]

WHY ARE FILIPINO AMERICANS "INVISIBLE"?

First of all, what was a Filipina back then? Filipina girls, we didn't even register on the radar. None of you registered on the radar, you know: straight, long black hair; dark skin; Chinese eyes; buck teeth; and a Mexican last name. *(changes voice)* You're not on the chart. You're not on the chart. You don't exist. You're *other."*
—Comedian Rex Navarrete

An examination of the ways Jocelyn Enriquez's appearance has been pushed between expectations of what makes one "look" Latina, black, or Asian reveals

FIGURE 11.5. Various Artists/
Freestyle–Greatest Beats: The
Complete Collection, Volume 10
(TBCD 1191)/Tommy Boy/Timber!
Records 1997.
Source: Courtesy of Joey Gardner

the constructed nature of racial categories and their mediation through cultural forms such as music, photographs, Web sites, and music videos. A narrative of Enriquez's performance of various dance-music genres foregrounds the social context wherein racial interpretation takes place.[2] But the onus of responsibility is placed solely on the Filipino American subject in the few Asian Americanist observations of the Filipino American experience with racial ambiguity, or the instigation of the questioning of a person's racial background. When one Asian American sociologist claims that "Filipinos look like other races," his statement places on the defensive those who do not conform to the "look" of the Asian American category to which Filipino Americans are assigned (Liu). Filipino American racial ambiguity is attributed not to the specificities of context, social construction, and mediation, but to hybridity. A consequence of centuries of colonial and trade encounters between Filipinos and everyone else, hybridity offers a partial explanation for their racial ambiguity, but it becomes insufficient when one considers that others of alleged belonging—be they black, white, Latino, or Native American—are no less interracial than Filipino Americans. Anatalio C. Ubalde, in an essay about his white-Filipino background and not being recognized as Filipino, surmises that his dilemma comes not from his being mestizo but from the absence of a categorical "Filipino" physical appearance (Ubalde, "Mestizo"). In discussing racial ambiguity, it helps to bear in mind Omi and Winant's definition of "race," that "although the concept of race invokes biologically based human characteristics (so-called 'phenotypes'), selection of these particular human features for purposes of racial signification is always and necessarily a social and historical process" (55). Hybridity in relation to the rigidly defined categories of race in the United States then becomes understood not as a biological condition, but as the category to which a marginal group is assigned when that group has yet to achieve the hegemony to project a monolithic image of itself, or when the hegemonic group has yet to recategorize the marginal "hybrid" group into a singular race.[3]

Asian Americanists are unable to address the constructedness of race because their notion of panethnic identity relies upon an inadequate conception of "racial lumping," or white hegemony's inability to distinguish between persons of different ethnicities and national origins. One effect of lumping becomes the elision of instances that challenge a panethnicity based on a perception of Asian Americans as "Asian." Deviations are treated as evidence of heterogeneity within a liberal pluralist model of Asian America rather than as symptoms of the limitations of its racial discourse.[4] The presence of racial ambiguity does not by itself invalidate lumping as a conceptual tool for understanding the position of Filipino Americans within Asian American panethnicity. Racial lumping, insofar as Filipino Americans continue to be classified by state institutions as "Asian American," will at certain registers cast them similarly to other Asian Americans. But the many instances of their misrecognition challenge assumptions regarding its dynamics. To explain the contradiction that they pose to racial lumping, the critique must shift from Filipino Americans to the processes of racial interpretation. To perceive and interpret a person's racial identity does not necessarily yield that identity, unless information confirming the person's ethnicity or race is immediately at hand. Rather, racial interpretation operates through the confluence of several factors: preconceived notions of race; immediate context; and perceived information such as skin color, facial features, dress, hair, accent, name, social class background, education, or neighborhood. The point at which one's ethnic or racial identity must be inferred from these factors we may call *perception*. Where one's ethnic or racial identity is known and confirmed, that point we may call *cognition*.[5] Perception and cognition represent mechanisms within the conceptual mapping of race; when this racial mapping is accepted as unchanging and essential, it creates and reproduces the structures of domination known as racism (Omi and Winant, 71). Cognition often leads directly to racial identification; however, information attained perceptually may contradict cognitive information and delay such identification. For example, someone who knows another person is Filipina American but does not understand why, if she "looks Asian," she has a Spanish last name, may be unable to place the other in her racial mapping.

While perception and cognition (or, respectively, "you all look alike" and "you all are alike") as components of racial identification may or may not lead hegemonic thinking about different Asian Americans to the same conclusion, Asian

Americanists treat perception and cognition as interchangeable cogs and assume their results are always identical in all cases. But perception can outweigh cognition in how one is identified, as well as in how one identifies. Katya Gibel Azoulay, writing on the identities of individuals of Jewish and black descent, argues for a dynamic model of identity formation which emphasizes the context of racial interpretation, representation, and politics over racial descent (30–31): "I do not think one can overstate that how one identifies and how *one is identified by others* have a mutual impact on the range of identities from which one chooses a position. The question of physical appearance—phenotype—in the United States has had a significant impact on how people identify and are identified, as evidenced by laws, social practices, and attitudes affecting people who in the past were involuntarily but officially categorized as "Negro" or "Colored" (8). Racial ambiguity rather than passing (which connotes an individual's deliberate assimilation into another racial community through physical appearance, the performance of race, avoidance of family, and the erasure of memory) has become the dominant concern for those of interracial descent (101, 104). Azoulay offers an anecdote about her two sons' divergent experiences at a black student camp. The darker-skinned son had deliberately taken up the gestures, dress codes, and hairstyle of "blackness," which "facilitated [his] entry into the Black student camp without the subtle pressure of proving himself demanded of his older, lighter-skinned brother" (25). This son insisted as well "that his Black friends respect the fact that he was Jewish and that his white friends respect his being Black." Their experiences with racial ambiguity refute notions of race defined exclusively by ancestry. As Azoulay puts it: "The very expression 'to look white' indicates the explicit invention of a category whose meaning cannot exist on a visual level but only as an ideological construct" (91).

Those of interracial background share with Filipino Americans chronically misrecognized as not Asian a mercurial sense of how they are perceived. Yet because a Filipina American often has Filipino parents, racial identity at the level of cognition is settled and she has the possibility of an unconditional Filipino identity and an unworried Asian American identity. Cognitively certain what she is, she remains perceptually undefined. It is in this rupture between the instability of perception and the certainty of cognition that we begin to identify the racial discourse for Filipino Americans. This rupture finds its expression in a Filipino's testament to racial discrimination as reported in the *San Francisco Examiner*: "When I applied for a job with Kaiser, they weren't very friendly with me until they found out I was Filipino. When they thought I was Hispanic, the treatment was quite different" (Nakao). Perceptually she is Hispanic; cognitively she is Filipina. Not recognized as Filipina until she identifies herself, she is racialized according to any of the other acknowledged racial groups she approximates—in this case, as Latina. In other words, her invisibility takes the shape of *perceptual absence,* that though categorized as Asian American, she is not recognized or treated as such.

Granted particular confluences of bodily presentation and context, Filipinas can defy the perceptual display expected of Asian Americans.

If perceptual absence helps account for the social condition that Filipino Americans call more commonly "invisibility," why is this the case? What is at stake in excluding Filipino Americans from the racial discourse by classifying them as Asian American but treating them as otherwise? To see how and why it is possible to be oblivious to the second-largest Asian American group, the moment at which Filipino Americans become subject to perceptual absence must be located in the Asian American historical narrative and more broadly in a genealogy of U.S. race relations. An insistence on Filipino Americans as cognitively Asian American despite perceptual contradictions is ideologically necessary to a hegemonic conception of relations between different nonwhite groups, especially after the civil rights movements of the late 1950s through the early 1970s. But because this ideological investment in Filipino American invisibility is shared both by white hegemony and by a liberal pluralist construction of Asian American panethnicity, an alternative historical genealogy of Asian America must be offered. Before the civil rights movements of the mid–twentieth century, in the white imagination not all Asians were alike or described in similar terms. And Filipinos were not "invisible"—they existed palpable and distinct. During the U.S. Senate debates over Philippine annexation and the Philippine-American War, Filipinos were represented similarly to Native Americans and portrayed in the same racist caricatures as blacks (Williams). During the late 1920s and early 1930s, as tens of thousands of *manongs* migrated to the West Coast, state laws were amended to segregate and disenfranchise so-called Malays (San Buenaventura). During the "race riots" over Filipino men's consorting with white women, articles and editorials in white newspapers showed that those opposed to "miscegenation" thought themselves capable of distinguishing between various Asian immigrants and colonial subjects (Wood). The photograph of a Stockton boarding house sign which reads, "Positively No Filipinos Allowed" encapsulates the pre–civil rights racialization of Filipinos as Filipino (Cordova, book jacket).

After World War II began what Omi and Winant call "the great transformation" of the U.S. racial order. Through the civil rights movements, nonwhites gained access to political systems and brought about social change through "the interaction of racially based social movements and the racial state" (Omi and Winant, 88). Seeking institutional recognition in reaction to racial lumping, various Asian ethnicities joined together and created the term "Asian American," a cultural nationalism that helped to "link distinct groups who were racialized as one monolithic entity" (109). But whites protective of the privileges of hegemony reacted to nonwhite struggles for recognition by altering the racial discourse. As Adrian Piper has observed: "Stereotypes change in accordance with changes in the objects of political discrimination, as different populations seek access to the goods, services and opportunities enjoyed by the advantaged" ("Two Kinds," 50). White hegemony drew upon stereotypes of Chinese and Japanese as industrious and docile workers, racist perceptions present in the United States since the nineteenth century and invoked to pass various Asian exclusion acts, and reconceptualized Asian Americans into the "model minority" who succeeds in the United States despite being nonwhite and who is held up as an example to blacks, Latinos, and Native Americans (Takaki, *Iron Cages*, 219–40; *Strangers*, 474–84, 497–502). In tandem with the "model minority" stereotype, its corresponding perceptual expectations developed: straight black hair, yellow skin, slanted eyes, an "oriental" last name. Asian Americanists reacted against the "model minority" stereotype and attempted to refute it. However, the construction of Asian American panethnicity upon racial lumping led Asian Americans to accept the perceptual expectations of the "model minority." In fact, to better gain access to the racial state of the post–civil rights era, it was in the interest of Asian Americans to internalize the structure of racial categories, consent to hegemony's perceptual expectations of Asians, and represent Asian Americans as such. In order to assert their presence in the racial state, Asian Americans along with white hegemony began privileging those who met the rigid demands of racial lumping: racial lumping does not mean "you all look alike," but "we *make* you all alike."

Asian Americans pliable to orientalist notions of Asian difference are favored in regard to representation, and subjects such as Filipino Americans are not seen as Asians but misrecognized for other nonwhites according to the individual's perceptual display and immediate context. Since race as an ideological construct makes it inconceivable that an Asian can "look Native American," "look Latino," or "look black," the individual is called Asian American even as she is treated otherwise. Her body is erased between its perceptual and cognitive acknowledgments, and she becomes lost within the Asian American category. It is this fissure between race as visible phenomenon and race as ideological invention that now characterizes the Filipino American experience: that as blacks are made hypervisible through the "one drop" mandate; as Asian Americans are "model minorities" and Latinos are expendable cheap labor, and both are subject to irrevocable foreignness, Filipino Americans experience perceptual absence or, metaphorically speaking, invisibility. In the post–civil rights U.S. racial order, Filipino Americans do not and cannot exist.

Filipina/o Americans as Neocolonial/Asian American Subjects

Filipino Americans have thus far two complementary responses to their metaphorical invisibility. When looking for historical moments to mark the beginning of their vanishing, they invoke not the post–civil rights coalescence of the "model minority" stereotype but the arrival in the Philippines first of Magellan, then of the U.S. Navy, attributing their invisibility to Spanish and U.S. imperialism. The Spanish destroyed pre-Hispanic Philippine culture and imposed Roman Catholicism and, in many cases, Spanish surnames; then the U.S. colonial project of "benevolent assimilation" brought U.S. institutions and popular culture. So when Filipinos immigrated to the United States, they found themselves readily misrecognized as Latino and acclimated to a U.S. culture incapable of acknowledging its "little brown brothers" as neocolonial subjects (Campomanes, "Filipinos in the United States"; Balce-Cortes and Gier, 70; Espiritu, *Filipino American Lives*, 1; Lowe, 11). Oscar V. Campomanes, who first identified the trope of invisibility in Filipino American culture as an actively generated ideological effect, sees discourses of U.S. imperialism overdetermining the Filipino American "incommensurable sense of nonbeing": "The invisibility of the Philippines became a necessary historiographical phenomenon because the annexation of the Philippines proved to be constitutionally and culturally problematic for American political and civil society around the turn of the century and thereafter" ("Filipinos in the United States," 50, 53). Campomanes calls invisibility both symptom and mechanism of a culture of U.S. imperialism, that the domestic national culture of the "mainland" must deny the presence of neocolonial subjects in order to maintain its historical and moral alibis for empire abroad.

The second response to invisibility involves a categorical assertion, even in the face of perceptual and cognitive contradictions, that Filipino Americans are Asian American. The homogeneous racial representation of Asians as the "model minority" is refuted with a liberal pluralist model of Asian American panethnicity, an umbrella broad and diverse enough to cover all Asians, including Filipinos. In spheres where they are not underrepresented compared to other Asian Americans and have at least the same cultural capital and access to resources, Filipino Americans take the Asian American mantle without hesitation. Such has been the experience of Filipino Americans in popular music, like Jocelyn Enriquez. After countering the accusations of racial infidelity which followed her early in her career, she became not solely a Filipino American but an Asian American idol. The major-label distribution of her second album and her brief association with Tommy Boy had boosted her national visibility to make her a staple of Asian American festivals and collegiate conferences, including some at elite institutions where few Filipino Americans are enrolled as students. So at places like Northwestern University, where in 2000 its Asian American Advisory Board brought Enriquez to perform before a student audience of East Asian Americans, whites, and gay men, her exhortations "Asians make some noise!" was received with the same raucous energy that young Filipino Americans had reciprocated at Summer Fest three years earlier.

These two responses together gird the most widely accepted refutation of invisibility—that Filipino Americans are Asian Americans with multiple colonial legacies—and inform Filipino American assertions of visibility through cultural practices that appeal to a construction of Philippine indigeneity. They attempt to resolve racial ambiguity into fixed and definitive signs of Filipino identity and provide a means for Filipino Americans to announce themselves to non-Filipinos and each other. Leny Mendoza Strobel, calling the pervasiveness of this strategy the "born-again Filipino" movement, catalogs their activities:

> They write in *alibata*, the ancient alphabet still used by the Mangayan tribe in the Philippines; they sport *alibata* tattoos that say "*kayumanggi*" (brown skin) or *taga-ilog* (Tagalog, or "from the river"); they learn *kali* and *escrima* (indigenous martial arts); they write poetry in Pilipino and do research on the anti-colonial resistance movements. Through e-mail, they circulate lists of "what makes a truly Filipino home," referring to the traditions brought over to the U.S. Student groups print T-shirts with indigenous images framed by quotations from Jose Rizal, and proverbs like "*Ang hindi marunong lumingon sa kanyang pinanggalingan ay hindi makakarating sa paroroonan*" (Whoever does not look back to where he came from will not get to where he is going). (39)

Enacting such an ethnic identity satisfies a demand implicit in the critique of Western imperialism's influence on a "colonial mentality"–stricken Filipino American, namely that it be anticolonial. More significantly, indigeneity mimics those aspects of Asian American identity that both establish cultural alterity and locate Filipinos on a cognitive map of race shaped by U.S. orientalism. In these representations of the indigenous, observes Barbara Gaerlan: "Filipino Americans found a merging of Hollywood and the broader Orientalist conception of American culture which very effectively belies the exceptionalist argument that the United States escaped the legacy of colonialism" (258).[6] A Philippine representation to parallel East and South Asian ones as the "East" is created and an orientalist notion of difference fulfilled (Prashad). If Filipino Americans cannot "look Asian," they can enact a cultural difference that proves they have an ancient, exotic, mysterious, spiritual civilization, just like other Asians.

By foregrounding the influence of Western imperialism on Filipino American identity, the neocolonial theory of invisibility accounts for the difference between Filipino American and Asian American identities at the register of cognition and explains why even individual Pinoys whose appearances approximate Asian phenotypes—Filipinos who "look Asian"—may find it difficult to identify with an orientalized notion of Asian American culture. Their objection—that they are seen as Asian, but never as Filipino—addresses a cognitive map of race that orientalizes Asian Americans and cannot account for a neocolonial identity whose resonance in the United States is one of hybridity. The neocolonial framework, however, does not work consistently with other minority groups who also claim a colonial relationship with the United States. If the culture of U.S. imperialism must efface

colonial subjects because their presence contradicts the national mythology of anticolonial origins, then Filipino Americans alone should not suffer invisibility. But
one group of colonial subjects, Puertoriqueños, do not see themselves as chronically misrecognized due to imperialism. Their colonial identities are elided when
domestic-based racism lumps Puerto Ricans with other Latinos and relabels these
U.S. nationals as foreigners, but such an elision does not result in de facto invisibility (Rivera). This counterexample suggests that the neocolonial explanation, in
citing empire in a foreign geography to account for the domestic experiences of
neocolonial subjects (who may have never stepped foot in their ancestral land),
misses a critical step and needs to reconsider the neocolonial subjects' experience
of the culture of U.S. imperialism within national boundaries. Amy Kaplan reminds
us that challenging the denial of American empire by examining culture in the history of U.S. imperialism includes "relating those internal categories of gender,
race, and ethnicity to the global dynamics of empire-building" and seeing "how,
conversely, imperialism as a political or economic process abroad is inseparable
from the social relations and cultural discourses of race, gender, ethnicity, and class
at home" (16). A theorization of invisibility as an imperial discourse pins down one
variable that affects Filipino American identity, but it says little about what happens to them in the more immediate context of U.S. race relations. This omission
pertains especially to Filipino Americans who identify with communities based
in the United States and who may recognize themselves in a second-generation
Pinay poet like Jean Vengua Gier: "I am interested in the predicament of second,
third, fourth and even fifth generation Filipino American writers who have come
to identify with a specific American landscape and locus of culture(s), who speak
English as their first language, whose parents or grandparents decided to settle
in the U.S., yet who still continue to feel set apart, foreign" (6). One "locus of
culture(s)" includes the terrain of struggle for justice and civil rights on the part of
racial minorities. Such history is mutually constituted by struggles abroad against
imperialism; but for racial discourse–deprived Filipino Americans, a language that
allows them to understand themselves as racially constituted subjects as do other
people of color is yet emergent. In other words, Filipino Americans experience
the culture of U.S. imperialism through a domestic, post–civil rights discourse of
race (or, rather, the absence thereof). Without these additional terms, the insuffi-
ciency of the neocolonial framework becomes apparent when one considers, for
example, that an African American/Afro-Carribean/Puertoriqueño convergence in
hip-hop, not a notion of Philippine indigeneity, informs Filipino American DJs.
Their activities, institutions, and achievements signify something more than Pinoys
assimilating into a more dominant cultural practice and (something Filipino American hip-hop heads have been accused of) trying to "act black." Guided solely by
a neocolonial critical hand, the ancestral line between José Rizal and Mixmaster
Mike looks sketchy.

A second problem with the neocolonial theory of Filipino American invisibility is a fault shared with the categorical assertion of Filipino Americans as Asian American. It is as well the elephant in the Asian American studies room that most continue to ignore. With the exception of the work of E. San Juan, Jr., the "critique of Western imperialism" approach has yet to challenge the Asian American institutional neglect of Filipino Americans.[7] Asian America, to cite Viet Thanh Nguyen, is "a hegemonic construction built in response to the dynamics of racial formation and complicit in reproducing racial formation's management of power through an inadequate representative categorization that ignores issues of domination, rivalry, antagonism, and inequality" (239). One could easily imagine an addendum to the imperialism argument: in replicating the racial categories of the imperial nation-state, Asian American cultural nationalism excludes Filipino Americans and reenacts a colonial relationship in which they are absorbed into yet another's (cultural) national vision and the subaltern subject again cannot speak for herself. Instead, the neocolonial framework confines its attacks to Western imperialism and its white agents and leaves Asian Americans unscathed by criticism. This silence is troubling. It speaks volumes about the conditions under which Filipino Americans, already underrepresented and marginalized, negotiate Asian American institutions and about their understandable reluctance to criticize the powers that be. If the purported means to visibility for Filipino Americans is through representing oneself as Asian American, one can ill afford to offend those who control the means to cultural production and institutional legitimacy.

And why do Filipino Americans, those designated the second-largest Asian American group, protest too little? Their grievances against Asian Americans range from institutional exclusion and marginalization (such as in elite academic institutions, compared to Asian Americans) to events reifying hierarchy and inequality (the *Blu's Hanging* controversy within the Association for Asian American Studies) to outright bigotry (by virtue of "looking Asian," becoming privy to a Chinese American's denigrating view of Filipinos) to unwittingly offensive encounters (being asked to speculate why Filipino Americans are not like Asian Americans, as if one had a choice in the matter, or being told that her concern for her own people is insignificant and an obstacle to unity).[8] Though Filipino Americans may identify with Asian Americans and even participate in their activities, the disparity of representation, material resources, and cultural capital and the subsequent interethnic hierarchy makes Asian America insidious. As these institutions' discourses extend to Filipino Americans and describe those who lack a racial discourse in the negative ("unlike other Asians . . ."), Filipino Americans meet with a shame and inferiority similar to the feelings provoked in colonial subjects. That they struggle with this post–civil rights manifestation of "benevolent assimilation" does not disturb me as much as does the failure of Asian Americans to acknowledge this crisis, even as Asian Americans assume that Filipino Americans have no recourse beyond panethnicity and insist on speaking on our behalf. The panethnic coalition is predicated upon equality and mutuality; the reality of the coalition is one of the privileged speaking without self-reflection for the underrepresented. At "On the Verge: Conversations on Pilipino American Studies," a 9 February 2002 conference held in Berkeley that protested the exclusion of Filipino Americans from Asian American studies, Anatalio C. Ubalde said: "We are not Asian American at others' convenience." To that I would add that we are not, as Asian Americans often see us, disruptions to be contained. In light of the structural differences, Asian Americans' willful blindness, and the silence of Filipino Americans, I doubt that Filipino American agency or emergence can be fostered in Asian American studies as the discipline is presently constituted.

Theorizing Filipino American identities demands an extreme skepticism of the process of racial interpretation—we know much, much less about others than we think we know.[9] One must lose the breezy, quotidian confidence that the stranger seen in passing is of one background when, in fact, s/he may be of another. The confirmation of the other's identity does not restore confidence in the certain knowledge of racial categories; rather, the act of terminating racial ambiguity exposes, however briefly, the perceptual absence imposed upon Filipino Americans. Acknowledging this invisibility as a post–civil rights condition can initiate attention to the underestimated impact of misrecognition and the consequences of being shut out of representation: the construction of racial categories and the unmasking of their permeable, fluid boundaries; Filipino Americans' exclusion from racial discourse and the absence of a language to comprise their racial representation; the heightened urgency of context and specificity in demarcating the range of identities accessible to an individual Filipino American. Invisibility is as well a condition of a culture of U.S. imperialism; that it is articulated through a neocolonial framework, however, does not make a domestic-oriented one such as race less compelling. Through the terms of an internal category, the elision of neocolonial subjects can be understood as facilitated by both racial lumping and a hegemony of rigidly defined racial categories and experienced by Filipino Americans as perceptual absence. In order to theorize invisibility as an imperial discourse, critical approaches concerned with international relations and empire must be accompanied if not preceded by another that addresses directly the social construction of race at home. Such a framework exists readily in mixed-race studies, a focus on the experiences of a group of individuals made invisible and hybrid by virtue of straddling racial categories. (Alternately, mixed-race individuals, whether or not their backgrounds include a Filipino one, find uncanny acceptance among Filipino Americans and they themselves wonder at the lack of anxiety in Pinoy attitudes toward hybridity.) With misrecognition and racial ambiguity as their central concerns, the narratives of mixed-race persons chart the protagonist's coming to terms with the dissonance between perception and cognition: a cognizance that others do not see her as she sees herself, experiences of rejection by those with whom she otherwise shares a common background, the struggle to master bodily presence and gain fluency with various racial discourses, and the attainment of a maturity defined by the ability to shape others' perception and racial interpretation. Such narratives may serve as rich and versatile models for Filipino Americans as they begin to describe an experience of hybridity yielded from the fissures between racial categories.

How does one escape a circumstance akin to an early-twenty-first-century, Asian American version of the tragic mullata? How can Filipino Americans create tangible representations of themselves when they are denied a language with which to talk about being Pinoy? One could attempt to fight invisibility by talking about one's absence, but continuing to reference absence only reinforces that incommensurable sense of nonbeing and leaves one muddling about the nothingness of Pinoy identity. How does one spin gold out of air?

I Mix So Fast, I Scratch So Sweet: The Shape of a Filipino American Racial Discourse

> Race is really nothing but a state of mind. If I'm at a party and there's a cute Korean girl, guess what? I'm Korean. If there's a cute Latina, then I'm Latino. If there's a cute white girl, then I'm black.
>
> —Comedian Tim Tayag

Filipino Americans may form mutual collaborations by virtue of their shared condition of perceptual absence—alienated from whites (for being nonwhite), blacks and Latinos (for being Asian), and Asian Americans (for being insufficiently Asian)—and resist invisibility by demanding they be acknowledged as Filipino American. Their inclusion in the U.S. racial discourse and the creation of a distinct category, however, entails hegemony's reciprocating this recognition of difference, something I don't see happening short of a historical trauma that thrusts Filipinos into current affairs or the organization of both Filipino Americans and non-Filipinos into a movement to extract state recognition. For the time being, our most practical means to representation may be through the very racial categories that generate our invisibility. A couple of movies and several fictional narratives have recently appeared in which Filipino American characters escape racial drift and discover provisional agency in passing or enacting another ethnic identity (Cajayon and Castro; Ong; Roley, *American Son*; *Slow Jam King*; Tenorio). However, like Jocelyn Enriquez's own interpretation of her not having control over her image as a neophyte's hard lessons, these narratives are offered as cautionary tales. I know of but a couple of works in which the absence of a Filipino American racial discourse itself is served up for parody (Manalo, Camia, and Cachapero; Pulido). Leave it to the forementioned Filipino American comedian to propose that chronic misrecognition allows for a playful (albeit socially opportunistic) post–civil rights mode of being.

For a cultural practice that can serve as a model for other modes of Filipino American expression, I look to the mobile DJs, specifically the hip-hop DJs. During the 1990s, Filipino American DJs from the San Francisco Bay Area and Los Angeles dominated hip-hop DJ competitions; popularized the DJ crew; invented new techniques and refined turntable and mixer technologies; produced mixtapes, instructional/variety show videos, DJ battle footage, and break beat records; collaborated and toured with highly visible MCs; established new organizations, conferences, and competitions; and in short influenced hip-hop so massively that their transformation of the DJ arts merited a new name: turntablism (Chonin, "Dilly"). The claim of Filipino American DJs on turntablism, noted Melanie Cagonot, curator of an exhibition on Filipino American DJs and herself a Pinay MC, represented "the first time young Filipino Americans have had something that's ours" (Chonin, "Turning the Tables"; *Tales of the Turntable*).

Their success has been attributed to their distance from the East Coast hip-hop scene and to the similarities between the fusion character of hip-hop DJing and neocolonial Filipino culture (Chonin, "Turning the Tables"; Cook). Juliana Snapper, who develops a precise and textured lexicon of turntablist practices and reads turntablism through a critical discourse of postcolonial temporality, cites U.S. subnationals' "ambivalent relationships to imperial models of linearity and progress": "In their reconstruction of musical texts and their use of antiquated technology and found sound objects, turntablists speak to the inadequacy of imperial constructs of modernity, agency and progress. Toying with musical time and pirating technology becomes a powerful mode of creative control" (12, 13). But I would like to filter the questions "Why, of the four pillars of hip-hop, DJing?" and "Why, of all ethnic/racial groups, Filipino Americans?" through the prism of invisibility.

Music, however it may be perceived and circulated socially, remains formalistic and devoid of inherent semantics, especially as a song's cumulative elements are isolated, ensembles broken down into discrete instruments, bars parsed into phrases into notes and beats and shouts. This tendency toward abstraction is cherished by the founding African American hip-hop DJs like Afrika Bambaataa, who established as one of the hallmarks of a master DJ the ability to throw different genres—electro, rock, salsa, funk, reggae, European classical, country-western, children's songs, to name a few—into the mix and get the crowd moving to music it would otherwise sit out (Rivera, 57; Rose, 51–52; *Scratch;* Webber, 94):

> I used to like to catch the people who'd say, "I don't like rock. I don't like Latin." I'd throw on Mick Jagger—you'd see the blacks and the Spanish [Latinos] just throwing down, dancing crazy. I'd say, "I thought you said you didn't like rock." They'd say, "Get out of here." I'd say, "Well, you just danced to the Rolling Stones." "You're kidding."

I'd throw on "Sergeant Pepper's Lonely Hearts Club Band"—just that drum part—one, two, three, BAM! and they'd be screaming and partying. I'd throw on The Monkees, "Mary Mary"—just the beat part where they'd go "Mary, Mary, where are you going?"—and they'd start going crazy. I'd say, "You just danced to The Monkees." They'd say, "You liar. I didn't dance to no Monkees." I'd like to catch people who categorize records. (qtd. in Toop, 66)

When music as a relatively social discourse–free cultural form was taken up by Filipino Americans, two conditions—perceptual absence and their concentration in racially segregated neighborhoods around San Francisco's southern city limits—had shaped a unique subjectivity such that Filipino American DJs and their Filipino American audiences, excluded from racial discourse, could listen to different musical genres without memory of categorical belonging, nor with feelings of attachment or territorial possession over genres as racial property. They possessed, instead, an acutely developed sense of the Duke Ellingtonian spirit of music: there are two kinds of music, good and bad (and who is to say that a clever DJ cannot salvage an outro or a bridge of the bad?). As exclusion became liberation from an inhibiting ideology, Filipino American DJs discovered their freedom within the groove and fulfilled Afrika Bambaataa's representation of the break as something beyond its technical definition as the segment of a record where the rhythmic and percussive elements are foregrounded over the thematic to "that [place] you look for in a record that lets your God-self just get wild" (*Scratch*). DJ QBert, a Filipino American member of the Invisibl Skratch Piklz whose virtuosity rivals Charlie Parker's, compares turntablism to speech—"It's kinda like talking, you just speak what you're saying; . . . each technique is a word, so the larger your vocabulary the more articulate[ly] you can speak" (*Scratch*). He attests to the fluency Filipino Americans are denied by language but have attained in the reconstruction of samples, beats, and percussive elements played on the turntable proper into autonomous, free-standing works. The products themselves, however, are not a music identified as Filipino American—the condition of perceptual absence forecloses their racial categorization. Rather, it is the reconstructive process—to select samples from disparate sources, to decompose them through any of the hundreds of turntable techniques, and to resequence the discrete elements—that offers a model of Filipino American representation, a vehicle of Pinoy genius such that DJ QBert's 1994 *Demolition Pumpkin Squeeze Musik* remains hip-hop's most celebrated mixtape and the Invisibl Skratch Piklz performance of "Da Klamz uv Deth" routine stands as both a hip-hop landmark and the greatest cultural production, musical or not, by Filipino Americans to date (DJ QBert; *Invisibl Skratch Piklz versuz Da Klamz uv Deth*). What improvisation is to African American culture, mixing is to Filipino Americans.

Still, while turntablism is the prototype of Filipino American culture and the mobile DJ crew its organizing unit, as mediums of Filipino American representation they are hardly complete or ideal. The abstract character of music that otherwise lends itself to the creativity of those listening from outside racial discourse impedes the ability of Filipino Americans to confront their invisibility via the turntable (though their massive success has made issues about Filipino American participation in hip-hop unavoidable). Indeed, some of the premier Filipino American DJs are adamant about the meritocratic nature of turntablism: hard work, not identity, they argue, makes a battle champ (Friar, "QBert"). Moreover, their exclusion from racial discourse has had a strange effect on Filipino American DJs when they attempt to narrate themselves. African American DJs easily connect their craft with a history-laden sense of time and place, invoking hip-hop's origins in South Bronx housing projects as a response to racial segregation, gang violence, and urban decay (Rivera; Rose; *Scratch*). In contrast, Filipino American DJs asked to identify their music's origins and influences speak of future time and outer space. While spaceships, eight-armed extraterrestrials, and other figments of science fiction serve as what Oliver Wang calls a "Filipino-futurism," an alternative discourse that compensates for the absence of race (Wang, e-mail), it is not as if Filipino Americans did not have their own neighborhoods, institutions, and social practices amidst racial isolation and hierarchy (*Tales of the Turntable*). And these DJs, far from evading their ethnic identities, are proud Pinoys: in one segment of the Invisibl Skratch Piklz' *Turntable TV* series, QBert pretends to beat Toadman with an *eskrima* stick (*Turntable T.V. Version 3.0*); in another, Q-Bert and Yogafrog cruise a shopping mall in that most Pinoy of cities, Daly City, and find that despite the Piklz' front-page coverage in the *San Francisco Chronicle*, none of the Pinays they approach recognize them (*Turntable T.V. Annual 2*).[10] Again, the condition of perceptual absence denies them a language with which to make meaning of their ethnic identities, communities, and culture. If it is the case that Filipino Americans are lost between their perceptual and cognitive acknowledgments, they must become as agile with the existing racial discourses as their DJs are with recordings from different musical genres to create a language for themselves within that racial fissure.[11]

WORKS CITED

A.M. "Jocelyn." *Old School Freestyle, Volume One.* CD album. Various artists. Critique, 1996.

Amirrezvani, Anita. "Filipino Pride: Artists Create a New Aesthetic Amid Cultural Contradictions." *Contra Costa Times,* 4 October 1998, C1–2.

Azoulay, Katya Gibel. *Black, Jewish, and Interracial: It's Not the Color of Your Skin, but the Race of Your Kin, and Other Myths of Identity.* Durham, N.C.: Duke University Press, 1997.

Balce-Cortes, Nerissa, and Jean Vengua Gier. "Filipino American Literature." In *New Immigrant Literatures in the United States: A Sourcebook to Our Multicultural Literary*

Heritage, ed. Alpana Sharma Knippling. Westport, Conn.: Greenwood Press, 1996, 67–89.

Cajayon, Gene, and John Manal Castro. *The Debut: The Making of a Filipino American Film.* Chicago: Tulitos Press, 2001.

Campomanes, Oscar V. "Afterword: The New Empire's Forgetful and Forgotten Citizens: Unrepresentability and Unassimilability in Filipino American Postcolonialities." *Critical Mass* 2, 2 (Spring 1995): 145–200.

———. "Filipinos in the United States and Their Literature of Exile." In *Reading the Literatures of Asian America,* ed. Shirley Geok-lin Lim and Amy Ling. Philadelphia: Temple University Press, 1992, 49–78.

Chonin, Neva. "A Dilly of a Career: The Bay Area's Invisibl Skratch Piklz Have Become World Stars of Turntablism." *San Francisco Chronicle,* 1 November 1998.

———. "Turning the Tables: Vibrant Bay Area DJ Culture Celebrated in Clubs, Museum." *San Francisco Chronicle,* 27 September 2001.

Consul, Wilma. "Filipinos in the U.S. Music Industry." *Filipinas Magazine,* July 1994, 38–41.

Cook, Dave "Davey D." October 1995. www.daveyd.com/filipinodjs.html.

———. "Filipino DJs of the Bay Area (Why Are They So Successful?)." 1 March 1999. www.daveyd.com/filipinodjs.html.

Cordova, Fred. *Filipinos: Forgotten Asian Americans.* Dubuque, Iowa: Kendall Hunt, 1983.

DJ QBert. *Preschool Break Mix.* Cassette mixtape. Dirt Style, 1994.

The Debut. Dir. Gene Cajayon. 5 Card Productions, 2000.

Enriquez, Jocelyn. "Do You Miss Me: The Remixes." CD maxi-single. Classified/Tommy Boy/Timber!, 1996.

———. "I've Been Thinking About You." CD maxi-single. Classified, 1994.

———. *Jocelyn.* CD album. Classfied/Tommy Boy/Timber!, 1997.

———. "A Little Bit of Ecstasy." CD maxi-single. Classified/Tommy Boy/Timber!, 1997.

———. *Lovely.* CD album. Classified, 1994.

Espiritu, Yen Le. *Filipino American Lives.* Philadelphia: Temple University Press, 1995.

The Flip Side. Dir. Rod Pulido. Puro Pinoy Productions, 2001.

Freestyle—Greatest Beats: The Complete Collection, Volume Ten. CD album. Various artists. Timber!/Tommy Boy, 1997.

Friar, William. "Making a Place for Themselves." *Contra Costa Times,* 4 October 1998, C3.

———. "QBert (a k a Richard Quitevis): The Turntable Pioneer Takes a Solo Spin." *Contra Costa Times,* 4 October 1998, C3.

Fujikane, Candace. "Sweeping Racism under the Rug of 'Censorship': The Controversy over Lois-Ann Yamanaka's Blu's Hanging." *Amerasia Journal* 26, 2 (2000): 158–94.

Gaerlan, Barbara S. "In the Court of the Sultan: Orientalism, Nationalism, and Modernity in Philippine and Filipino American Dance." *Journal of Asian American Studies* 2, 3 (1999): 251–87.

Gier, Jean Vengua. "'. . . to have come from someplace': *October Light, America Is in the Heart,* and 'Flip' Writing after the Third World Strikes." *Critical Mass: A Journal of Asian American Cultural Criticism* 2, 2 (Spring 1995): 1–33.

Gilmore, Samuel. "Doing Culture Work: Negotiating Tradition and Authenticity in Filipino Folk Dance." *Sociological Perspectives* 43, 4 (2000): S21–41.

Gonzalves, Theodore S. "The Day the Dancers Stayed: On Pilipino Cultural Nights." In *Filipino Americans: Transformation and Identity*, ed. Maria P. P. Root. Thousand Oaks, Calif.: Sage, 1997, 163–82.

———. When the Walls Speak a Nation: Contemporary Murals and the Narration of Filipina/o America." *Journal of Asian American Studies* 1, 1 (February 1998): 31–63.

Gonzalves, Theodore S., Josh Kun, and Elizabeth H. Pisares. "Sounds Like 1996: An Annotated Take-Out Menu of Recent Asian American Music." *Hitting Critical Mass* 4, 2 (Summer 1997): 49–60.

Invisibl Skratch Piklz versuz Da Klamz uv Deth. Dir. Philip Fierlinger. Turntable/Dasein, 1997.

Jam, Billy. "Filipino Freedom." *BAM*, 12 September 1997, 28.

Kaplan, Amy. "'Left Alone with America': The Absence of Empire in the Study of American Culture." In *Cultures of United States Imperialism,* ed. Amy Kaplan and Donald E. Pease. Durham: Duke University Press, 1993, 3–21.

Liu, John. Association for Asian American Studies roundtable discussion, American Studies Association conference. Seattle, 20 November 1998.

Liwanag: Literary and Graphic Expressions by Filipinos in America. San Francisco: Liwanag Publications, 1975.

Llamas, Lizet. "The Ultimate Sound: Jocelyn Enriquez." *Santa Clara*, 29 May 1997, 19.

Lowe, Lisa. "The Power of Culture." *Journal of Asian American Studies* 1, 1 (1998): 5–29.

Mabalon, Dawn Bohulano. Review of *Filipino American Lives* by Yen Le Espiritu. *Amerasia* 22, 1 (Spring 1996): 279–82.

Manalo, Allan S., Kevin Camia, and Patty Cachapero. "PCN Salute." *Zyzzyva* 8, 3 (Winter 1997): 171–76.

Meno, Gwendlynn. "Jocelyn Enriquez: The Look of Lovely." *BAM*, 12 September 1997, 28–29.

Nakao, Annie. "'Subtle' Racism, Sexism Reported in the City." *San Francisco Examiner,* 28 December 1998.

Nguyen, Viet Thanh. Review of *An Interethnic Companion to Asian American Literature* edited by King-kok Cheung. *Amerasia Journal* 24, 3 (1998): 236–39.

Omi, Michael, and Howard Winant. *Racial Formation in the United States: From the 1960s to the 1990s.* 2d ed. New York: Routledge, 1994.

Ong, Han. *Fixer Chao.* New York: Picador USA, 2001.

Piper, Adrian. "Passing for White, Passing for Black." *Transition* 58 (1992): 4–32.

———."Two Kinds of Discrimination." *Yale Journal of Criticism* 6, 1 (1993): 25–74.

Prashad, Vijay. *The Karma of Brown Folk.* Minneapolis: University of Minnesota Press, 2000.

Pulido, Rod. *The Flip Side: A Filipino American Comedy.* Chicago: Tulitos Press, 2002.

Rabaya, Violet. "I Am Curious (Yellow?)." In *Roots: An Asian American Reader*, ed. Amy Tachiki, Eddie Wong, and Franklin Odo, with Buck Wong. Los Angeles: UCLA Asian American Studies Center, 1971, 110–11.

Rex Navarette Is Hella Pinoy: A Life Comedy Concert. Dir. Rex Navarette. Kakarabaw Productions, 2004.

Rivera, Raquel Z. *New York Ricans from the Hip Hop Zone.* New York: Palgrave Macmillan, 2003.

Rodrigues, Darlene. "Imagining Ourselves: Reflections on the Controversy over Lois-Ann Yamanaka's Blu's Hanging." *Amerasia Journal* 26, 2 (2000): 195–207.

Roley, Brian Ascalon. *American Son.* New York: Norton, 2001.

———. "Filipinos: The Hidden Majority." *San Francisco Chronicle*, 20 August 2001.

Root, Maria P. P. "Multiracial Asians: Models of Ethnic Identity." *Amerasia Journal* 23, 1 (1997): 29–41.

Rose, Tricia. *Black Noise: Rap Music and Black Culture in Contemporary America.* Middletown, Conn.: Wesleyan University Press, 1994.

San Buenaventura, Steffi. "The Colors of Manifest Destiny: Filipinos and the American Other(s)." *Amerasia Journal* 24, 3 (1998): 1–26.

San Juan, Jr., E. "Beyond Identity Politics: The Predicament of the Asian American Writer in Late Capitalism." *American Literary History* 3, 3 (Fall 1991): 542–65.

———. *Exile to Diaspora: Versions of the Filipino Experience in the United States.* Boulder, Colo.: Westview, 1998.

———. "Multiculturalism vs. Hegemony: Ethnic Studies, Asian Americans, and U.S. Racial Politics." *Massachusetts Review* 32, 3 (Fall 1991): 467–78.

———. *The Philippine Temptation: Dialectics of Philippines-U.S. Literary Relations.* Philadelphia: Temple University Press, 1996.

Scratch. Dir. Doug Pray. Darkhorse Entertainment, 2001.

Slow Jam King. Dir. Steven E. Mallorca. Slow Jam King Productions, 2004.

Snapper, Juliana. "Scratching the Surface: Spinning Time and Identity in Hip-Hop Turntablism." *European Journal of Cultural Studies* 7, 1 (2004): 9–25.

Spickard, Paul R. "What Must I Be? Asian Americans and the Question of Multiethnic Identity." *Amerasia Journal* 23, 1 (1997): 43–60.

Strobel, Leny Mendoza. "'Born-Again Filipino': Filipino American Identity and Asian Panethnicity." *Amerasia Journal* 22, 2 (Spring 1996): 31–53.

Takaki, Ronald. *Iron Cages: Race and Culture in 19th-Century America.* 1979. New York: Oxford University Press, 1990.

———. *Strangers from a Different Shore: A History of Asian Americans.* New York: Penguin, 1989.

Tales of the Turntable: Filipino-American DJ's of the San Francisco Bay Area. Curator Melanie Cagonot. Redwood City: San Mateo County History Museum, 29 September 2001–25 February 2002.

Tenorio, Lysley A. "Superassassin." *Atlantic Monthly*, October 2000, 105–17.

Toop, David. *Rap Attack 2: African Rap to Global Hip Hop.* London: Serpent's Tail, 1991.

Turntable T.V. Annual 2. Dir. Yogafrog and QBert. Invisibl Skratch Piklz, 1999.

Turntable T.V. Version 3.0: The Smegma Returns. Dir. D-Styles, QBert, and Yogafrog. Invisibl Skratch Piklz, 1997.

Ubalde, Anatalio C. "Jocelyn Enriquez: Filipinos, Make Some Noise!" *Hoy!/Excuse Me Magazine* 1, 2 (1996): 3–5.

————. "Mestizo." *Maganda* 6 (1993): 50–53, 66.

Wang, Oliver. "Brown and Proud." *San Francisco Bay Guardian*, 11 November 1998. www.sfbg.com/AandE/33/06/skratch.html.

————. E-mail to the author, 13 March 2004.

————. "Funk Phenomenon: Bay Area Turntablism Spins into Decade Two." *San Francisco Bay Guardian*, 11 November 1998. www.sfbg.com/AandE/33/06/funk.html.

Webber, Stephen. *Turntable Technique: The Art of the DJ.* Boston: Berklee Press, 2000.

Williams, William A. "United States Indian Policy and the Debate over Philippine Annexation: Implications for the Origins of American Imperialism." *Journal of American History* 66:4 (March 1980): 810-31.

Wood, James Earl. *Material Concerning Filipinos in California, Collected ca. 1929–1934.* The Bancroft Library, University of California, Berkeley.

12   A Different Breed of Filipino Balikbayans

The Ambiguities of (Re-)turning

INTRODUCTION

Over the last decade, a marked shift has been noted in Filipino American youth's orientation from what has been a predominantly assimilationist mode of survival to one foregrounding their separate Filipino identity vis-à-vis the U.S. mainstream. Fueled by an opening (up) to formerly repressed cultural and historical memory, mainly through the instrumentality of a homeland discursive export called Sikolohiyang Pilipino (Filipino psychology),this newly assertive form of cultural nationalism has led a number of Filipino American youth to undertake not merely a symbolic (re)turn to a forgotten or previously unknown native land, but a literal one. Mostly a phenomenon among college students who are encountering for the first time a radically different narrative of Filipino history and subjectivity, this nostalgic longing among second-, third-, and fourth-generation Filipino Americans to reconnect with a formerly disavowed historical past has given rise to the phenomenon of a different breed of *balikbayans*, or homeland returnees. Caught up in the fervor of a Fanonian moment of decolonization, these youths begin to manifest a diasporic identity signified by participation in various Balik-Aral (back-to-study) summer programs and other kinds of visits to the homeland. These programs, jointly coordinated by Filipino American faculty and their Philippines counterparts, are designed to take these youth returnees to the Philippines to study Philippine history, society, and culture as well as to learn basic Filipino. Other more individualized homeland explorations likewise become avenues for exploring further their newfound Filipino subjectivity.

The result, however, is far from singular and unambiguous, ranging from extreme shock and disillusionment to decisions to stay longer than originally intended. This essay examines the roots in the political and historical imaginary of such ambivalent gestures of returning among second-, third-, and fourth-generation Filipino American youth and their implications for the dynamics of transformation among a minoritized population seeking a new sense of purpose within a (re-)discovered ethnic subjectivity.

New Balikbayans: Encountering
the Diaspora in Reverse

In the summer of 1999 I went home to the Philippines for two months of field research for a dissertation, aided by a small grant from Arizona State University.[1] My goal, after four years away, was to reacquaint and immerse myself once more in efforts within the Philippine academy that were seeking new ways to constitute local knowledge within the Western-style social science disciplines that were the legacy of centuries of Spanish and U.S. colonial education. This was part of the core of my dissertation project. As a Filipina only temporarily sojourning in the United States, I was what one would term in Filipino a "balikbayan" (*balik*, literally, to return, and *bayan*, homeland). It didn't matter that I was there for only two months; I was a bona fide balikbayan, welcomed and embraced as a true home-grown daughter.

But what of U.S.-born Filipino Americans who travel to the Philippines for the first time? Surely, they could not be balikbayans in the same sense of the word? Given that such persons—save perhaps for the color of their skin—would not be marked by a "native" identity, it isn't likely that their (re-)turn would be imbued with the same sense of originary connection to the homeland and thereby hailed with the same "authenticity" as a native born like me? And yet, on another level, might one not say that a virtual (re-)turn is possible even for Pinoys who have never set foot on Philippine soil? It is with this breed of returnees that I had the most interesting encounter that summer while conducting research at the Diliman campus of my alma mater, the University of the Philippines (UP).

"Bagong estudyanteng gradwado ako dito sa Sikolohiyang Pilipino. Nag lipat ako dito sa Pilipinas itong June lang" [I am a new graduate student here in Filipino psychology. I moved here to the Philippines only this June]. Thus did Jorge Intal introduce himself to me by e-mail in broken Filipino. He mentioned that Elizabeth de Castro (formerly Elizabeth Protacio-Marcelino), a professor of psychology at UP, had given him my e-mail address and shared with him a piece I had written on the indigenization movement in the Philippine academy. Intrigued by the essay, he wanted to discuss it with me. Auspiciously, the paper was an attempt to create spaces of dialogue around issues of belonging, nationhood, and identity between Filipino scholars in the homeland and their diasporic counterparts in the United States—my notion of what an intercultural communication project might look like. Located in the interstitial spaces between the homeland and the diaspora, I wanted to make sense of the competing constructions of "Filipino-ness" coming from either side of the geographic divide. In his e-mail, after two sentences in Filipino, Jorge shifted to English. When we met, he apologized that his Filipino "is still so basic," explaining that he was still trying to learn the language.

Jorge is a second-generation Filipino American whose parents immigrated to Virginia in 1969. Born and raised in the United States, he studied in a boarding school in Michigan and dreamed of becoming a musician. Instead, he earned a Bachelor of Science degree in neuroscience. When I learned how young he was—twenty-one? twenty-two? I don't remember—I wondered, What on earth is he doing here? Does he have family? Relatives? A girlfriend, perhaps? "No, none of the above," he assured me. "I came from Brown," he explained, "and although there are many [FilAm scholars] there, . . . many of us did not know much about SP [Sikolohiyang Pilipino] or other parallel indigenization movements in other academic disciplines in the Philippines.

He told me he got interested in comparative cultures during his last year in the Psychology Department at Brown University. Later, his interest found a specific focus in Filipino psychology through a course taught by Eric Reyes in Filipino American cultures, part of the newly established ethnic studies program at Brown, in which the class discussed issues of globalization, modernity, and colonization. That course also introduced Jorge to the thinking of Sikolohiyang Pilipino founder and pioneer Virgilio Enriquez, whose works, happily enough, Jorge found in the university library. Enriquez's work triggered Jorge's decision to come to the Philippines and take his graduate studies in Sikolohiyang Pilipino. He sensed that he was staking his future on an unknown arena whose full implications he had yet to explore, but Filipino "liberation psychology" (the alternative term Enriquez employed) ignited something powerful in the depths of Jorge's being.

SIKOLOHIYANG PILIPINO AND OTHER NARRATIVES OF (RE-)TURN

The narrative import of Sikolohiyang Pilipino that Filipino American scholar E. M. Strobel notes in "'Born-Again Filipino'" largely constitutes the impetus behind such gestures of (re-)turning—not only in Jorge's case but in others' as well—is embedded in a wider movement in the homeland, the Philippine indigenization movement (see Mendoza, *Between the Homeland*).[2] Although social and political activist movements existed within the Filipino American community, only with this new discourse did student youths gain access—in theoretically legitimated ways—to the more expressive forms of Filipino culture(s), which then served to provide the raw material for the reinvention of self as "Filipino."[3] Indigenous concepts such as *kapwa* (the unity of self and others, with its implications for a radically different way of being-with-others), *loob* (depth of being or interiority), and *pahiwatig* (the complex of indirect verbal and nonverbal patterns of communication rooted in a keenly nuanced sensitivity for the other's feelings) gave substance to the formerly emptied and negated Filipino "identity" category, providing not only a historical but also a cultural base from which to (re-)claim a different way of being as *Filipino* Americans—this time with the emphasis on the first word.

In the Philippine academy, where "identity" has become a site of struggle for both historical and cultural resignification, the indigenization movement has found the need to constitute a national discourse on civilization separate from the West.[4] A collaborative endeavor spanning decades and disciplines, it sought to undertake what Fanon refers to as "a passionate search for national culture" (*The Wretched*, 209). Comprised of several strands of interdisciplinary narratives, this project envisions the work of nationhood as of necessity beginning with the revision of theory as the very instrument of knowing. At the core of the movement's anticolonialist thrust is an attempt to deconstruct centuries of the colonial Euro-Western epistemological legacy by rejecting its premises and rethinking theorizing practices in the academic disciplines. A massive cultural reclamation project, the indigenization movement intends to recover (read: uncover) "indigenous" ways of knowing and being.

This project began with the early works of Filipino anthropologists who reconstructed Philippine prehistory and culture and posited an "organic" nation; works of Filipino linguistic philosophers who asserted a distinct indigenous Filipino philosophy; works of Filipino psychologists who retheorized "the" Filipino "personality" and challenged the universalist assumptions of a Western-oriented psychology; and the perspectives of Filipino historians who undertook to rewrite Philippine history. More contemporary developments in Philippine studies include the programmatic trilogy of Sikolohiyang Pilipino (liberation psychology), Pantayong Pananaw (a new ethnocentered framework for Philippine historiography) and Pilipinolohiya (a newly emergent discourse on civilization intended to serve as an indigenously conceived academic discipline).[5]

Sikolohiyang Pilipino, an important strand in this multiple discourse on indigenization, found its way into the Filipino American scholarly community in the early 1990s through the work of movement pioneer and University of the Philippines professor Virgilio Enriquez, who came to Northern California as a visiting professor at University of California, Berkeley. It is this discourse, which provided a legitimating framework for a more positive reading of Filipino culture and subjectivity, that Strobel in "'Born-Again Filipino'" credits for the nationalist resurgence in the 1990s among both Filipino American youth in colleges and health professionals and cultural workers in Filipino American communities: "This development of decolonizing discourse in the social sciences and humanities in the Philippines has influenced the discourse within the Filipino American community in the 1990s. As this perspective is integrated into community discussions, it provides a medium for the articulation of cultural identity that is rooted in indigenous consciousness" (39). This renewed sense of subjectivity, according to Strobel, gave rise to what was later dubbed the Born-Again Filipino Movement, which adopted Filipino "indigenous" experience as the new interpretive principle in its worldview and everyday life, launching careers in the academy and inspiring an influx of Filipino American students to graduate school in unprecedented numbers. The transforming impact of that cultural encounter with a lost past through the power of discourse gave a tremendous boost to second-, third-, and fourth-generation U.S.-born Filipino Americans whose assimilationist orientation had for decades earned the community the unflattering sobriquet "the invisible minority" (Campomanes, "Institutional Invisibility").

The indigenization movement in the Philippine academy developed among sectors of the intelligentsia enthused by a nationalist imperative. Its roots lie in a long tradition of resistance movements, first against centuries of Spanish domination of the Philippines and subsequently of U.S. colonial domination. Despite this long nationalist tradition and the country's observance of its centennial in 1998 (celebrating recognition of the Philippine Republic as the first independent republic in Asia), a systematic undoing of more than four centuries of the colonial legacy of epistemic violence begins only in the later 1970s.[6] Since colonial domination was secured most effectively through a colonial system of education, the academy became the logical site for Filipino nationalist intellectuals' contestation and critical intervention.[7]

The project to undo colonization, then, began mainly as a contest over historical representation and interpretation. From the late 1950s to the 1970s, Filipino nationalist scholars saw it as their primary task to rectify what they considered gross and systematic distortions in the colonial historical narratives, meant to secure the colonial order. Examples include the denial that a strong and sustained anticolonial revolutionary tradition among Filipinos ever existed, and the consequent dismissal of the now well-documented widespread popular uprisings throughout the colonial era as nothing more than sporadic outbreaks or aberrations in what were otherwise "peaceful civilizing missions" by Spain and the United States. The colonizers depicted these revolutionary uprisings as the demented rioting of weak-minded individuals cracking up under the stress of culture change, the greedy opportunism of ordinary "bandits" and "criminals," or the misguided zeal of uneducated, ignorant, and irrational "troublemakers" who knew nothing of the civilized rule of law. In addition, they hailed assimilationist and reform-minded members of the elite class as the "true Filipino heroes" and promoted Americans as "benevolent saviors," "benefactors," and "allies." Among many other glaring factual distortions and deliberate misrepresentations, these remain firmly lodged to this day in the Filipino popular imagination.

Historiography played a significant part in uncovering the goal of the blatantly racist/colonialist discourse of the academic disciplines introduced in the Philippine educational system during the colonial era: to secure compliance, loyalty, and the willing self-subjection of a people via the internalization of their ascribed helplessness, ignorance, immaturity, and lack of humanity. Degraded (and degrading) colonial narrative representations enabled this process.[8] By the early 1970s, the impetus that began within the discipline of history found an echo in psychology with the significant pioneering work of Enriquez, who developed "liberation psychology" as a way of doing psychology differently than the West. His goal was not merely to counter the effects on the Filipino psyche of the degrading colonial representations but to build a more adequate framework for understanding Filipino "indigenous" culture.

Within this framework, Enriquez distinguishes between two approaches to indigenization: "indigenization from without" and "indigenization from within" (*Colonial to Liberation Psychology*, 101). He defines indigenization from without as originating in the exogenous (colonial) culture; the West is the source of theoretic constructs, and the indigenous (Filipino) culture is the target recipient of culture flow. Its main method or strategy is "content indigenization, test modification and translation of imported materials" (85). From this starting point, nationalist Filipino psychologists attempted to indigenize Philippine psychology. However, despite efforts to deepen theoretical understanding of the inner dynamics of the indigenous culture, this model failed to dislodge the implicitly racist cultural assumptions and biases of Western psychology's analytic constructs.

Indigenization from within, by contrast, uses the indigenous culture as at once the starting point and the source and basis of concepts, methods, and theories. Its goal is not to build upon exogenous constructs and indigenize their use and application but to develop its own analytical tools, instruments, and conceptual frameworks using the indigenous culture as the main reference point. The resulting potent formulation called into question the universalist assumptions of Western experimental psychology as the only legitimate "science." Called Sikolohiyang Pilipino, it represented a distinctive critique of the negative framing of the so-called essential Filipino personality. Filipino psychology rejects the degrading images inscribed in the colonial narratives as little more than the ethnocentric shadow projections of Western colonial scholarship. It is this strand of the indigenization narrative that was to take root among Filipino American youths in Northern California when Enriquez served as a visiting professor at UC Berkeley.

In anthropology, a rethinking of disciplinary perspectives began with the works of F. Landa Jocano, which reacted to studies by U.S. anthropologists H. Otley Beyer and Robert Fox (see Bennagen, "Indigenization"). Jocano (*Philippine Prehistory*), along with Filipino anthropologists Zeno Salazar ("Ang pagpapasakasaysayang") and Ponciano Bennagen ("Mirror"), among others, challenged what they deemed the unimaginative explanations of Filipino origins based on "wave migration" and "diffusionist" theories. These theories tended to identify everything in the Philippines, including the early inhabitants and their material and symbolic culture, as derived or adapted from neighboring continents. From this unidirectional tracing of influence came the unstated implication that everything Filipino is borrowed and unoriginal. The Filipino anthropologists saw this portrayal of Philippine prehistoric culture and civilization as just one more base-less interpretation that needed countering, all the more because old textbooks presented it as fact, with the slide from theory to fact obscured by the lack of alternative interpretations.

A further contribution in this regard is the firsthand research work of humanities scholar Felipe de Leon, Jr., who explores the surviving indigenous art forms of ethnic communities nationwide. Belying allegations of cultural deficiency among Filipinos prior to contact with the purportedly superior cultures of the West, he documented a vast array of rich, diverse, and unique Philippine precolonial art forms. These, he argued, persisted through time, in spite of colonization and West-ernization. Using art as a projective tool, he combined rigorous cultural analysis of Philippine traditional arts with insights from Sikolohiyang Pilipino to establish an alternative "image of the Filipino in the arts."[9]

In political science, Renato Constantino's nationalist writings delivered the most scathing denunciation of the systematic process by which the colonial stereotypes and representations of Filipinos, their culture, and their history were naturalized in the popular imagination through the colonial educational system. His ground-breaking 1977 essay "The Miseducation of the Filipino" in particular criticized neocolonial conditions in the Philippines that continued long after the formal end of U.S. rule. In unmasking the vested interests that have fueled the maintenance of a dependent Philippine economy through educational policies that catered more to foreign than to Filipino interests, he helped end, once and for all, the view of education and knowledge production as innocent, neutral enterprises. This realiza-tion underscored the strategic need to recapture agency in determining the kind of education essential for Filipinos to win the struggle for independence, particularly in the ideological arena.

In all these efforts, the challenge went beyond the need to change the sub-ject content of the disciplines from foreign to Philippine material ("indigeniza-tion from without") to, more critically, the need to change the conceptual tools of analysis ("indigenization from within"). Conducted at first within each aca-demic discipline, the search for new concepts, categories, instruments, and the-oretical frameworks better suited to Philippine cultural and social realities in-evitably grew into an intensely interdisciplinary endeavor. Scholars became aware of each other's works and of an emerging consensus (more amazing because arrived at semi-independently) on an indigenous (versus colonial) framework across the disciplines.

Thus, one may conclude that the impetus for the indigenization movement in the Philippine academy arose out of the need to reject Western impositions on Philippine scholarship, which had sought to squeeze Philippine realities into a cer-tain mold using a colonial framework of analysis. Indeed, within this framework, there was no way for Filipinos to speak (among themselves or with each other) or to make sense of their everyday experiences without constant intrusion and self-disparagement from an internalized dominant Other's point of view inscribed in the very instruments of learning. This was deemed the most serious and detrimental consequence of a colonial education. As Prospero Covar laments in this regard:

> We were made to hope that western education was going to liberate our minds and elevate our quality of life, but the opposite happened—we became captive to western ways of thinking and system of economy. Our thinking, culture and society became virtually westernized, when we were, in fact, Asians. The categories we used to make sense of our world were not ours; they were borrowed and offered by the academic disciplines. We became mesmerized and awed by the claim and promise of universalism. We disparaged and marginalized our own indigenous view as "ethnic," "parochial," and "provincial." Who would not be appalled by such insult? ("Pilipinolohiya," 40; my translation)

Indigenization then, as it originated, appears to be mainly a decolonizing move. It initially turned on the functional need to separate out what were considered the repressive impositions from without from the relatively more spontaneous, self-directed, autonomous ways of being (Filipino). More recent developments in indigenous theorizing, however, have sought to move beyond this reactive phase of the struggle for national self-determination and to begin building a national discourse on civilization (in contrast to official state nationalism) outside and apart from the normalizing gaze of the colonially oriented and racialized academic disciplines.[10]

New Narratives, New Subjectivities

Jorge is but one of a growing number of bright, idealistic U.S.-born second-, third-, or even fourth-generation Filipino American youths influenced by this renewed sense of history and cultural memory as mediated through the discourse of Sikolohiyang Pilipino to trek (back) to a homeland unknown or disavowed. This is a nation, only now beginning to be acknowledged in U.S. public discourse as "America's first Vietnam," whose bloody pacification at the turn of the century left the United States so traumatized by the dark side it revealed of its noble and heroic self-image that it determined never again to take another formal colony (alas, a resolve observed more in the breach than in compliance as the United States undertook one military intervention after another in numerous countries in the years to follow). Curiously enough, this is the homeland that these U.S.-born Filipino American youths are seeking to (re-)turn to—whether in the imaginary or in actual space and time. It is a place that, for all its griefs and unending sorrows (and, some say, its perversely high happiness quotient), they seem to actively, proudly, desire to get to know.

To facilitate such (re-)turns, Balik-Aral (returning-to-study) programs, also known as "reality tours," have proliferated in the United States this past decade on an unprecedented scale. Some are organized as visits, some undertaken as personal or individual projects or in collaboration with activist or Philippine-based nongovernmental organizations to participate in militant student conferences and artist workshops and performances—all aimed at learning more about the nation's repressed history. One that I am familiar with was a collaborative Summer Study-Abroad Program in 1992 between San Francisco State University (SFSU) and the University of the Philippines (UP), in which twelve SFSU Filipino American students enlisted to attend a Philippine language and culture class for ten weeks at UP. SFSU faculty Dan Gonzales and Antonio "Tony" de Castro coordinated the U.S. end of the program, while UP psychology professor Elizabeth "Beth" Protacio-Marcelino took charge of the Philippine end. The program gave the students a chance to tour various parts of the country, which introduced them to different cultural communities, while the professors lectured and conducted discussions along the way. At the conclusion of the program, Protacio-Marcelino (*Identidad*) conducted an in-depth study of the student participants' narratives of transformation for her dissertation project at the UP Department of Psychology. What emerged as a significant finding in the students' experiences is the impact of a colonized consciousness on their process of identity construction. On the other hand, their exposure to Sikolohiyang Pilipino as an alternative discourse on Filipino subjectivity, coupled with their experience in the study-abroad program, became vehicles for their subsequent transformation of consciousness through the twin processes of decolonization and indigenization. The study in effect supported the thesis that these two processes are indispensable to Filipino Americans' critical negotiation of their identities in a highly racialized environment such as that of the United States.

The program ran a second year with an enrollment of about fifteen students carefully selected from what was usually a larger pool of applicants. It was discontinued, however, according to Protacio-Marcelino, "due to campus politics": the program's resounding success—and its high-profile publicity in a two-part cover story in Makati City's September 1993 *Sunday Inquirer Magazine*—attracted interest from top-level people in the two participating institutions, and apparently "credit-grabbing and interference with its administration and disposition of the funds became a problem." With Protacio-Marcelino and de Castro out of the program, the Philippine side lost the breadth of field contacts Protacio-Marcelino had established, field trips became logistically impossible, and the approach became more classroom than field based.

Currently, however, several other independent groups have picked up where UP-SFSU left off. A program organized by freelance consultant Susan Kimpo in collaboration with Ateneo de Manila University on the Philippine side runs a three-week version whose main focus is learning the Filipino language. In the course of language learning, however, the students are taught Philippine society, history, and culture. A group from UC Berkeley manages another program through the International Studies Center. Both consult Protacio-Marcelino and de Castro, now a husband-and-wife team, who conduct some of the lectures. Finally, UP sociology professor Nanette Dungo runs a similar program with students from Virginia Polytech in Maryland, where she had taught for a year.

Asked what lessons came out of conducting such programs, Protacio-Marcelino wrote me in March 2001 that "it is important to do advocacy and promotions work back there in the U.S. The students ask a lot of questions that need to be addressed. It should also be sustainable. There is really no support group for them when they go back there so whatever gains are achieved in the Philippines are lost when they get back because they are not understood by those who did not go through the experience."

Overall, however, she considers such programs "very promising," she wrote— that is, "if the Filipino American community will recognize the importance of this experience for young people and set up a strong organization that will seriously implement this program in coordination with schools and universities there." While she grants that individuals like herself and de Castro could run such programs without institutional support, it could be "very, very intense and time consuming; it might well be a full time job." Jorge himself names a number of his Filipino American friends who have literally "gone back," at least two of whom still work as volunteers in Subic, Olongapo, where one of the largest U.S. naval installations left behind a deadly trail of toxic waste material after the bases pullout in 1992.

THE AMBIVALENCES OF HOMELAND (RE-)TURNINGS

Just as nationalism is being hailed in the West as passé and a severely mistaken project, we find this curious and belated awakening to nationalism in both the Philippine homeland and the diaspora—a phenomena that ought to call attention to the gross unevenness of processes of globalization currently sweeping the world. That this is happening among a generation of Filipino American youths whose formerly assimilationist orientation made erasure of the past a normative precondition for success in the United States is both significant and complex. As Jorge learned quickly enough, (re-)turning is never a simple matter of mere physical relocation or even of psychic reversal (never a simple move from there to here or from a default orientation to one's dominant other to a definitive turning to self).

In the very university that spawned liberation psychology, the University of the Philippines, Jorge is surprised to find that the discourse of Sikolohiyang Pilipino appears marginalized (once more) with the noted return to dominance of a more Western experimental psychology—"a conservative backlash," indigenization scholars would say. Jorge is learning, too, the delicate negotiations he needs to make as one deemed to stand outside the (Filipino) community he longs to be part of. He comments wryly to me in a 1999 e-mail, partly quoting my essay:

> [Indigenization scholars] argue for Pilipinos to communicate freely "in their own terms, in their own language, using their own thought patterns and manner of relating..." [yet this] exclusionary vision is kind of painful for me because of my background (not being born or raised here) and because of my intentions to pursue *sikolohiyang pilipino*, a discourse I'm sure [they] feel I have no right to engage in. Basically, the old question, "who am I," returns as I try to negotiate who is to be included among Salazar's "*tayo*": Pilipinos who speak the language in which he [Salazar] writes (i.e., Tagalog-Pilipino)? Pilipinos all over the world? Pilipinos in the Philippines? And who then are the "outsiders"?[11]

In a way, Jorge's presence breaches the normative imaginary enclosure around the category "*bayan*" (cultural nation or "place of belonging") and the more elusive identity category "Filipino." In a sense, he is the diaspora-come-near, the ambivalent signifier of an "other" that is not wholly other. Such disruptions, one might venture, present an exciting challenge for both Filipino and Filipino American scholars committed to understanding their complex, multisited locations and varied social positioning. On the one hand, the "nation" can no longer pretend to exclude from its business the countless Filipinos scattered abroad not only in the United States, but in every nook and cranny in the world. For not only do the faithful remittances of these overseas Filipinos to the homeland constitute a substantial portion of the country's annual gross national earnings, but also their self-projections, representations, and performances of Filipino-ness cast a reflective image upon the homeland constituents, even as homeland notions of Filipino-ness react upon them. On the other hand, those seeking reconnection with the homeland need to consider that the geographically circumscribed national community has pressing problems and agendas all its own. To seek to enter that community, even only discursively, requires acknowledging its peculiar contexts, struggles, logics, and normative priorities.

In the end, I believe it is good for Filipino scholars in the homeland, as for Filipino American would-be balikbayans, to disrupt each other's narratives and normative conceptions of the "nation" and its past and question what stakes and mutual investments there are in each community's laying claim to the belated signifier "Filipino"—particularly in the double inscription of the present moment that invokes at once nationhood and transcendence of nationhood as requisites for survival in an increasingly fraught global environment. It may be that only by opening up a space for dialogue might we forge a common ground for a multisited struggle aimed at redressing the injustices of the past as well as the insults of the present. Such a common ground need not be based on any one essentialized definition of the identity term "Filipino," but on knowledge of the infinite negotiations and renegotiations being made of that signifier as Filipinos both at home and abroad actively, critically engage their differing contexts and locations, conscious of the historic tie that binds them despite their differences.

In a way, I feel lucky. As Jorge reflected in a 1999 e-mail (and, I surmised, not without a tinge of envy) on what I had once regarded as my impossible location in the limbo between the homeland and the diaspora (being neither here nor there):

> Your discussion [in your paper] reflects the care with which we must socially negotiate the political terrain of translation; but more importantly it speaks about your own personal journey and experiences too which I may be able to relate to now that I am here in the Philippines and we are in opposite situations.... Your attempts at understanding the cultural barriers that separate Pilipino and American academic discourses is really tremendous and I am glad that you are doing this, especially because you can speak Pilipino and it privileges you with access "sa loob" [to the Filipino inner self] as Prof. Marcelino says.

THE RETURNS OF RETURNING

I spoke with Jorge in April 2000 when I learned that he was vacationing from school at his parents' home in Virginia. It had been almost a year since he and I met in the Philippines, and I was curious to find out how his year of study at the University of the Philippines had been. His first words to me over the phone were: "A lot of things have changed, . . . mellowed out a lot." As expected, I thought. He continued,

> I had thought of returning to the Philippines not just for a vacation. When I got there, I had so much on my mind . . . I wanted to dive into my graduate work. I felt disappointed. I felt I was up against too much. There was so much I wasn't accustomed to . . . I couldn't find my own flow, my own energy. It was kind of sad because I felt my energy dissipated. I had a hard time engaging. I couldn't find an academic community with similar pursuits and interests, no great place for graduate students to find each other. In the Psychology Department itself, there weren't many who were interested in *SP*, only some. We didn't really talk much about *SP*. Rather, I found things to be very western—experimental designs, statistics, et cetera unrelated to what I wanted to pursue.

It turns out that there were only three students enrolled in the Sikolohiyang Pilipino program. The other two, frustrated, had moved on to Philippine studies.[12] Despite the note of disappointment, however, Jorge did have gratifying things to say. (I was impressed that his experience wasn't entirely disillusioning—fairly common in such idealistic returnings.) Most of his positive comments had to do with his opportunity to experience life outside the academy, as in "I really feel that I pacified a lot of my curiosities, especially when I started traveling around and saw first-hand what Filipinos are like...their lives in the provinces. It was important for me to get out from Manila."

He said he was able to spend some time in the Cordilleras in Northern Philippines and in Ifugao, Mountain province. He also traveled around Mindanao, the southernmost part of the country, to "see a lot of things, experience things firsthand." He noted that it was really important for him to "mobilize" himself for the past six months and that when he did, he ended up having the rewarding experience of "seeing the different Filipino cultures." Obviously resourceful, he was able to connect and make friends with people who helped make these trips possible.

With regard to his university experience, Jorge had a productive relationship with at least one psychology faculty member, Professor Marcelino, in her research on an educational program for children of human rights victims. According to Jorge, it was a "Sikolohiyang Pilipino-based program" he found challenging and meaningful, as he told me over the phone:

> If there's one thing that *SP* has done for me, it is its perspective on methodological approaches to conducting research, that is, the need for very informal ways of talking to people in the form of *pagtatanong-tanong* [asking around], *pakikipagkuwentuhan* [exchanging stories], *pakikisalamuha* [getting involved versus being a detached observer], and so on. I guess I didn't really understand how deeply-seated that importance is. These methods of doing research have been criticized as "unscientific," but the thing is, they work! They [the critics] don't realize how difficult it is for social scientists to get rich data without practicing the value of *kapwa* [taking the other as also part of oneself].

This, Jorge said, is the most important learning he takes away from Sikolohiyang Pilipino, and he could only imagine how far this notion of *kapwa* could make a difference for social workers and other professionals once they truly employ it in their practice.

While Jorge does not think the formal study of Sikolohiyang Pilipino (which he found close to nil in the University of the Philippines anyway) is enough to bring him back to the Philippines, he said he is drawn to research projects like the one he worked on with Beth Marcelino. At the moment, however, his thoughts were turning toward transferring to a program in anthropology in one of the schools in California "where there are large communities of Filipino Americans." He then plans on returning to the Philippines to conduct ethnographic work, possibly in one of the local cultural communities.

Reflecting on his Philippine experience, Jorge wondered about the many other Filipino American students (a number of whom he knows personally) who, like him, are coming "back," most of them enrolling in medical schools such as University of the East and the University of Santo Tomas. A problem he mentioned with these individually initiated (re-)turns, given his own experience, is the lack of preparation of these numerous Filipino American youths for the experience of culture—as well as reentry—shock. He noted that most of them just up and leave for the Philippines in a burst of nationalistic fervor, and there are many he knows "who never quite make it." This is something, he says, that Philippine host schools and universities are looking into to prevent such premature dropping.

In a related conversation, Sikolohiyang Pilipino proponent Leny Mendoza-Strobel noted (personal e-mail communication, February 2000) the importance for students who go on such "return journeys" (particularly short-term ones, no more than two to three months) to have someone go through a "debriefing process" with them. Otherwise, she warns, they come back to the United States with the colonizer's gaze, having seen how "backward" and "primitive" Filipinos back home are, or, entirely disillusioned that all the things they were told about how "wonderful" Filipino culture is are, after all, "nothing but a bunch of lies." Three of her students who attended summer school in one of the private universities in Manila, for instance, returned with all sorts of anecdotes and stories about how they "knew so much more about Philippine history and decolonization stuff" than their Filipino classmates, saying, "Leny, they don't know a thing, the students there!" When Strobel pointed out how such an attitude was an unconscious taking on of the colonial gaze, she said, they became "repentant" and realized it is not that Filipino students know less, "they just know different things." As Strobel told me (personal e-mail communication, June 1998) when she later reflected on the potential for massive disillusionment for such returning Filipino American students unless provided with some guidance: "I guess for a FilAm there is a temptation to want to think of the Philippines as the unspoiled mother country where one can go for nostalgia, as source of the indigenous, the nonwestern, therefore non-corrupt, non-commercial, etc., . . . and yet for them over there they have no choice, they are saturated with images, and their appetites stimulated for anything 'stateside.'"

Yet one might venture to say that such potential for disillusionment may be what is needed to facilitate what Hall calls the difficult process of "entry into the politics of criticism" ("New Ethnicities," 448). That is, with the revalorized sign "Filipino" failing to deliver its expected signified (the true, the pure, the authentic) or the automatic nativist guarantee of all that is good and all that is to be cherished as a source of pride and (nationalist) edification, such disillusionment can have the salutary effect of inviting one to think in more complex ways. It can lead one to reevaluate the fraught interrelationships of history, memory, and desire and realize the slipperiness and instability all identity projects cast simultaneously against the still lingering shadows of colonial memory, on the one hand, and on the other, in fetishistic response to the competing attraction of "cool," borderless identities produced in the glitter of the global capitalist market.[13] In the end, in the search for self and recognition, there are no final guarantees. This is in no way to diminish the significance of such belated cultural awakenings but precisely to mark their import as a defining moment in the overall struggle for subjectivity that, at the same time, never really comes to an end.

I suggest that, in and of themselves, the implications of the "Jorges" of the Filipino diaspora and their belated homeland (re-)turnings constitute a rich site for the continuing theorization of an emergent cultural politics whose shape and direction may impact both homeland and diasporic communities' struggles to make a space for themselves within an increasingly tenuous, cacophonous, and confusing world.

Works Cited

Agoncillo, T. A., and M. Guerrero. *History of the Filipino People.* 5th ed. Quezon City: R. P. Garcia, 1977.

Bennagen, P. L. "The Indigenization and Asianization of Anthropology." In *Indigenous Psychology: A Book of Readings*, ed. V. G. Enriquez. Quezon City: Akademya ng Sikolohiyang Pilipino, 1990, 1–30.

———. "Mirror, Mirror on the Wall, Are We Human After All? (Towards a Humanist Anthropology)." In *The Social Responsibilities of the Social Scientist as an Intellectual*, ed. A. G. Carlos and A. R. Magno. Quezon City: University of the Philippines Press, 1977, 42–50.

Campomanes, O. V. "The Institutional Invisibility of American Imperialism, the Philippines, and Filipino Americans." *Maganda S,* 7–9 (January 1994): 60–62.

Canieso–Doronila, M. L. *The Limits of Educational Change: National Identity Formation in a Philippine Elementary School.* Quezon City: University of the Philippines Press, 1989.

Constantino, R. *A History of the Philippines: From the Spanish Colonization to the Second World War.* New York: Monthly Review Press, 1975.

———. "The Miseducation of the Filipino." In *Rediscovery: Essays in Philippine Life and Culture*, ed. C. N. Lumbera and T. Gimenez–Maceda. [Quezon City]: Department of English, Ateneo de Manila and National Book Store, 1977, 125–45.

———. *The Philippines: A Past Revisited.* Quezon City: Tala Publishing Services, 1975.

Covar, P. R. "Pilipinolohiya." In *Pilipinolohiya: Kasaysayan, pilosopiya at pananaliksik*, ed. V. V. Bautista and R. Pe-Pua. Manila: Kalikasan Press, 1991, 37–45.

De Leon, F. M., Jr. "The Roots of a People's Art in Indigenous Psychology." In *Indigenous Psychology: A Book of Readings*, ed. V. G. Enriquez. Quezon City: Akademya ng Sikolohiyang Pilipino, 1990, 311–27.

———. "Towards a People's Art." *Lipunan* 3 (1981): 1–15.

Enriquez, V. G. *From Colonial to Liberation Psychology: The Philippine Experience.* Diliman, Quezon City: University of the Philippines Press, 1992.

———. "Kapwa: A Core Concept in Filipino Social Psychology." *Philippine Social Sciences and Humanities Review* 42 (1978): 1–4.

———. "Mga Batayan ng Sikolohiyang Pilipino sa Kultura at Kasaysayan." [Cultural and historical bases of Filipino psychology]. In *Sikolohiyang Pilipino: Batayan sa kasaysayan, perspektibo, mga konsepto at bibliograpiya* [Filipino psychology: Historical Bases, Perspectives, Concepts, and Bibliography], ed. V. G. Enriquez. Diliman, Quezon City: University of the Philippines, 1975, 1–20.

———. "Pakikisama o pakikibaka? [Getting along or waging a struggle?]: Understanding the Psychology of the Filipino." Paper presented at the Conference on Philippine Culture, Bay Area Bilingual Education League. Berkeley, California, 29–30 April 1977.

Fanon, F. *The Wretched of the Earth.* New York: Grove Press, 1963.

Hall, S. "New Ethnicities." In *Stuart Hall: Critical Dialogues in Cultural Studies*, ed. D. Morley and K-S. Chen. London: Routledge, 1996, 441–49.

Jocano, F. L. *Philippine Prehistory: An Anthropological Overview of the Beginnings of Filipino Society and Culture.* Diliman, Quezon City: Philippine Center for Advanced Studies, University of the Philippines, 1975.

———. "Rethinking Filipino Cultural Heritage." *Lipunan* 11 (1965): 53–72.

Lynch, F. "Social Acceptance Reconsidered." In *Four Readings on Philippine Values*, ed. F. Lynch and A. de Guzman. IPC Papers No. 21–68. 4th ed. rev. Quezon City: Institute of Philippine Culture, Ateneo de Manila University, 1973.

Mendoza, S. L. *Between the Homeland and the Diaspora: The Politics of Theorizing Filipino and Filipino American Identities.* New York: Routledge, 2002.

———. "Bridging Theory and Cultural Politics: Revisiting the Indigenization-Poststructuralism Debates in Filipino and Filipino American Struggles for Identity." In *Intercultural Alliances: Critical Transformation*, ed. Mary Jane Collier. International and Intercultural Communication Annual 25. Thousand Oaks, Calif.: Sage, 2003, 249–77.

———. "Nuancing the Discourse on Anti-Essentialism: A Critical Genealogy of Philippine Experiments in National Identity Formation." In *Between Law and Culture: Relocating Legal Studies*, ed. David Theo Goldberg, Michael Musheno, and Lisa C. Bower. Minneapolis: University of Minnesota Press, 2001, 224–45.

Pratt, M. L. "Transculturation and Autoethnography: Peru 1615/1980." In *Colonial Discourse/Postcolonial Theory,* ed. F. Barker, P. Hulme, and M. Iversen. Manchester: Manchester University Press, 1994, 24–46.

Protacio-Marcelino, E. "Identidad at Etnisidad: Karanasan at Pananaw ng mga Estudyanteng Filipino Amerikano sa California." [Identity and ethnicity: Experiences and perspectives of Filipino American students in California]. Ph.D. diss., University of the Philippines, 1996.

Salazar, Z. A. "Ang pagpapasakasaysayang Pilipino ng nakaraang pre–Spaniko." [Historicizing the Philippines' pre-Spanish past]. Typescript. Author files. 1974–1975.

Strobel, E. M. "'Born-Again Filipino': Filipino American Identity and Asian Panethnicity." *Amerasia Journal* 22, 2 (1996): 31–53.

Notes

INTRODUCTION: CRITICAL CONSIDERATIONS

The epigraph is from Oscar V. Campomanes, "The New Empire's Forgetful and Forgotten Citizens: Unrepresentability and Unassimilability in Filipino-American Postcolonialities," *Critical Mass: A Journal of Asian American Cultural Criticism* 2, 2 (Spring 1995): 150–51.

1. Yen Le Espiritu, for example, deploys the term "differential inclusion" to underscore the violent and differential incorporation of groups of color into the national community but also to describe a process whereby a group of people is deemed integral to the building and sustaining of the nation precisely because of its subordinate status. Yen Le Espiritu, *Home Bound: Filipino American Lives across Cultures, Communities, and Countries* (Berkeley and Los Angeles: University of California Press, 2003).

2. Our use and understanding of the notion of cultural aphasia is informed by the work of Ryan Bishop and Lillian S. Robinson, who deploy the term to make sense of the elision of the Thai sex-tourist industry from that country's public discourse and consciousness. Bishop and Robinson, *Night Market: Sexual Cultures and the Thai Economic Miracle* (New York: Routledge, 1998).

3. William Appleman Williams, *Empire As a Way of Life: An Essay on the Causes and Character of America's Present Predicament along with a Few Thoughts about an Alternative* (New York and Oxford: Oxford University Press, 1980); Amy Kaplan, "Left Alone with America: The Absence of Empire in the Study of American Culture," in *Cultures of United States Imperialism*, ed. Kaplan and Donald E. Pease (Durham, N.C.: Duke University Press, 1993).

4. For a more detailed discussion, see Oscar V. Campomanes, "New Formations of Asian American Studies and the Question of U.S. Imperialism," *positions* 5, 2 (1997): 523–50.

5. That the debate over whether or not the United States has been or is a bona fide imperial power continues is both remarkable and telling to us, symptomatic of the pervasiveness of cultural aphasia in this nation with regards to this history.

6. The phrase "spectre of invisibility" comes from Oscar V. Campomanes, "Filipinos in the United States and Their Literature of Exile," in *Reading the Literatures of Asian America*, ed. Shirley Geok-lin Lim and Amy Ling (Philadelphia: Temple University Press, 1992), 53.

7. For a discussion of the elision of the Philippine-American War in historical accounts, see Angel Velasco Shaw and Luis H. Francia, eds., *Vestiges of War: The Philippine-American War and the Aftermath of an Imperial Dream, 1899–1999* (New York: New York University Press, 2002); Luzviminda Francisco, "The First Vietnam: The Philippine-American War, 1899–1902," taken from *The Philippines Reader: A History of Colonialism, Neocolonialism,*

Dictatorship, and Resistance, ed. Daniel B. Schirmer and Stephen Rosskamm Shalom (Boston: South End Press, 1987). For a discussion of the construction of Filipinos as ungrateful recipients of U.S. beneficence, see Roxanne Lynn Doty, *Imperial Encounters: The Politics of Representation in North-South Relations* (Minneapolis: University of Minnesota Press, 1996); Richard Drinnon, *Facing West: The Metaphysics of Indian-Hating and Empire Building* (Minneapolis: University of Minnesota Press, 1980).

8. A number of scholars have commented on the limitations of conceptual frameworks that have historically informed the study of Filipinos within Asian American studies. Campomanes, for example, asserts that these frameworks tend to be United States–centric, relying on assimilationist frameworks and conceptualizing Filipino migration to the United States in terms of immigration and settlement. He also points out that a similar logic and set of tendencies operate in Filipino American studies (Campomanes, "New Formations of Asian American Studies"); Campomanes addresses similar themes in "Filipinos in the United States." See also Kandice Chuh, *imagine otherwise: on Asian Americanist critique* (Durham, N.C.: Duke University Press, 2003), for her critique of Asian American studies, namely its continued reliance on nation as a critical frame. For a critique of the paradigmatic claims and assumptions of postcolonial studies, particularly its Eurocentric focus, see C. Richard King, ed., *Postcolonial America* (Urbana: University of Illinois Press, 2000), especially the essay by E. San Juan, Jr., "Establishment Postcolonialism and Its Alter/Native Others: Deciding to Be Accountable in a World of Permanent Emergency"; see also Kaplan and Pease, *Cultures of United States Imperialism.* The term "postcolonial" itself has come under critical scrutiny, particularly in relation to the legacies of colonial powers like Britain and the United States. See Anne McClintock, "The Angel of Progress: Pitfalls of the Term 'Post-colonialism,'" *Social Text* 31–32 (1992): 84–98; Ella Shohat, "Notes on the 'Post-Colonial,'" *Social Text* 31–32 (1992): 99–113.

9. For a more detailed account and critique of what transpired at the 1998 meeting, see Chuh, *imagine otherwise.* See also Candace Fujikane, "Sweeping Racism under the Rug of 'Censorship': The Controversy over Lois-Ann Yamanaka's *Blu's Hanging,*" *Amerasia Journal* 26, 2 (2000): 158–94; Darlene Rodrigues, "Imagining Ourselves: Reflections on the Controversy over Lois-Ann Yamanaka's *Blu's Hanging,*" *Amerasia Journal* 26, 2 (2000): 195–207.

10. E. San Juan, Jr., *Racial Formations/Critical Transformations*, 125.

11. Kandice Chuh and Karen Shimakawa, "Introduction," in *Orientations: Mapping Studies in the Asian Diaspora*, ed. Chuh and Shimakawa (Durham, N.C., and London: Duke University Press, 2001), 10.

12. For a discussion of how the deployment of the "trope of exclusion" to describe the experiences of Asian Americans is problematic, see Chuh, *imagine otherwise.*

13. In this volume, see the interview with Campomanes, who gestures toward shared experiences of colonization, conquest, and displacement between Filipinos and other colonized subjects as a possible point of departure for narrating Filipino history and subjectivity. But as Saranillio points out in his contribution to this volume, we also need to account for particular histories of colonization and especially the different relations of colonized groups to imperial projects. Joanne L. Rondilla has also written about this issue, calling for a reassessment of connections between Filipinos and Pacific Islanders, connections rooted in

analogous histories of colonization. Rondilla, "The Filipino Question in Asia and the Pacific: Rethinking Regional Origins in Diaspora," in Paul Spickard, Joanne L. Rondilla, and Debbie Hippolite Wright, eds., *Pacific Diaspora: Island Peoples in the United States and across the Pacific* (Honolulu: University of Hawaii Press, 2002). See also Leti Volpp, "American Mestizo: Filipinos and Antimiscegenation Laws in California," *UC Davis Law Review* 33 (2000): 795–835.

14. E. San Juan, Jr., *Racial Formations/Critical Transformations*, 117.

15. William J. Pomeroy, *An American-Made Tragedy: Neo-Colonialism and Dictatorship in the Philippines* (New York: International, 1974), 5.

16. King, "Introduction," in King, *Postcolonial America*, 4–5.

17. Sharon K. Hom, "Cross-Discipline Trafficking: What's Justice Got to Do with It?" in Chuh and Shimakawa, *Orientations*, 77.

18. For a discussion of law as a constitutive or generative force, see David Theo Goldberg, Michael Musheno, and Lisa C. Bower, eds., *Between Law and Culture: Relocating Legal Studies* (Minneapolis: University of Minnesota Press, 2001). See especially the essay by Rosemary J. Coombe, "Sports Trademarks and Somatic Politics: Locating the Law in a Critical Cultural Studies," which focuses on the constitutive power of law in relation to and within the context of contemporary sports culture. See also Lisa Lowe, *Immigrant Acts: On Asian American Cultural Politics* (Durham: Duke University Press, 1996), for an incisive discussion of the constitutive power of law in relation to Asian Americans.

19. For a consideration of Filipino labor organizing in the canning industry, see Chris Friday, *Organizing Asian American Labor: The Pacific Coast Canned-Salmon Industry, 1870–1942* (Philadelphia: Temple University Press, 1994). For a history of the pivotal role that Filipinos played in the revitalization of the farmworkers' movement in the 1960s, see Craig Scharlin and Lilia V. Villanueva, *Philip Vera Cruz: A Personal History of Filipino Immigrants and the Farmworkers Movement* (Los Angeles: UCLA Labor Center, Institute of Industrial Relations and UCLA Asian American Studies Center, 1992). For a discussion of the emergence of what came to be known as the anti–martial law movement in the United States, see Barbara Gaerlan, "The Movement in the United States to Oppose Martial Law in the Philippines, 1972–1991: An Overview," *Pilipinas* 33 (Fall 1999): 75–98. See also Helen Toribio, "We Are Revolution: A Reflective History of the Union of Democratic Filipinos (KDP), *Amerasia Journal* 24, 2 (Summer 1998): 155–77. Theodore S. Gonzalves has written extensively on Filipino cultural politics, including an essay on murals and their significance as visual markers of Filipinoness but also as places where Filipinos can narrate history on their own terms as well as consolidate conventional ways of telling history. Gonzalves, "When the Walls Speak a Nation: Contemporary Murals and the Narration of Filipina/o America," *Journal of Asian American Studies* 1, 1 (February 1998): 31–63. See also his essay on the politics of culture shows, "The Day the Dancers Stayed: On Pilipino Cultural Nights," in Maria P. P. Root, ed., *Filipino Americans: Transformation and Identity* (Thousand Oaks: Sage, 1997).

20. For a discussion of the contours of Asian American politics in which electoral politics constitutes just one form of political activity that Asian Americans have pursued, see Gordon H. Chang, ed., *Asian Americans and Politics: Perspectives, Experiences, Prospects* (Stanford, Calif.: Stanford University Press, 2001). For a discussion of the need to break away

from conventional notions of politics in relation to black politics, see Robin D. G. Kelley, *Race Rebels: Culture, Politics, and the Black Working Class* (New York: Free Press, 1996).

21. In addition to the emerging scholars we solicited contributions from for this volume, we want to acknowledge an emerging cohort of young scholars producing what we consider exemplary work: Kimberly Alidio, Rick Baldoz, Lisa Cacho, Catherine Ceniza Choy, Linda N. Espana-Maram, August Espiritu, Candace Fujikane, Eleanor Jaluague, Eric Reyes, Darlene Rodrigues, Dorothy Fujita Rony, Karin Aguilar-San Juan, Neferti Tadiar, Charlene Tung, and Sunny Vergara. We also want to acknowledge the core members of the Critical Filipina and Filipino Studies Collective (CFFSC) for producing intellectually and politically compelling work: Nerissa Balce (one of our contributors), Lucy San Pablo Burns, Richard Chu, Peter Chua, Gladys Nubla, Robyn Magalit Rodriguez, Joanne L. Rondilla, Jeffrey Santa Ana, and Rowena Tomaneng. Finally, we would be remiss not to mention the names of more established scholars who provided the impetus and inspiration for this project: Walden Bello, Steffi San Buenaventura, Sharon Delmendo, Yen Le Espiritu, Luis H. Francia, Jessica Hagedorn, Reynaldo C. Ileto, Luzvimida Francisco, Martin F. Manalansan IV, Jonathan Y. Okamura, Vincente L. Rafael, Maria P. P. Root, Ninotschka Rosca, E. San Juan, Jr., Helen C. Toribio, and Leti Volpp.

22. The phrase "vigorous pursuit of 'Filipino American' critique" is a paraphrase of Lisa Lowe's apt characterization of the project in the Foreword.

CHAPTER ONE: PATTERNS OF REFORM, REPETITION, AND RETURN IN THE FIRST CENTENNIAL OF THE FILIPINO REVOLUTION, 1896–1996

This article was originally delivered as the opening address to the second annual UC Berkeley Filipino and Pilipino American Studies Symposium, 12–13 April 1996.

1. For a record of Rizal's travel notes and impressions of the United States, see *Publicaciones de la Comisión Nacional del Centenario de José Rizal, Escritos de José Rizal*, vol. 1, *Diarios y memorias* (Manila: Comisión Nacional del Centenario de José Rizal, 1961); the quotes are on 217–19, 219.

2. W.E.B. DuBois gave the name "double-consciousness" to the predicament of the U.S. black intellectual at the turn of the century (see "Of Our Spiritual Strivings" in *The Souls of Black Folk* [1903], www.bartleby.com/114/1.html). For a reading of Rizal's own reflection on this condition, see Benedict Anderson, *The Spectre of Comparisons* (London: Verso, 1998), 2.

3. The question of the privileged object(s) of investigation in the field of Asian American and ethnic studies has been a subject of debate in recent years. Some key texts include Sau-ling Wong, "Denationalization Reconsidered: Asian American Cultural Criticism at a Theoretical Crossroads," *Amerasia Journal* 21, 1 and 2 (1995): 1–27; Lisa Lowe, *Immigrant Acts* (Durham: Duke University Press, 1996); and Arif Dirlik, "Asians on the Rim: Transnational Capital and Local Community in the Making of Contemporary Asian America," in *Across the Pacific: Asian Americans and Globalization*, ed. Evelyn Hu-DeHart (Philadelphia: Temple University Press, 1999), 29–60. For the ramifications of this debate

on Filipino and Filipino American studies, see Oscar Campomanes, "The New Empire's For-getful and Forgotten Citizens: Unrepresentability and Unassimilability in Filipino American Postcolonialities," *Critical Mass* 11, 2 (Spring 1995): 145–200.

4. This projection was based on the 1990 U.S. Census. The 2000 U.S. Census shows that the Chinese population is the largest detailed Asian group in the United States (2.7 million), with Filipinos (2.4 million) and Asian Indians (1.9 million) as the next largest Asian groups.

5. Ninotchka Rosca, *State of War* (New York and London: Norton, 1988).

6. In 1999, the *Los Angeles Times* reported that "nearly 46% of Filipina high school girls who were surveyed five years ago by the San Diego Unified School District said they had seriously contemplated suicide during the previous 12 months. The teenagers cited the pain of trying to mesh cultures and a lack of Filipino American role models as key sources of conflict in their lives." See Julie Tamaki, "Cultural Balancing Act Adds to Teen Angst," jrn.Columbia.edu/workshops/Asians2_LATIMES.htm; see also Yen Le Espiritu and Diane L. Wolf, "The Paradox of Assimilation: Children of Filipino Immigrants in San Diego," migration.ucdavis.edu/cmpr/feb99/espiritu.html, especially 10–13, 20.

7. For a critique of structural adjustment programs and their failure in most coun-tries who adopted free market policies at the insistence of the IMF and World Bank, see Walden Bello (with Shea Cunningham and Bill Rau), *Dark Victory: The United States, Structural Adjustment, and Global Poverty* (Oakland: Food First, 1994). See also Merlin M. Magallona's analysis of the dismantling of Philippine state administration to facilitate the monopoly of U.S. and Japanese trusts and corporations, *The Dismantling of the Philippine State and the Impact on Civil Society* (Quezon City: Institute of International Legal Stud-ies, 1996). The U.S. government has yet to fully reverse the 1945 Rescission Act denying Filipino veterans (drafted by the United States to fight in World War II) compensation and benefits equal to that of their U.S. counterparts.

8. For statistics of the UC Berkeley population by ethnicity (fall 1996), see osr2.berkeley.edu/cgi-bin/Access/DB/Programs/handlesql2.pl. A statement of concern was published by members of undergraduate and graduate student groups; for a summary of its contents, see Jonathan Y. Okamura and Amefil R. Agbayani, "Pamantasan: Filipino American Higher Education," in *Filipino Americans: Transformation and Identity*, ed. Maria P. P. Root (Thousand Oaks, Calif.: Sage, 1997).

9. For a history of the legacy of the anti-Marcos movement based in the United States, see Helen Toribio, "We Are Revolution: A Reflective History of the Union of Democratic Filipinos (KDP), *Amerasia Journal* 24, 2 (Summer 1998): 155–77.

10. For a comparative analysis of Philippine poverty, U.S. international trade policies, and labor migration, see Linda Basch, Nina Glick Schiller, and Cristina Szanton-Blanc, *Na-tions Unbound: Transnational Projects, Postcolonial Predicaments, and Deterritorialized Nation-States* (Amsterdam: Gordon and Breach Science Publications, 1994).

11. See *Publicaciones de la Comisión Nacional*, 214, 216, 226.

12. Ibid., 226.

13. Ibid., 230.

14. "El mundo [da] la razon al más fuerte, almás violento! . . . allí está el Norte con su libertad egoista, su ley de Lynch, sus engaños políticos" (chap. 33). José Rizal, *El*

filibusterismo (Manila: National Historical Society, 1990), 250; for a description of Simoun, see page 8. Sharon Delmendo has critically examined the influence of U.S. politics on José Rizal; see "The American Factor in José Rizal's Nationalism, *Amerasia* 24, 2 (Summer 1998): 35–63.

15. For "structure of feeling," see Raymond Williams, *Marxism and Literature* (London: Oxford University Press, 1977), 128–32; for "haecceity," see Gilles Deleuze and Félix Guattari, *A Thousand Plateaus*, trans. Brian Massumi (Minneapolis: University of Minnesota Press, 1982), 260–65.

16. On the concept of the "care chain" of international domestic labor, see Rhacel Salazar Parreñas, *Servants of Globalization: Women, Migration, and Domestic Work* (Stanford: Stanford University Press, 2001).

17. See Karl Marx, *The Eighteenth Brumaire of Louis Bonaparte* (1852; repr., New York: International, 1990). For a history of identity struggles formed in and around the politicization of Filipino identity, see John D. Blanco, "Vernacular Counterpoint: Filipino Enlightenment in a Late Colonial Context, 1837–1896" (Ph.D. diss., UC Berkeley, 2001), especially chaps. 5 and 6.

18. See the letter correspondence concerning Filipino revolutionary diplomat Mariano Ponce, Cuban revolutionary Gonzalo de Quezada, and Puerto Rican revolutionary Ramón Emeterio Betances in *Cartas sobre la Revolución 1897–1900* (Manila: Bureau of Printing, 1932), 167–86 passim.

19. For an analysis of the correspondence between racism and imperialism, see the early pamphlet by anti-imperialist Kelly Miller, "The Effect of Imperialism upon the Negro Race," *Anti-Imperialist Broadside*, No. 11 (Boston: New England Anti-Imperialist League, n.d. [1900]), in *Anti-Imperialism in the United States, 1898–1935*, ed. Jim Zwick, www.boondocksnet.com/ai/ (accessed 26 April 2002).

20. This is the enduring message behind Ernst Bloch's *Natural Law and Human Dignity*, trans. Dennis J. Schmidt (Cambridge: MIT Press, 1986); and more recently, Michael Hardt and Antonio Negri, *Empire* (Cambridge: Harvard University Press, 2000).

21. On the relationship between Filipino *ilustrado* thought, particularly Rizal, and (Spanish) constitutional republicanism, see Cesar Adib Majul, *The Political and Constitutional Ideas of the Philippine Revolution* (1967; rpt. Quezon City, Manila: University of the Philippines Press, 1996), 22–32, 62–63; Manuel Sarkisyanz, *Rizal and Republican Spain and Other Rizalist Essays* (Manila: National Historical Society, 1995), 18, 111–30.

22. Toribio, "We Are Revolution."

23. Arjun Appadurai, *Modernity at Large: Cultural Dimensions of Globalization* (Minneapolis: University of Minnesota Press, 1996), 33–34, 48–65.

24. Salud Algabre, a female organizer in the Sakdal peasant uprising of 1935, qtd. in Reynaldo Ileto, *Pasyon and Revolution: Popular Movements in the Philippines, 1840–1910* (Quezon City, Manila: Ateneo de Manila University Press, 1979).

25. Carlos Bulosan, letter to Wilfredo Bulosan, 1 April 1948, *Philippine Studies* 39 (1991): 347–50. See also Oscar Campomanes and Todd Gernes's introduction to the letters in the same volume, "Two Bulosan Letters from America" (337–41).

26. See the important contribution to a legal analysis and history of antimiscegenation laws by Leti Volpp, "American Mestizo: Filipinos and Anti-Miscegenation Laws in California," *UC Davis Law Review* 79, 5 (Summer 2000): 795–835.

27. See Oscar Campomanes, "Filipinos in the United States and Their Literature of Exile," in *Discrepant Histories: Translocal Essays on Filipino Cultures*, ed. Vicente Rafael (Philadelphia: Temple University Press, 1995), 163–64.

CHAPTER TWO: ON FILIPINOS, FILIPINO-AMERICANS, AND U.S. IMPERIALISM

Oscar Compomanes responded in writing to the written questions for this interview.

1. See James Thomson, Peter Stanley and John Curtis, *Sentimental Imperialists* (New York: Harper and Row, 1982).

2. Oscar V. Compomanes, "1898 and the Nature of the New Empire," *Radical History Review*, Winter 1999, 130–46.

3. I think to bear out this point, you must consult the highly engaging account of U.S. Filipino formation in Rick Bonus's book, *Locating Filipino Americans: Ethnicity and the Cultural Politics of Space* (Philadelphia: Temple University Press, 2000).

4. Compomanes, "1898 and the Nature."

5. See Antonio Gramsci, "America and Fordism," in *The Antonio Gramsci Reader: Selected Writings, 1916–1935*, ed. David Forgacs (New York: New York University Press, 2000); Octavio Paz, "Imperial Democracy," in *One Earth, Four or Five Worlds: Reflections on Contemporary History* (New York: Harcourt Brace Jovanovich, 1985); Nick Joaquin, Culture and History: Occasional Notes on the Process of Philippine Becoming (Manila: Solar, 1988); Gilles Deleuze and Felix Guattari, *A Thousand Plateaus* (Minneapolis: University of Minnesota Press, 1983); Michael Hardt and Antonio Negri, *Empire* (Cambridge: Harvard University Press, 2000).

6. Seward qtd. in Walter LaFeber, *The American Age: U.S. Foreign Policy at Home and Abroad since 1750* (New York: Norton, 1989), 5.

7. William Pomeroy, *American Neo-Colonialism: Its Emergence in the Philippines and Asia* (New York: International, 1970), 5.

8. Michael Hunt has a long helpful chapter on this kind of political ethnocentrism in *Ideology and U.S. Foreign Policy* (New Haven: Yale University Press, 1987); see chapter 9, "The Perils of Revolution."

9. Bill Ashcroft, Gareth Griffiths, and Helen Tiffin, eds., *The Empire Writes Back: Theory and Practice in Post-Colonial Literatures*, 2d ed. (New York: Routledge, 2002).

10. Benedict Anderson, "Hard to Imagine: A Puzzle in the History of Philippine Nationalism," in *Cultures and Texts: Representations of Philippine Society*, ed. Paul Pertierra and Eduardo Ugarte (Quezon City: University of the Philippines Press, 1999), 81–119.

11. Frantz Fanon, "The Negro and Recognition," in *Black Skin, White Masks* (1952; New York: Grove Press, 1967), 219.

12. Ibid.

CHAPTER THREE: FILIPINO BODIES, LYNCHING, AND THE LANGUAGE OF EMPIRE

An abridged early version of this essay was read in two colloquia in April and May 1999, the first version at the St. Clair Drake Cultural Studies colloquium at the University of California-Berkeley organized by the African American Studies department, the second in a colloquium organized by the East Bay Filipino American National Historical Society. Many thanks to Fidelito C. Cortes and my colleagues Caroline A. Streeter, Vernadette Gonzalez, and Jody Blanco for their helpful critiques of this essay. I am indebted to John, Livy, and Anna More, who were my gracious hosts when I conducted research in Washington, D.C.

1. For an excellent cultural and sociological discussion of Filipino American identities and the formation of Filipino immigrant communities, see Rick Bonus, *Locating Filipino Americans: Ethnicity and the Cultural Politics of Space* (Philadelphia: Temple University Press, 2000). Selected new writings on Filipino American communities and culture that examine the colonial past and/or neocolonial present include: Yen Le Espiritu, *Home Bound: Filipino American Lives across Cultures, Communities, and Countries* (Berkeley and Los Angeles: University of California Press, 2003); Dorothy B. Fujita-Rony, *American Workers, Colonial Power: Philippine Seattle and the Transpacific West, 1919–1941* (Berkeley and Los Angeles: University of California Press, 2003); Catherine Ceniza Choy, *Empire of Care: Nursing and Migration in Filipino American History* (Durham, N.C.: Duke University Press, 2003); S. Lily Mendoza, *Between the Homeland and the Diaspora: The Politics of Theorizing Filipino and Filipino American Identities: A Second Look at the Poststructuralism-Indigenization Debates* (New York: Routledge, 2002); E. San Juan, Jr., *After Postcolonialism: Remapping Philippines–United States Confrontations* (Lanham, Md.: Rowman and Littlefield, 2000); Barbara M. Posadas, *The Filipino Americans* (Westport, Conn.: Greenwood Press, 1999); Jonathan Y. Okamura, *Imagining the Filipino American Diaspora: Transnational Relations, Identities, and Communities* (New York: Garland, 1998).

2. By the 1930s, thousands of Filipinos worked as migrant farmworkers in states such as California, Oregon, and Washington. According to the 1930 census, there were 45,208 Filipinos living in the United States. See Bureau of Insular Affairs, War Department, *Filipino Immigration into the Continental United States and Occupations Followed by Filipinos in the States of California, Oregon, and Washington and in the Continental United States as a Whole*, January 14, 1932, National Archives, Maryland, RG 350, Folder 51, BIA files. Historian Sucheng Chan has argued that by the late 1920s, Filipinos suffered the "last major round of violence against Asians." In the summer of 1930, five hundred white American youths picketed a newly opened dance hall in Palm Beach, California, frequented by Filipino farmworkers. That same summer, a second riot occurred with four hundred white men attacking the Northern Monterey Filipino Club. Dozens of Filipinos were beaten and two were killed. See Chan, *Asian Americans: An Interpretative History* (Boston: Twayne, 1991), 53.

3. Carlos Bulosan, *America Is in the Heart* (1946; rpt. Seattle: University of Washington Press, 1973), 206–8, ellipses mine.

4. Emory Bogardus, "American Attitudes towards Filipinos," James Earl Wood Papers, Bancroft Library, University of California, Berkeley, microfiche, reel 4, 0261–0262. Even

Mexican farmworkers resented competition from Filipino farmworkers and contemptuously nicknamed them *chonggo*, Spanish for "monkey." See Bogardus, Wood Papers, reel 4. Filipino labor activist and United Farm Workers' leader Philip Vera Cruz recalls that white communities used the term "monkey" to refer to Filipinos. White communities were threatened by Filipino men who had relationships with white immigrant or working-class women who worked in the dance halls frequented by Filipinos. See *Philip Vera Cruz: A Personal History of Filipino Immigrants and the Farmworkers Movement*, ed. Craig Scharlin and Lilia V. Villanueva (Los Angeles: UCLA Labor Center, 1992), 9–11. On anti-Filipino violence, see Howard De Witt, *Violence in the Fields: California Filipino Farm Labor Unionization during the Great Depression* (Saratoga, Calif.: Century Twenty One Publications, 1980); Gladys Hennig Waldron, "Anti-Foreign Movements in California, 1919–1929" (Ph.D. diss., University of California, 1956), 266–79; Generoso Pacificar Provido, "Oriental Immigration from an American Dependency" (M.A. thesis, University of California, 1931), 17–21.

5. Critics have interpreted Bulosan's *America Is in the Heart* in different ways but none have discussed this torture scene as a lynching. For critics' reception of Bulosan, see Tim Libretti's incisive discussion in "*America Is in the Heart* by Carlos Bulosan," in *A Resource Guide to Asian American Literature*, ed. Sau-ling Cynthia Wong and Stephen H. Sumida (New York: Modern Language Association, 2001), 22–23.

6. Critic Rachel C. Lee, in *The Americas of Asian American Literature: Gendered Fictions of Nation and Transnation* (Princeton, N.J.: Princeton University Press, 1999), 17–43, offers an interesting but problematic discussion of women (Filipinas, white women, and women of color) in Bulosan's text that deserves space in another forum. Lee discusses a scene where a Filipina bride and the groom were tied to trees, whipped, and stoned by the Filipino villagers because they were suspected of having sexual relations outside marriage (17). It is important to note that the scene was described by Bulosan as a "fast-dying custom, in line with other backward customs in the Philippines" (*America Is in the Heart*, 7). In other words, Bulosan acknowledged the brutality of this ritual—in line with his Marxist ideals of critiquing the "feudal" past—but Lee omits this in her discussion and excises the quote altogether. Lee fails to historicize the contradictory position of Filipino men as hypersexualized and feminized subjects. She also does not account for the suffering woman as a nationalist trope in the Filipino literary tradition, which Bulosan draws from. In my view, Bulosan invoked gendered images and ideas of "brotherhood" as a rhetorical and political strategy. It was the author's strategy of reminding his U.S. readers, who were reading him in postwar America, of the historical ties between the Philippines and the United States, recalling the discourse of the Philippines as a young ward and as a "little brown brother" of the United States. The origin of this filial relationship was empire, which I discuss in this essay.

7. William Loren Katz, preface to *The Black Press Views American Imperialism (1898–1900)*, ed. George P. Marks III (New York: Arno Press/New York Times, 1971), viii. Orlando Patterson echoes this observation in his study of lynching as a blood ritual influenced by ideas of Christian religion, human sacrifice, and cannibalism. Charts used by Patterson show a dramatic increase in lynchings of African Americans in the 1890s; see Patterson, *Rituals of Blood: Consequences of Slavery in Two American Centuries* (Washington, D.C.:

Civitas, 1998), 175, 177 for charts and, for a discussion of lynching, ritual, and religion, 171–232.

8. Etienne Balibar, "Racism and Nationalism," in *Race, Nation, Class: Ambiguous Identities*, ed. Balibar and Immanuel Wallerstein (London: Verso, 1991), 45. I thank Nikhil Singh for suggesting Balibar's discussion on racism and nationalism.

9. See Stuart Creighton Miller, *"Benevolent Assimilation": The American Conquest of the Philippines, 1899–1903* (New Haven: Yale University Press, 1982), 104–28.

10. The conceptual framework and ideas of this essay have largely been informed by the writings of Hazel V. Carby, who claims that writers like Anna Julia Cooper had a global perspective on domestic racial oppression and U.S. expansion in the Pacific, though I would add that Cooper wrote her prescient ideas seven years before the Philippine-American War. Carby views the 1890s as an intense and productive time for black women intellectuals such as Frances Harper (*Iola Leroy*), Anna Julia Cooper (*Voice from the South*) and Ida B. Wells (*Southern Horrors: Lynch Law in All Its Phases*). She argues that lynching, the common occurrence of the rape of black women by white men in the South, and U.S. expansion were all attempts to regain control of emancipated nonwhite bodies. See Carby, " 'On the Threshold of Woman's Era': Lynching, Empire, and Sexuality in Black Feminist Theory," in *"Race," Writing, and Difference*, ed. Henry Louis Gates, Jr. (Chicago: University of Chicago Press, 1986), 301–16; also by Carby, *Reconstructing Womanhood: The Emergence of the Afro-American Woman Novelist* (New York: Oxford University Press, 1987), 95–120.

11. Carby, "On the Threshold," 304. While Harper, Cooper, and Ida B. Wells published their works before the Philippine-American War and the annexation of the Philippines as a new U.S. colony, their writings illustrate the origins of a contemporary feminist aesthetic of viewing global issues through a domestic lens, a literary aesthetic and political principle that we find a century later in the writings of feminist women of color from the 1970s who wrote against the Vietnam War, for example in the 1970s community newspaper *Triple Jeopardy*, published by the Third World Women's Alliance. I am grateful to Tiya Miles for introducing me to this source.

12. Kristin L. Hoganson, *Fighting for American Manhood: How Gender Politics Provoked the Spanish-American and Philippine-American Wars* (New Haven: Yale University Press, 1998), 134–38.

13. Judson and Woolsey, qtd. in "Three Views of the Philippine Problem," *Literary Digest* 18 [1] (January–June 1899): 1, 2.

14. "The White Man's Burden versus the Brown Man's Burden," ibid., 18 [8]: 219.

15. Labouchere qtd. in ibid.

16. Ernest H. Crosby qtd. in ibid.

17. *Literary Digest* 18 [5]: 142. Succeeding quotes from this journal are cited by volume, issue, and page number in the text or notes.

18. The *Literary Digest* quotes Professor Blumentritt in the *Vienna Tageblatt*; whether he is the German scholar who was a publisher and a personal friend of the Filipino nationalist José Rizal is uncertain.

19. Amy Kaplan, "Black and Blue on San Juan Hill," in *Cultures of United States Imperialism*, ed. Kaplan and Donald E. Pease (Durham, N.C.: Duke University Press, 1993), 219.

20. From W.E.B. DuBois's objection to U.S. intervention in Korea in the 1950s to criticism of the Vietnam War in the mid-1960s by Martin Luther King, Jr., Stokely Carmichael, and Eldridge Cleaver, black voices have sounded the connection between imperialism and racism. See Katz, preface, vii.

21. Marks, *The Black Press*, 51, 52, 53, 67.

22. Vicente L. Rafael, "White Love: Surveillance and Nationalist Resistance in the U.S. Colonization of the Philippines," in *Cultures of United States Imperialism*, ed. Kaplan and Pease, 185.

23. See Kenneth Mostern, "Three Theories of the Race of W.E.B. DuBois," *Cultural Critique*, Fall 1996, 39.

24. Sandra Gunning, *Race, Rape, and Lynching: The Red Record of American Literature, 1890–1912* (New York: Oxford University Press, 1996), 31; Paul Alexander Kramer, "Jim Crow Science and the 'Negro Problem' in the Occupied Philippines, 1898–1914," in *Race Consciousness: African-American Studies for the New Century*, ed. Judith Jackson Fossett (New York: New York University Press, 1997), 227–46.

25. Editorial, qtd. in Marks, *The Black Press*, 150.

26. Leon F. Litwack, *Trouble in Mind: Black Southerners in the Age of Jim Crow* (New York: Vintage Books, 1998), 405.

27. Marks, *The Black Press*, xvii, xviii. Unless otherwise noted, succeeding page number citations in the text are from this source.

28. Walter L. Williams, "United States Indian Policy and the Debate over Philippine Annexation: Implications for the Origins of American Imperialism," *Journal of American History*, March 1980, 810–31. Williams gives a revealing list of U.S. generals in the Philippines who were "Indian veterans." Notables include Thomas Anderson, whose personal papers are in the University of California Bancroft Archives, and Arthur McArthur, the father of General Douglas McArthur, who would be immortalized as a World War II hero by Filipinos (828).

29. Marks, *The Black Press*, 106.

30. Cited in William B. Gatewood, Jr., *"Smoked Yankees" and the Struggle for Empire: Letters from Negro Soldiers, 1898–1902* (Fayetteville: University of Kansas Press, 1987), 258–59. See also Marks, *The Black Press*, 155. For details on the lynching of Sam Hose, see Litwack, *Trouble in Mind*, 280–83.

31. Gatewood, *Smoked Yankees*, 15.

32. Ibid., 268.

33. Ibid., 280.

34. Morse qtd. in Reginald Horseman, *Race and Manifest Destiny: The Origins of American Racial Anglo-Saxonism* (Cambridge: Harvard University Press, 1981), 86.

35. See Oscar V. Campomanes, "1898 and the Nature of the New Empire," *Radical History Review* 73 (Winter 1999): 130–46.

36. Gail Bederman, *Manliness and Civilization: A Cultural History of Gender and Race in the United States, 1880–1917* (Chicago: University of Chicago Press, 1995), 223, 226, 225.

37. Mostern, "Three Theories," 28. For a summary of debate on DuBois's adherence to Stalinism, which affected his position among scholars, see William E. Cain, "From

Liberalism to Communism: The Political Thought of W.E.B. DuBois," in Kaplan and Pease, *Cultures of United States Imperialism*, 456–71. Succeeding quotations from W.E.B. DuBois, *Darkwater*, in *The Oxford W.E.B. DuBois Reader*, ed. Eric J. Sundquist (New York: Oxford University Press, 1996), are cited in the text by page number.

38. John Carlos Rowe, *Literary Culture and U.S. Imperialism: From the Revolution to World War II* (New York: Oxford University Press, 2000), 215; and see 204–16.

39. Mostern, "Three Theories," 31.

40. Eric Sundquist, "W.E.B. DuBois and the Autobiography of Race," introduction to *The Oxford W.E.B. DuBois Reader* (New York: Oxford University Press, 1996), 27.

41. Ibid., 31.

CHAPTER FOUR: "JUST TEN YEARS REMOVED FROM A BOLO AND A BREECH-CLOTH"

1. Andrea Dworkin, *Pornography: Men Possessing Women* (New York: Putnam, 1979), 17.

2. Yen Le Espiritu, *Asian American Women and Men: Labor, Laws, and Love* (Thousand Oaks, Calif.: Sage, 1997), 7.

3. *Manong* means "big brother" and refers to members of the predominately male first wave of Pilipino migrants to the United States.

4. Lisa Lowe, *Immigrant Acts: On Asian American Cultural Politics* (Durham, N.C., and London: Duke University Press, 1996), 26.

5. Avery P. Gordon, *Ghostly Matters: Haunting and the Sociological Imagination* (Minneapolis: University of Minnesota Press, 1997).

6. Here, I am incorporating Avery Gordon's understanding of Raymond William's term, about which she writes: "I have not endeavored to establish transhistorical or universal laws of haunting per se but rather to represent the structure of feeling that is something akin to what it feels like to be the object of a social totality vexed by the phantoms of modernity's violence. What does it mean? It means following the insights that come to those who see all these forces operating at once. Such a way of seeing can make you a bit crazy and imprecise and wary of shorthands. While it may be true that the constellation of social forces all collide in various ways, that social life's complication is, to use an often overused phrase, overdetermined, the obvious task of the critic or analyst is to designate the precise contours of experience and causality in particular instances" (ibid., 18–19).

7. Honorante Mariano, *The Filipino Immigrants in the U.S.* (Eugene: University of Oregon Press, 1933), 4.

8. Carlos Bulosan, *America Is in the Heart* (1943; rpt. Seattle: University of Washington Press, 1973), 69–70.

9. Daniel B. Schirmer and Stephen R. Shalom, "Colonization," in *The Philippines Reader: A History of Colonialism, Neocolonialism, Dictatorship, and Resistance*, ed. Shirmer and Shalom (Boston: South End Press, 1987), 45–47.

10. Raymond Williams, *Marxism and Literature* (Oxford: Oxford University Press, 1977), 118.

11. Ronald Takaki, "Dollar a Day, Dime a Dance: The Forgotten Filipinos," in *Strangers from a Different Shore: A History of Asian Americans* (New York: Penguin, 1989), 315.

12. Linda N. Espana-Maram, "Brown 'Hordes' in McIntosh Suits: Filipinos, Taxi Dance Halls, and the Performing Immigrant Body in Los Angeles," in *Generations of Youth: Youth Cultures and History in Twentieth-Century America*, ed. Joe Austin and Michael Nevin Willard (New York: New York University Press, 1998), 5.

13. Takaki, "Dollar a Day," 318.

14. Mariano, *Filipino Immigrants in the U.S.*, 31.

15. Takaki, "Dollar a Day," 320.

16. Lowe, *Immigrant Acts*, 11.

17. Homi K. Bhabha, "The Other Question . . ." *Screen* 24, 6 (November–December 1993): 18–36.

18. Espana-Maram, "Brown 'Hordes' in McIntosh Suits," 5.

19. Judge Sylvain Lazarus, interview with *Time* magazine (1929), qtd. in Takaki, "Dollar a Day," 328.

20. Takaki, ibid.

21. Emory S. Bogardus, "Anti Filipino Race Riots," in *Letters in Exile*, ed. Bogardus (Los Angeles: UCLA Asian American Studies Center, 1976), 52–53.

22. Takaki, "Dollar a Day," 329.

23. Howard A. DeWitt, "The Watsonville Riot of 1930: The Nadir of Anti-Filipino Sentiment in California," in *Anti-Filipino Movements in California: A History, Bibliography, and Study Guide* (San Francisco: R and E Research Associates, 1976), 48.

24. Legal and political actors officially resisted the same "penetration" and attempted to speed the exclusion of the Pilipino from the United States through antimiscegenation laws. The earliest court cases concerning the intermarriage of Pilipinos with white women were determined according to the presiding judge's interpretation of the racial classification of Pinoys. If the judge decided that Pilipinos, who were Malays, were also Mongolians, then previous legislation prohibited these unions. If he decided that "when speaking of the 'Mongolians,' reference is had to the yellow and not to the brown people," then the marriages were allowed. The racial identity of Pilipinos was not legally determined until 1933, in *Salvador Roldan v. Los Angeles County*, when Pilipinos were officially granted the right to marry whites in California. But this legal "victory" was sabotaged by two bills that amended the Civil Code to include the Malay race in the nonwhite groups already prohibited from marrying whites. These bills provided for the retroactive invalidation of any white intermarriage. See Henry Empeno, "Anti-Miscegenation Laws and the Pilipino," in Bogardus, *Letters in Exile*, 63–71.

25. H. Brett Melendy, "California's Discrimination against Filipinos, 1927–1935," in *The Filipino Exclusion Movement, 1927–1935: Occasional Papers No. 1*, ed. Josefa M. Saniel (Quezon City: Institute of Asian Studies, University of the Philippines, 1967), 9.

26. Teun van Dijk, *Elite Discourse and Racism* (Newbury Park, Calif.: Sage, 1993), 50.

27. Raymond Williams, *Marxism and Literature* (Oxford: Oxford University Press, 1977), 108.

28. U.S. Cong., 34–38.

29. Ibid., 35.

30. Ibid., 35–36.

31. C. M. Goethe, "Filipino Immigration Viewed as a Peril," *Current History*, June 1931, 353–56.

32. Melendy, "California's Discrimination against Filipinos," 9; Samuel Dickstein, qtd. in ibid., 10.

33. Melendy, ibid.

34. Takaki, "Dollar a Day," 333.

35. Royal F. Morales, *Makibaka: The Pilipino American Struggle* (Los Angeles: Mountainview, 1974), 58.

36. Benedict Anderson, *Imagined Communities: Reflections on the Origin and Spread of Nationalism*, rev. ed. (London: Verso, 1991); and see Bhabha, "The Other Question."

37. Anderson, *Imagined Communities*, 149.

38. See Bhabha, "The Other Question."

39. Honi Fern Haber, *Beyond Postmodern Politics: Lyotard Rorty Foucault* (New York: Routledge, 1994), 30 (emphasis mine).

40. Donna Harraway, "Situated Knowledges: The Science Question in Feminism and the Privilege of Partial Perspective," in *Human Geography: An Essential Anthology*, ed. John A. Agnew (Oxford: Blackwell, 1996), 187.

41. Gordon, *Ghostly Matters*, 20.

CHAPTER FIVE: LOSING LITTLE MANILA

For their invaluable assistance, advice, and inspiration, the author would like to thank Ernesto Tirona Mabalon, Christine Bohulano Bloch, Concepcion Bohulano, Adeline B. Suguitan, Carmen Saldevar, Jose Bernardo, Ted Lapuz, Leslie Crow, Gordon Chang, Allyson Tintiangco-Cubales, Marisela Chavez, Kim Warren, the Little Manila Foundation, the Filipino American National Historic Society, Stockton chapter and national office, the archivists at the University of the Pacific and the Office of the City Clerk in Stockton, California, and the editors of this volume.

1. Carmen Saldevar, interview by author, Stockton, California, September 2002.

2. Addressing or referring to older men as *manong* and older women as *manang* in Ilokano, Visayan, and Tagalog shows respect. Filipina/o Americans began using the terms in the 1960s to refer to Filipinas/os who entered the United States before World War II.

3. Saldevar interview, September 2002.

4. Kenneth Jackson's *Crabgrass Frontier* remains the most comprehensive history of suburbanization in the United States during the twentieth century. See Jackson, *Crabgrass Frontier* (Oxford University Press: New York, 1985), 173–75.

5. Ibid., 175. The prewar emergence of subdivisions and shopping centers far from the downtown core hinted at rapid suburbanization and the proliferation of suburban sprawl that would characterize U.S. landscapes from World War II to the present.

6. Paul Groth, *Living Downtown: The History of Residential Hotels in the United States* (Berkeley: University of California Press, 1994), 253.

7. Jackson, *Crabgrass Frontier*, 215. FHA loan programs afforded middle-class whites in Stockton the opportunity to buy single-family homes. Suburbanization was further

spurred by the demand in homes among veterans and their families; the GI Bill created a Veterans' Administration program that helped veterans purchase homes after the war. Jackson notes that no other agency has had more impact on the lives of ordinary Americans than the Federal Housing Administration, established as part of the New Deal. As a result of FHA loans, families had to pay only 10 percent down on a home; owning a single-family detached home on a large lot in a low-density neighborhood became the ideal, as well as a goal within easy reach for middle-class families. Generous tax subsidies on mortgage interest made homeowning even more feasible.

8. Olive Davis, *Stockton: Sunrise Port on the San Joaquin* (Sun Valley, Calif.: American Historical Press, 1989), 88.

9. Richard Bastear, lecture, Political Science 10, San Joaquin Delta College, Fall 1991. On the FHA and restrictive covenants, see Jackson, *Crabgrass Frontier*, 208–9.

10. Lillian Galedo, "Roadblocks to Community Building: A Case Study of the Stockton Filipino Community Center Project," University of California, Davis, Asian American Studies Division, 1970, 4–5.

11. See Groth, *Living Downtown*, 151. In Stockton's West End, as in other single laborers' zones in other West Coast cities (Seattle, San Francisco, and Los Angeles all had sizable zones), single residential occupancy hotels, cheap rooming houses, and businesses catering to working-class people and families abounded.

12. The FHA lending programs were zealous in their rush to build suburban, middle-class neighborhoods; FHA officials preferred to make loans in all-white subdivisions and officially refused to guarantee loans in neighborhoods that were mixed racially and in downtown districts in which mixed use was common. Jackson, *Crabgrass Frontier*, 208.

13. Ibid.

14. John A. Jakle and David Wilson, *Derelict Landscapes: The Wasting of America's Built Environment* (Savage, Md.: Rowan and Littlefield, 1992), 131.

15. Critiques of postwar federal urban renewal policy abound, one of the most powerful from social critic Jane Jacobs, whose *Death and Life of Great American Cities* (New York: Random House, 1961) remains one of the most influential books in U.S. city planning and urban studies. For a conservative viewpoint, see Martin Anderson, *The Federal Bulldozer* (Cambridge: MIT Press, 1964). See also the essays in James Q. Wilson, ed., *Urban Renewal: The Record and the Controversy* (Cambridge and London: MIT Press, 1966); Chester Hartman, *City for Sale: The Transformation of San Francisco* (Berkeley: University of California Press, 2002); Jakle and Wilson, *Derelict Landscapes*.

16. Stockton City Planning Commission, "Redevelopment: A Report Prepared by the City Planning Commission for the City Council, the City of Stockton, February 1952," Harold S. Jacoby Papers, University of the Pacific Holt-Atherton Collection. Across the nation, city leaders and real estate developers saw the new federal urban redevelopment programs as a boon for remaking downtowns and eliminating slums and ghettoes. To get federal money for urban redevelopment projects, a city had to create a local redevelopment agency in order to be eligible for funds, then designate an area as a urban renewal zone and send renewal plans to Washington, D.C., for approval. City officials, under the power of eminent domain, could obtain land in the redevelopment zone. As slum clearance

became commonplace in U.S. cities, the Supreme Court ruled that eminent domain could be used if the projects were deemed beneficial to the public good. Once the city owned the land, demolitions could commence. To attract investment, cities then sold the land at less than acquisition cost to private developers. The federal government provided two-thirds of the cost of the redevelopment, usually funds for acquisition and demolition. Each municipality had to meet the remainder of the cost, usually with funds for public works improvements, such as roads, sewers, parks, parking lots, and public facilities. Proponents believed that taxes from the rebuilt areas would compensate for this outlay. See ibid.

17. Ibid.

18. Jakle and Wilson, *Derelict Landscapes*, 122.

19. Minutes of the City Council Meeting, 26 September 1955, Office of the City Clerk, Stockton, California (hereafter, Clerk's Office).

20. Letter from John C. Lilly, City Manager, to the City Council, Minutes of the City Council, 10 October 1955, Clerk's Office.

21. R. Coke Wood and Leonard Covello, *Stockton Memories: A Pictorial History of Stockton, California* (Fresno, Calif.: Valley, 1977).

22. Anderson, *The Federal Bulldozer*, 4.

23. Jane Jacobs and Herbert Gans were two of the earliest and most influential critics of urban redevelopment policies. See Jacobs, *Death and Life*, and Herbert Gans, *The Urban Villagers: Group and Class in the Life of Italian Americans*, rev. and expanded ed. (New York: Free Press, 1982). See also the essays in Wilson, *Urban Renewal*.

24. Minutes from meeting of the Stockton City Council regarding the creation of the Urban Renewal Committee, 21 November 1955, Clerk's Office.

25. Minutes of the City Council Meeting, 23 July 1956, Clerk's Office.

26. *Stockton Record*, 10 April 1963, West End Redevelopment Project Press Clippings Notebooks, Clerk's Office.

27. Davis, *Stockton*, 105; "Just Kindling Now," *Stockton Record*, 14 February 1966, 23.

28. Davis, *Stockton*, 105.

29. Chester Hartman, "The Housing of Relocated Families," in *Urban Renewal: The Record and the Controversy*, ed. James Q. Wilson (Cambridge and London: MIT Press, 1966), 321.

30. "West End's People Are Relocating," *Stockton Record*, 3 April 1964, 1.

31. Hartman, "The Housing of Relocated Families," 359. For a description of the impact of total clearance of the West End on the Italian American community of Boston, see Gans, *The Urban Villagers*.

32. Saldevar interview, September 2002.

33. Ibid.

34. Jackson, *Crabgrass Frontier*, 248–49. In 1916, with the Federal Highway Act, the federal government began to shift its focus from mass transit to freeway construction. The passage of the 1956 Interstate Highway Act, a result of relentless pressure from powerful auto, oil, rubber, and asphalt lobbies, funded the construction of more than forty thousand miles of highways and freeways, further spurring the growth of suburbs.

35. "West Side Freeway Path Set," *Stockton Record*, 30 January 1960, 10.

36. Raymond A. Mohl, "Shifting Patterns of American Urban Policy Since 1900," in *Urban Policy in Twentieth Century America*, ed. Arnold R. Hirsch and Raymond A. Mohl (New Brunswick, N.J.: Rutgers University Press, 1993), 16.

37. Andres Duany, Elizabeth Plater-Zyberk, and Jeff Speck, *Suburban Nation: The Rise of Sprawl and the Decline of the American Dream* (New York: North Point Press, 2000), 130.

38. Galedo, "Roadblocks to Community Building," 4.

39. "Washington-Lafayette Route for Freeway Is Opposed," *Stockton Record*, 2 June 1961, 26.

40. Angelina Bantillo Magdael, interview by author, Stockton, California, 17 August 2001.

41. "Washington-Lafayette Route for Freeway," 17.

42. "Crosstown Freeway Site Decision Near: Washington St., Lafayette Route Proposal Made," *Stockton Record*, 15 November 1961, 17.

43. "Washington-Lafayette Route Is Approved by City Council," *Stockton Record*, 27 December 1961.

44. "10 Get Paid for Moving Costs," *Stockton Record*, 1 October 1965.

45. "Rooms with a View," *Stockton Record*, 9 February 1968, 34.

46. "Crosstown Freeway Plans Take Shape," *Stockton Record*, 4 February 1970, 22.

47. "Crosstown Freeway's Ecological Impact," *Stockton Record*, 6 June 1971, 11.

48. "Pathway for the Freeway," *Stockton Record*, 4 April 1972, 1.

49. Carmen Saldevar, interview by author, Stockton, California, 7 October 2002.

50. "'Sweet and Sour' of Business Relocation," *Stockton Record*, 2 May 1971, 8.

51. "People in Freeway's Path: The Human Side of Relocation," *Stockton Record*, 3 May 1971, 1, 14.

52. Saldevar interview, 7 October 2002.

53. "Fund Delays Stall Crosstown Freeway until 1974," *Stockton Record*, 2 May 1971, 1.

54. "Pathway for the Freeway"; "No Federal Aid: Crosstown Freeway Stalled," *Stockton Record*, 20 October 1972, 1.

55. City official, interview by author, Stockton, California, 26 August 2002 (name withheld by request).

56. Saldevar interview, 7 October 2002.

Chapter Six: Filipino Americans, Foreigner Discrimination, and the Lines of Racial Sovereignty

1. W.E.B. DuBois, *The Souls of Black Folk* (Chicago: A. C. McClurg, 1903).

2. *Shelley v. Kraemer*, 334 U.S. 1, 21 n. 26.

3. Leti Volpp, "American Mestizo: Filipinos and Antimiscegenation Laws in California," *U.C. Davis Law Review* 33 (2000): 822–23.

4. *Wards Cove Packing Company v. Atonio*, 490 U.S. 642, 663 (1989) (Stevens, J., dissenting).

5. Michael Omi and Howard Winant, *Racial Formation in the United States: From the 1960s to the 1990s*, 2d ed. (New York and London: Routledge, 1994).

6. Angelo N. Ancheta, *Race, Rights, and the Asian American Experience* (New Brunswick, N.J.: Rutgers University Press, 1998), 64–66.

7. *Statutes at Large* 48 (1934): 456.

8. John Higham, *Strangers in the Land: Patterns of American Nativism, 1860–1925* (New York: Atheneum, 1970).

9. H. Brett Melendy, "The Tydings-McDuffie Act of 1934," in *Asian Americans and Congress: A Documentary History*, ed. Hyung-Chan Kim (Westport, Conn.: Greenwood Press, 1996), 287.

10. *Chae Chan Ping v. United States (The Chinese Exclusion Case)*, 130 U.S. 581 (1889); *Fong Yue Ting v. United States*, 149 U.S. 698 (1893).

11. *Fong Yue Ting v. United States*, 717.

12. Approximately 95 percent of Filipinos living in the United States chose to reject the offer. Yen Le Espiritu, *Filipino American Lives* (Philadelphia: Temple University Press, 1995), 13–14.

13. *Statutes at Large* 79 (1965): 911.

14. U.S. Department of State, Bureau of Consular Affairs, Visa Bulletin, August 2005.

15. Greg B. Macabenta, "Filipinos under Fire," *Business World*, 22 May 2002, 4.

16. *Statutes at Large* 1 (1790): 103.

17. The U.S. Supreme Court confirmed the racial bar in two cases: in *Ozawa v. United States*, 260 U.S. 178 (1922), the Court ruled that the common definition of the Caucasian race precluded a Japanese immigrant's gaining citizenship, and in *United States v. Thind*, 261 U.S. 204 (1923), the Court ruled that even scientific classification as Caucasian was not dispositive, since Asian Indians were readily distinguishable from white people.

18. *In re Alverto*, 198 F. 688 (D. Pa. 1912).

19. *In re Rallos*, 241 F. 686, 687 (E.D.N.Y. 1917).

20. *Toyota v. United States*, 268 U.S. 402, 410 (1925). The Supreme Court did indicate, however, that subsequent legislation that allowed the naturalization of Filipinos who served in the U.S. military would not be subject to the racial bar.

21. *Statutes at Large* 56 (1942): 182. The statute provided that "any person not a citizen, regardless of age, who has served or hereafter serves honorably in the military or naval forces of the United States during the present war, and who, having been lawfully admitted to the United States, including its Territories and possessions . . . may be naturalized."

22. *Statutes at Large* 60 (1946): 6, 14, and 221, 223.

23. Kevin Pimentel, "To Yick Wo, Thanks For Nothing! Citizenship for Filipino Veterans," *Michigan Journal of Race and Law* 4 (1999): 459, 472–77.

24. *Statutes at Large* 104 (1990): 4978.

25. Richard Simon, "Filipino Veterans of WWII Win a Battle in Struggle for Benefits," *Los Angeles Times*, 17 December 2003.

26. Even though the racial bar on naturalization was relaxed after World War II, the numbers of immigrants from the Philippines had already been severely limited, making the naturalization of Filipinos already in the United States of less consequence.

27. The Washington Supreme Court acknowledged that Filipinos were covered under the 1937 amendments to the alien land law, but the court struck down the amendments as exceeding the legislature's constitutional powers. *DeCano v. State*, 110 P.2d 627 (Wash. 1941).

28. Ronald Takaki, *Strangers from a Different Shore: A History of Asian Americans* (Boston: Little, Brown, 1989), 332.

29. Alan Gathright, "U.S. Screeners Oust Private Workers; Guards Protest, Cry Racism at San Jose, Oakland Airports," *San Francisco Chronicle*, 1 October 2002.

30. *Sugarman v. Dougall*, 413 U.S. 634 (1973) (civil service); *In re Griffiths*, 413 U.S. 717 (1973) (law); *Examining Board v. Flores de Otero*, 426 U.S. 572 (1976) (civil engineering); *Bernal v. Fainter*, 467 U.S. 216 (1984) (notaries public).

31. *Foley v. Connelie*, 435 U.S. 291 (1978) (state troopers); *Ambach v. Norwick*, 441 U.S. 68 (1979) (public school teachers); *Cabell v. Chavez-Salido*, 454 U.S. 432 (1982) (probation officers).

32. 441 U.S. 68, 87 (1979) (Blackmun, J., dissenting).

33. *Statutes at Large* 110 (1996): 2,105.

34. Ibid., 3,009.

35. Christina M. Rodriguez, "Accommodating Linguistic Difference: Toward a Comprehensive Theory of Language Rights in the United States," *Harvard Civil Rights-Civil Liberties Law Review* 36 (2001): 133–223.

36. *Jurado v. Eleven-Fifty Corp.*, 813 F.2d 1406 (9th Cir. 1987).

37. *Dimaranan v. Pomona Valley Hospital Medical Center*, 775 F. Supp. 338 (C.D. Cal. 1991).

38. *Fragante v. City and County of Honolulu*, 888 F.2d 591 (9th Cir. 1989), *cert. denied*, 494 U.S. 1081 (1990).

39. National Asian Pacific American Legal Consortium, *1997 Fifth Annual Report, Audit of Violence against Asian Pacific Americans* (Washington, D.C.: National Asian Pacific American Legal Consortium, 1997), 24, 25.

40. "Moving beyond the Past," *Asian Week*, 25 May 2000, www.asianweek.com/2000_05_25/opinion_/leadedit.html; Henry Weinstein, "Furrow Gets 5 Life Terms for Racist Rampage Court: The White Supremacist Wounded Five People at a Valley Jewish Center and Murdered a Filipino American Postal Worker in 1999," *Los Angeles Times*, 27 March 2001.

41. U.S. General Accounting Office, *Immigration Reform* (1990).

42. Lina M. Avidan, *Employment and Hiring Practices under the Immigration Reform and Control Act of 1986: A Survey of San Francisco Businesses* (San Francisco: Public Research Institute, San Francisco State University, and Coalition for Immigrant and Refugee Rights and Services, January 1990), iii.

Chapter Seven: On the Politics of (Filipino) Youth Culture

Theodore S. Gonzalves responded in writing to the written questions for this interview.

CHAPTER EIGHT: COLONIAL AMNESIA

Thank you to the editors, Tony Tiongson, Ricardo and Edgardo Gutierrez. My deep appreciation also goes to Kēwaikaliko for allowing me to use his artwork. I would also like to thank the following people for their thoughtful comments at different stages of this project: Dean Alegado, Rosie Baldonado, Tracy Lachica Buenavista, Duane Champagne, Vicente Diaz, Candace Fujikane, Jason Luna Gavilan, Theodore Gonsalves, Eiko Kosasa, Roderick Labrador, Don Nakanishi, Jonathan Okamura, Christine Quemuel, Darlene Rodrigues, Sarita See, Haunani-Kay Trask, Julkipli Wadi, Erin Wright, Henry Yu, Dick and Drew Saranillio, Eloise Yamashita Saranillio, Shelley Takasato, and Sharon Heijin Lee. All errors are my own.

The epigraphs are from Renato Constatino, *The Philippines: A Past Revisited* (Manila: Renato Constantino, 1975), 9, and Kekuni Blaisdell, *Autobiography of Protest in Hawai'i*, ed. Robert H. Mast and Anne B. Mast (Honolulu: University of Hawai'i Press, 1996), 369.

1. See, for example, Ronald Takaki, *Pau Hana: Plantation Life and Labor in Hawaii, 1835–1920* (Honolulu: University of Hawai'i Press, 1983) and *Strangers from a Different Shore: A History of Asian Americans* (New York: Penguin Books, 1989).

2. See Haunani-Kay Trask, *From a Native Daughter: Colonialism and Sovereignty in Hawai'i* (1993; rpt., Honolulu: University of Hawai'i Press and the Center for Hawaiian Studies, 1999), 25.

3. Vicente Diaz, "Bye Bye Ms. American Pie: The Historical Relations between Chamorros and Filipinos and the American Dream," *ISLA: A Journal of Micronesian Studies* 3, 1 (1995): 160.

4. Ruben R. Alcantara, *Sakada: Filipino Adaptation in Hawaii* (Washington, D.C.: University Press of America, 1981); R. R. Cariaga, *The Filipinos in Hawaii: Economic and Social Conditions, 1906–1936* (Honolulu: Filipino Public Relations Bureau, 1937); Luis V. Teodoro, Jr., *Out of This Struggle: The Filipinos in Hawaii* (Honolulu: University of Hawai'i Press, 1981); Bernadette Suguitan Ledesma, *Ating Tao/Our People: The Filipinos in Hawaii* (Honolulu: General Assistance Center for the Pacific, 1976).

5. Jonathan Okamura, "Social Stratification," in *Multicultural Hawai'i: The Fabric of a Multiethnic Society*, ed. M. Haas (New York: Garland, 1998).

6. Haunani-Kay Trask, "Settlers of Color and 'Immigrant' Hegemony: 'Locals' in Hawai'i," *Amerasia Journal* 26, 2 (2000): 20.

7. Ibid.

8. Yen Le Espiritu, *Home Bound: Filipino American Lives across Cultures, Communities, and Countries* (Berkeley: University of California Press, 2003), 44.

9. Ibid., 24.

10. "Sakada" is a term used to describe the contract workers from the Philippines between 1906 and 1946.

11. Virgilio Menor Felipe, *Hawai'i: A Pilipino Dream* (Honolulu: Mutual, 2002), 29.

12. Ibid., 28.

13. Ibid., xvi.

14. Melinda Tria Kerkvliet, *Unbending Cane: Pablo Manlapit, a Filipino Labor Leader in Hawai'i* (Honolulu: University of Hawai'i Press, 2002), 47–48.

15. Dean Alegado, "The Legacy and Challenge of Ti Mangyuna" (Honolulu: Union of Democratic Filipinos [KDP], 1981), 5.

16. The epigraphs are from Joshua Agsalud, "My Perceptions of the Plantation Experience: Influences That Shaped My Views on the Americanization Process," paper presented at the Philippine Studies Conference, Center for Asian and Pacific Studies, University of Hawai'i, 28 June 1981; and Trask, "Settlers of Color," 2.

17. Agsalud, "My Perceptions."

18. Ibid., 12, 11.

19. The epigraph is from Helen Geracimos Chapin, *Shaping News: The Role of Newspapers in Hawai'i* (Hawai'i: University of Hawai'i Press, 1996), 4.

20. Zachary Labez, "Hawaiian Sovereignty and the 'Non-Hawaiian' . . . Another Viewpoint," *Hawaii Filipino Chronicle*, 16 March 1996, 13. Also see Labez, "On Statehood: Sovereignty and the Search for Justice," *Fil-Am Courier*, August 2003.

21. Zachary G. Labez, "The *Pinoys'* Quest for Political Empowerment in America," *Fil-Am Courier*, June 2001.

22. Felipe, *Hawai'i*, xix.

23. Kēwaikaliko, *"Benocide,"* in *Na Maka Hou: New Visions, Contemporary Native Hawaiian Art* (Honolulu: Honolulu Academy of Arts, 2001), 81.

24. Jeanette Wolfley, *"Rice v. Cayetano*: The Supreme Court Declines to Extend Federal Indian Law Principles to Native Hawaiians' Sovereignty Rights," *Asian-Pacific Law and Policy Journal* 3, 2 (Summer 2002): 360.

25. Mieke Bal, "Seeing Signs: The Use of Semiotics for the Understanding of Visual Art," in *The Subjects of Art History: Historical Objects in Contemporary Perspectives*, ed. March A. Cheetham, Michael Ann Holly, and Keith Moxey (Cambridge: Cambridge University Press, 1998), 81.

26. As cited in Ida Yoshinaga and Eiko Kosasa, "Local Japanese Women for Justice Speak Out against Daniel Inouye and the JACL,"*Honolulu Advertiser*, 6 February 2000, and reprinted in "Whose Vision? Asian Settler Colonialism in Hawai'i," special issue, *Amerasia Journal* 26, 2 (2000): 20.

27. Yoshinaga and Kosasa, ibid.

28. Haunani-Kay Trask, keynote address at the First International and Eleventh National Multi-Ethnic Literatures across the Americas and the Pacific (MELUS) Conference in Honolulu, reproduced in Haunani-Kay Trask, "Writing in Captivity: Poetry in Time of De-Colonization," in *Navigating Islands and Continents: Conversations and Contestations in and around the Pacific*, ed. Cynthia Franklin, Ruth Hsu, and Suzanne Kosanke (Honolulu: University of Hawai'i Press, 2000), 17.

29. In 1990 the Hawai'i State Legislature passed Act 304 to provide a mechanism for determining the amount of ceded-land revenues owed to OHA. This law specified that OHA was indeed entitled to 20 percent of revenue from the ceded lands. Three years later in 1993 the State paid OHA $19 million and agreed to make annual revenue payments. OHA filed a lawsuit in 1994 to resolve all remaining back-payment issues.

30. Debra Barayuga, "OHA Sues to Resume Land Revenues; The Agency Says That the State Failed in Its Fiduciary Duties as Trustee of the Lands," *Star Bulletin*, 22 July 2003.

31. Manulani Aluli Meyer, "Hawaiian Art: A Doorway to Knowing," in *Na Maka Hou: New Visions Contemporary Native Hawaiian Art* (Honolulu: Honolulu Academy of Arts, 2001), 12.

32. "President Arroyo Brings in $4 Billion in Pledges from U.S. Visit," *Hawaii Filipino Chronicle*, 1 December 2001, 9.

33. Darlene Rodrigues, an author and poet in Hawai'i, phone interview by author, 30 October 2003.

34. See Kyle Kajihiro, "The Militarizing of Hawai'i: Occupation, Accommodation, and Resistance," in *Whose Vision? Asian Settler Colonialism*, ed. Candace Fujikawe (Honolulu: University of Hawai'i Press, forthcoming).

35. Grace Alvara Caligtan, Darlene Rodrigues, Melisa S. L. Casumbal, Catherine Betts, Grace Duenas, Gigi Miranda, Cindy Ramierz, Sonya Zabala, Tamara Freedman, and Maile Labasan, "Filipinos Stand in Solidarity with Native Hawaiians in Opposing United States Military Expansion," posting to indyhawaii list, 15 March 2003, archives.lists.indymedia.org/imc-hawaii/2003-March/000715.html.

36. Jonathan Okamura, *Imagining the Filipino American Diaspora: Transnational Relations, Identities, and Communities* (New York: Garland, 1998), 8.

37. Eiko Kosasa, "Ideological Images: U.S. Nationalism in Japanese Settler Photographs," *Amerasia Journal* 26, 2 (2000): 83–84.

38. See Beverly Daniel Tatum, *"Why Are All the Black Kids Sitting Together in the Cafeteria?" and Other Conversations about Race* (New York: Basic Books, 1997), 105.

39. Reynaldo Ileto, *Filipinos and Their Revolution: Event, Discourse, and Historiography* (Manila: Ateneo De Manila University Press, 1999), 24.

CHAPTER NINE: "A MILLION DEATHS?"

1. Stanley Karnow, *In Our Image: America's Empire in the Philippines* (New York: Ballantine Books, 1989), 3–4.

2. Fred Cordova, *Filipinos: Forgotten Asian Americans* (Dubuque, Iowa: Kendall/Hunt, 1983), 217.

3. Ibid., 220.

4. Maria P. P. Root, ed., Introduction to *Filipino Americans: Transformation and Identity* (Thousand Oaks, Calif.: Sage, 1997), xiv.

5. Maria P. P. Root, "Contemporary Mixed-Heritage Filipino Americans," in ibid., 80.

6. Linda Revilla, "Filipino American Identity: Transcending the Crisis," in *Filipino Americans*, ed. Root, 96.

7. Frantz Fanon, *The Wretched of the Earth* (New York: Grove Weidenfeld, 1963), 210–11.

8. Ibid., 212.

9. Discussing such a shift in the political-economic modality of U.S. hegemony in the Philippines, E. San Juan, Jr., considers the aftermath of the much valorized People's Power insurrection of 1986 as a contingent opportunity for a more effective assimilation

into the emergent global structures of neoliberalism: "Scenes of this uprising were televised throughout the world, images exuding an aura of the miraculous. Few know that the restoration of neocolonial democracy—rule of transnationals through the comprador/oligarchic elite—after that event ushered in a new stage for the revival of neocolonial apparatuses of domination, agencies of hegemonic rule designed to protract the nation's subservience to transnational corporations and the IMF/World Bank." "One Hundred Years of Producing and Reproducing the 'Filipino,'" *Amerasia Journal* 24, 2: 3.

10. Omer Bartov, *Murder in Our Midst* (New York: Oxford University Press, 1996).

11. Luzviminda Francisco, "The First Vietnam: The U.S.-Philippine War of 1899," *Bulletin of Concerned Asian Scholars* 5, 4 (December 1973): 7.

12. Stuart Creighton Miller, "The American Soldier and the Conquest of the Philippines," in *Reappraising an Empire: New Perspectives on Philippine-American History*, ed. Peter W. Stanley (Cambridge: Harvard University Press, 1984), 20.

13. See, for example, Henry F. Graff, ed., *American Imperialism and the Philippine Insurrection: Testimony Taken from Hearings on Affairs in the Philippine Islands before the Senate Committee on the Philippines—1902* (Boston: Little, Brown, 1969).

14. Ward Churchill, *A Little Matter of Genocide: Holocaust and Denial in the Americas, 1492 to the Present* (San Francisco: City Lights Books, 1997), 410.

15. Qtd. in ibid., 411.

16. United Nations, Convention on the Prevention and Punishment of the Crime of Genocide, 9 December 1948, www.ohchr.org/english/law/genocide.htm.

17. Frank Chalk and Kurt Jonassohn, *The History and Sociology of Genocide: Analyses and Case Studies* (New Haven: Yale University Press, 1990), 11.

18. Churchill, *A Little Matter of Genocide*, 431–32.

19. Ibid., 433.

20. Barbara Gaerlan, "The Pursuit of Modernity: Trinidad H. Pardo de Tavera and the Educational Legacy of the Philippine Revolution," *Amerasia Journal* 24, 2: 101.

21. Arthur Kleinman, "The Violences of Everyday Life: The Multiple Forms and Dynamics of Social Violence," in *Violence and Subjectivity*, ed. Veena Das, Arthur Kleinman, Mamphela Ramphele, and Pamela Reynolds (Berkeley: University of California Press, 2000), 239.

22. Ludy Astraquillo Ongkeko, "When Being Filipino Is a Plus," *Philippine News*, 19–25 February 1997, A-5.

23. Alex A. Esclamado, "The Future Leaders," *Philippine News*, 19–25 March 1997, A-4.

24. E. San Juan, Jr., *After Postcolonialism: Remapping Philippines–United States Confrontations* (Lanham, Md.: Rowman and Littlefield, 2000), 13.

25. Frantz Fanon, "Chapter One: The Negro and Language," *Black Skin, White Masks* (New York: Grove Press, 1967), 17–18.

26. Ibid.

27. David Theo Goldberg, *Racist Culture: Philosophy and the Politics of Meaning* (Cambridge, Mass.: Blackwell, 1993), 4.

28. San Juan, Jr., *After Postcolonialism*, 74.

29. Brian McAllister Linn, *The U.S. Army and Counterinsurgency in the Philippine War, 1899–1902* (Chapel Hill: University of North Carolina Press, 1989), 169.

30. Linn writes in his preface: "Since this work relies heavily on Army operational records and personal papers, it is possible that the views of the officers and men serving in the provinces may have colored my own perceptions." Ibid., xiii.

31. Ibid., 170.

32. On whiteness, see Goldberg, *Racist Culture.*

33. Graff, *American Imperialism*, 64–65.

34. Nerissa Balce's incisive analysis of the entanglements between the racialization of Filipinos and contemporaneous antiblack and anti-Indian racial ideologies further resonates the context of American modernity's racialized conquest (see Chapter 3, this volume).

35. Francisco, "The First Vietnam," 4.

36. Luzviminda Francisco, "The First Vietnam: The U.S.-Philippine War of 1899," *Bulletin of Concerned Asian Scholars*, 1973, 10.

CHAPTER TEN: REFLECTIONS ON THE TRAJECTORY OF FILIPINO/A AMERICAN STUDIES

Rick Bonus responded in writing to the written questions in this interview.

CHAPTER ELEVEN: DO YOU MIS(RECOGNIZE) ME

Many *salamats* to the generous souls who've read versions of this essay and given me their support, critical insights, and encouragement: Anatalio C. Ubalde, Peter Bacho, Nerissa Balce, Jeannie Chiu, Michael Coleman, Mary Gamalinda, Theo Gonzalves, Tony Hale, Wesley Pua, Evelyn Rodriguez, Fabio Rojas, Jim Sabredo, John Scott, Tony Tiongson, Jean Vengua, Victor Viesca, and Oliver Wang. My gratitude goes as well to Glenn Gutierriez and Joey Gardner for reprint permission.

1. Jocelyn Enriquez's story should be brought up to date. In August 1997 Enriquez toured the Philippines, where she was welcomed as a star. Meanwhile, disagreements between Classified and Tommy Boy over artistic direction, album promotion, the release of singles, and operating costs came to a head, and in early fall 1997 the joint affiliation between the two labels was dissolved. Amidst the fallout, Tommy Boy offered Enriquez a contract; she accepted it, left Classified, and moved from the San Francisco Bay Area to Los Angeles. While Tommy Boy and Classified continued to share the album's profits, control over the single releases and promotion remained with Tommy Boy, which in spring 1998 released versions of "Get into the Rhythm" remixed by its own producers. The remixes did not fare well with mix DJs, radio stations, or Enriquez's fans. Her collaborations at this time included a cover of "If You Could Read My Mind" with dance-music artists Amber (Tommy Boy) and Ultra Naté (Strictly Rhythm), which was featured in the Miramax Films movie *54*, and "So Fabulous, So Fierce (Freak Out)," which superstar producers Thunderpuss 2000 recorded for Disney's *102 Dalmatians*. Tommy Boy, meanwhile, noted the decreasing popularity of dance/club music, and in 2000 the label dissolved the Timber! subdivision

and released Enriquez from her contract. After a hiatus from the music business to give birth to a son, marry her longtime boyfriend, Alain Macasadia, and relocate to San Diego, in 2003 Enriquez released through her own indie label a third album, *All My Life*; the album was produced by New York City–based DJ Rich Pangilinan (who had worked previously on a remix of "Get into the Rhythm" and mixed Tommy Boy's tremendously popular Dance Mix NYC series) and so far has yielded one *Billboard*-charting song, "No Way No How."

Freestyle fans lament the potential of *Jocelyn* lost upon the breakup between Classified and Tommy Boy. One song, "If I'm Falling in Love," showcased Enriquez's vocal mastery and could have become the most heralded freestyle song ever. According to Classified executives, it received much "attention on the street"; mix DJs in Texas spun it on their shows despite the absence of a single release; and out of Miami came reports of record shops selling bootlegged vinyl singles of the song. The columnists at *DMA* even called on Tommy Boy to release Glenn Gutierrez's freestyle remix. Alas, "If I'm Falling In Love" is relegated to the footnotes of essays by disappointed fans.

2. Enriquez's experience with racial ambiguity and misrecognition is hardly anomalous for a Filipina American. Though my own identification as a Filipina American has remained stable (due in part to the presence of a large Filipino community in the Northern California agribusiness city where I grew up), I have observed consistent patterns in my chronically being seen as anything but Filipina. During the summer, when my complexion gets darker, my straight black hair longer, and I'm less inclined to wear eyeglasses, my perceived ethnicity may switch to Native American; if the summer moment finds me in a setting that involves underrepresented minorities, my perceived ethnicity always switches to Native American, if not mixed-race. If identified only by my name, I become Latina (and later may get a query about why I don't look like what the inquirer thought I'd look like). I can pass for Latina when with my spouse, a *muy indio* Latino. Since there are many *india*-Latinas who "look Asian," those who would rather err on the side of caution have addressed me in Spanish. I have yet to be mistaken for black.

Most of the year, with my oval face, a complexion that on a Filipino scale would be described as light, and teaching positions in academia, a profession where there are few Pinays, I pass for Asian, specifically as Chinese. During graduate school at a California public institution with a huge Asian American student population but few Filipinos, more than several times professors addressed me by the names of Chinese American classmates. One day I was eating at a diner in the neighborhood of another elite research university, and in my presence a Chinese customer said, "When I'm fat, I look like a Filipino." I have spoken with several Pinoy and non-Pinoy friends about this incident; the only one who yet has been able to help me understand it is a man of Swedish and black descent.

Who can guess my ethnicity? Former Peace Corps volunteers or U.S. Navy personnel who had served in the Philippines or Guam, and a California Highway Patrol officer who once ticketed me for speeding near the San Francisco airport, which is amid several Filipino-concentrated suburbs. A couple of years teaching in Chicago at a private Roman Catholic university, where being Asian American was for all practical purposes being Filipino American, gave me the one extended period of time when I did not feel plagued by misrecognition.

3. Writing on the relevance of Asian American studies to interracial individuals of Asian descent, Maria P. P. Root has criticized likewise Asian Americanist models of race and racialization for their conflation of ethnicity/culture and race and called for studies of racial identification by phenotype and "colorism" among Asian Americans (34).

4. For example, sociologist Yen Le Espiritu presents one Filipino American's repeated misrecognition by others as evidence of Asian American heterogeneity. In her essay interpreting second-generation Filipino American ethnographic narratives, Espiritu cites a Filipino American saying, "There was a theme in the early part of my life of people asking me questions that I couldn't quite fully answer, like 'Where did you come from? I've never heard of that place.' 'Are you Mexican? Are you black? Are you Chinese?'" (Espiritu, 260). Another Filipina American is cited recalling a white boyfriend's parents, who forced the relationship to end because they thought she was Chinese (260). Espiritu calls these misrecognitions "symptomatic of a society that is racialized and yet indifferent to and ignorant of the racial differences and hybridization among its peoples" and acknowledges it causes Filipino Americans confusion. They are "key events, . . . a background against which (Filipino Americans) interpret subsequent incidents and reevaluate their assigned place in U.S. society" (260–61). But Espiritu understates the impact of these misrecognitions on Filipino American identity and toward the end of her essay contradicts her earlier examples of racial ambiguity in order to claim that "mindful that outsiders generally lump all Asians together, these Filipino Americans herald their common fate to build political unity with other Asian Americans" (266). Her second example—the Filipina American mistaken as Chinese—supports her defense of panethnicity, but her first contradicts it.

5. The use of the terms "perception" and "cognition" to characterize racial identification I borrow from the critical essays of Adrian Piper, a philosopher/conceptual artist and black woman who passes for white. In particular, I am indebted to her 1992 essay "Passing for White, Passing for Black," where "perceptual distortion" describes her being perceived as white by both whites and working-class blacks, and cognitive identification refers to the construction of black identity upon the "one-drop" rule (7). Of interest to me are her confrontations with others unable to reconcile the clash in perception and cognition that their conceptualization of blackness produces upon encountering someone like Piper (11).

6. Not all Filipino American representations of indigeneity, however, are ahistorical or uncritical. Out of the "born-again Filipino" movement have emerged a handful of mature, professionalized institutions with continuity and historical memory. Groups such as San Francisco's Bindlestiff Studio and Los Angeles's Kayamanan ng Lahi Philippine Folk Arts and long-established Pilipino Cultural Nights (PCNs) at academic institutions like San Francisco State University and the University of California, Berkeley are examples of how fetishes initially valued for their authenticity can become "living traditions," serve as mediums of self-critique, and ground Filipino Americans in an ethnic community while allowing them to connect with others invested as well in a hopeful spirit of history and agency (Gilmore; Gonzalves, "The Day the Dancers Stayed").

7. While Filipinos and Filipino Americans have long expressed discontent with the Asian American coalition (Rabaya; *Liwanag*), during the 1990s E. San Juan, Jr.'s criticisms of panethnicity became more pointed. He observes that the celebration of "heterogeneity" among Asian Americans evades a discussion of interethnic hierarchy, and he concludes that

while Asian American panethnicity exists, it does not include Filipinos ("Beyond Identity Politics"; "Multiculturalism vs. Hegemony"). Noting that the Asian American historical genealogy that bolsters panethnic coalition has no correspondence in present reality, San Juan rejects the political genealogy that links Chinese, Japanese, and Filipino immigrant workers as the historical basis for panethnicity (*Exile to Diaspora*, 180); he argues as well for removing Filipino Americans from the Asian American rubric ("this has, de facto, taken place through exclusion anyway") and recognizing them as a distinct group (*Philippine Temptation*, 90).

While not agreeing with San Juan overtly, other Filipino and Filipino American cultural critics tacitly concur via their work. Jean Vengua Gier notes Filipino American discomfort with Asian Americanists' unqualified claims on U.S. citizenship, given that such identification with the United States had been forced on Filipinos (4). Theo Gonzalves locates the assertion of Filipino American cultural production in the formation of ethnicity within race despite panethnicity (Gonzalves, "When the Walls Speak," 52; Gonzalves, Kun, and Pisares, 52). In her *Amerasia Journal* review of Yen Le Espiritu's 1995 ethnography of Filipinos and Filipino Americans, Dawn Mabalon corrects Espiritu's definitions of Filipino words and, where Espiritu attempts to claim the authority to speak for Filipinos by recounting moments when interlocutors told her she was "just like them," Mabalon dismisses her claims on the subject position as disingenuous (Mabalon, 281). Efren Padilla speaks for these Filipino American scholars when he says, "We are not against Asian panethnicity, if it means political coalition building" rather than the imposition of histories or identities that privilege East Asian Americans (qtd. in Strobel, 33).

8. On the *Blu's Hanging* controversy, see Fujikane, Rodrigues.

9. Most of us humans cannot not think of ourselves as subjects racialized by others' gazes any more than (to borrow a sociological quip) a fish can imagine not inhabiting water. I was reminded of the difficulty of such a cognitive leap at a 2004 discussion of Filipino American filmmaking by director Patricio Ginsela (whose best-known work to date includes the music video for the Black Eyed Peas' "The apl Song" and the movie *Lumpia*). After contrasting the exclusion of Filipino Americans from the big screen with the (relatively) more numerous roles for African Americans, he was questioned by an African American woman in the audience who observed that those roles were but racial stereotypes. Ginsela responded that at least both filmmakers and critical African American viewers could agree that the subject represented was black, even if there was a dispute over the merit of the racial representation.

10. Snapper as well observes a "performative ambiguity" when turntablists such as the Invisibl Skratch Piklz and DJ Symphony of the Beat Junkies deflect questions regarding the presence of Filipino Americans in turntablism (19–20).

11. One work that points the way to the demonstration of a Filipino American representation that does not involve music is Lysley A. Tenorio's short story "Superassassin." In this virtuoso telling of Pinoy invisibility and inner-city sadness, Tenorio throws down the discourses like a turntablist, mixing the languages of superhero comic books, academic history, junior-high slang, old-school pop songs, and embattled poor-urban institutions over the beat of the white mestizo narrator's perspective. With Tenorio presently at work on a collection of short stories and other artists like filmmaker Romeo Candido explicitly comparing their

creative processes to those of DJs, "Superassassin" represents nothing short of the shape of Filipino American narrative to come.

CHAPTER TWELVE: A DIFFERENT BREED OF FILIPINO BALIKBAYANS

1. What follows is an expanded version of a section that appears in Mendoza, *Between the Homeland*.

2. Some portions of this section have appeared in various forms in previous essays (see Mendoza, "Bridging," "Nuancing").

3. Among ongoing activist movements are efforts to deconstruct U.S. official historiography that masks U.S. imperial ambition in its occupation of the Philippines at the turn of the twentieth century as "benevolent assimilation" and to expose racist U.S. policies against Filipinos and Filipino Americans inscribed in antimiscegenation laws and the manipulation of Filipino immigrant quotas in the early 1900s.

4. Here, the term "national" is not taken unproblematically: careful distinction is made between a "cultural nationalism" constituted from below and the elitist discourse of state-sponsored nationalism, which the indigenization movement indicts as at the root of the Philippines' failure to move toward political self-determination and economic sufficiency.

5. For a more extensive and in-depth discussion of these developments in indigenous theorizing, see Mendoza, *Between the Homeland*.

6. Formally inaugurated on 12 June 1898 upon the defeat of the Spanish forces by the Philippine revolutionaries, the fledgling republic suffered a major setback when Spain, refusing the humiliation of conceding defeat at the hands of the native "*indios*," struck a deal with the invading U.S. forces, staged a mock battle, then ceded the Philippines to the United States for a token twenty million dollars in the now-infamous 1898 Treaty of Paris (see Constantino, *The Philippines*; Agoncillo and Guerrero, *History*). The four-century colonial legacy includes 350 years under Spain and more than half a century under the United States (with a three-year Japanese interlude from 1942 to 1945).

7. An alarming trend documented by Canieso-Doronila is that "as students progress through the grades, their preference for their own nationality decreases" (*Limits*, 72).

8. See Lynch, "Social Acceptance," for a discussion of the systematic disenfranchisement of the indigenous peoples of the Philippines during the Spanish regime through their effective representation as *indio* and the consequent abrogation of their legal status and rights under colonial state law. Lynch shows that the same policy continued in more subtle and dissimulated forms during the U.S. colonial regime.

9. I credit my own radical transformation of consciousness to a graduate course I audited at the University of the Philippines, Diliman, in 1982, which De Leon designed and incorporated into the humanities program there and which effected a new and decisive turn in my decolonization process.

10. See in-depth discussion of contemporary theoretical developments in indigenization in Mendoza, *Between the Homeland*.

11. The use of the letter *P* in "Pilipino" comes from the old Tagalog-based spelling of the term. One of the major Philippine regional languages, Tagalog does not include the

letter f in its alphabet. "Filipino," on the other hand, signals the expansion of the Tagalog-based alphabet to include sounds present in the other Philippine regional languages, "ef" being one of them. This is part of a move toward the construction of a Filipino national language. Jorge's reference to Salazar alludes to a particular construing of a normative Filipino community among indigenization scholars, that of anthropologist-historian Zeus Salazar.

12. Philippine studies is disavowed by indigenization scholars as reinscribing the colonial perspective inherited from the cold-war-era Area Studies orientation that treated the Philippines, its cultures, and its peoples as "objects" of study to serve foreign academic interests.

13. As Pratt describes the shadows of the colonized condition in this regard: "Under conquest social and cultural formations enter long-term, often permanent states of crisis that cannot be resolved by either conqueror or conquered" (Pratt, *Transculturation*, 26).

About the Contributors

ANGELO N. ANCHETA is a lecturer on law and director of the Legal and Advocacy Programs with the Civil Rights Project at Harvard Law School. He is the author of *Race, Rights, and the Asian American Experience* (1998).

NERISSA S. BALCE is an assistant professor of comparative literature at the University of Massachusetts–Amherst. She is preparing a book manuscript on U.S. imperialism, visual culture, and Philippine images.

JODY BLANCO is an assistant professor of comparative literature at the University of California, San Diego. His research focuses on Filipino literature, nineteenth-century Latin American and Caribbean literature, and anticolonial thought.

RICK BONUS is an associate professor of American ethnic studies at the University of Washington in Seattle. He is coeditor of *Contemporary Asian American Communities: Intersections and Divergences* (Temple University Press, 2002) and the author of *Locating Filipino Americans: Ethnicity and the Cultural Politics of Space* (Temple University Press, 2000).

OSCAR V. CAMPOMANES is a founding editor of the journal *American Studies–Asia* and teaches in the Department of English at Ateneo de Manila University and in the Graduate School of Santo Thomas (Manila). A recent contribution appeared in *Vestiges of War and the Aftermath of an Imperial Dream: 1899–1999* (2002), and the Development Academy of the Philippines recently published a volume he coedited and cowrote, *Culture and Governance* (2004).

THEODORE S. GONZALVES is an assistant professor of American studies at the University of Hawai'i at Manoa. He researches and teaches courses on Filipino/American cultures and histories, as well as on performance and cultural studies.

EDGARDO V. GUTIERREZ, is an engineer who earned his B.S. from Cal Poly San Luis Obispo and actively maintains his independent status in ethnic studies.

RICARDO GUTIERREZ, is a strategic consulting and investment management industry professional who earned his B.S. from San Francisco State University.

Lisa Lowe is a professor of comparative literature at the University of California, San Diego. She is coeditor of *The Politics of Culture in the Shadow of Capital* (1997) and the author of *Immigrant Acts: On Asian American Cultural Politics* (1996) and *Critical Terrains: French and British Orientalisms* (1991).

Dawn Bohulano Mabalon is an assistant professor of history at San Francisco State University and chair of Little Manila Foundation. Her research focuses on race, ethnicity, gender, and youth culture.

S. Lily Mendoza is an assistant professor in culture and communication at the University of Denver. She is the author of *Between the Homeland and the Diaspora: The Politics of Theorizing Filipino and Filipino American Identities* (2002).

Elizabeth H. Pisares has written essays published in *Hitting Critical Mass* and *MELUS*. Through Tulitos Press, she published the screenplays of the *Debut* and *The Flip Side*. Raised in Northern California, she lives in Bloomington, Indiana.

Dylan Rodríguez is an assistant professor in the Ethnic Studies Department at the University of California, Riverside. He is the author of the forthcoming book *Forced Passages: Imprisoned Radical Intellectuals and the Formation of the U.S. Prison Regime* (2006).

Dean Itsuji Saranillio is a doctoral candidate in Asian/Pacific Islander American Studies, Program in American Culture, at the University of Michigan. He is interested in the relationships between racial/ethnic minority groups and indigenous movements in the United States, specifically in Hawai'i during the territorial period and the movement for statehood.

Ruby C. Tapia is an assistant professor of women's studies at Ohio State University. Her research and teaching focus on women in/and visual culture, engaging the experiences, representations, and cultural production of women of color, as well as the theoretical formulations of critical race feminism and feminist media studies.

Antonio T. Tiongson, Jr., is a postdoctoral fellow at Mt. Holyoke College. His research focuses on Filipino youth cultural politics.

Index

Note: *Italicized* page numbers refer to illustrative material.

Also in the series *Asian American History and Culture*

Darrell Y. Hamamoto and Sandra Liu, eds., *Countervisions: Asian American Film Criticism*

Martin F. Manalansan, IV, ed., *Cultural Compass: Ethnographic Explorations of Asian America*

Ko-lin Chin, *Smuggled Chinese: Clandestine Immigration to the United States*

Evelyn Hu-DeHart, ed., *Across the Pacific: Asian Americans and Globalization*

Soo-Young Chin, *Doing What Had to Be Done: The Life Narrative of Dora Yum Kim*

Robert G. Lee, *Orientals: Asian Americans in Popular Culture*

David L. Eng and Alice Y. Hom, eds., *Q & A: Queer in Asian America*

K. Scott Wong and Sucheng Chan, eds., *Claiming America: Constructing Chinese American Identities during the Exclusion Era*

Lavina Dhingra Shankar and Rajini Srikanth, eds., *A Part, Yet Apart: South Asians in Asian America*

Jere Takahashi, *Nisei/Sansei: Shifting Japanese American Identities and Politics*

Velina Hasu Houston, ed., *But Still, Like Air, I'll Rise: New Asian American Plays*

Josephine Lee, *Performing Asian America: Race and Ethnicity on the Contemporary Stage*

Deepika Bahri and Mary Vasudeva, eds., *Between the Lines: South Asians and Postcoloniality*

E. San Juan, Jr., *The Philippine Temptation: Dialectics of Philippines-U.S. Literary Relations*

Carlos Bulosan and E. San Juan, Jr., ed., *The Cry and the Dedication*

Carlos Bulosan and E. San Juan, Jr., ed., *On Becoming Filipino: Selected Writings of Carlos Bulosan*

Vicente L. Rafael, ed., *Discrepant Histories: Translocal Essays on Filipino Cultures*

Yen Le Espiritu, *Filipino American Lives*

Paul Ong, Edna Bonacich, and Lucie Cheng, eds., *The New Asian Immigration in Los Angeles and Global Restructuring*

Chris Friday, *Organizing Asian American Labor: The Pacific Coast Canned-Salmon Industry, 1870–1942*

Sucheng Chan, ed., *Hmong Means Free: Life in Laos and America*

Timothy P. Fong, *The First Suburban Chinatown: The Remarking of Monterey Park, California*

William Wei, *The Asian American Movement*

Yen Le Espiritu, *Asian American Panethnicity*

Velina Hasu Houston, ed., *The Politics of Life*

Renqiu Yu, *To Save China, To Save Ourselves: The Chinese Hand Laundry Alliance of New York*

Shirley Geok-lin Lim and Amy Ling, eds., *Reading the Literatures of Asian America*

Karen Isaksen Leonard, *Making Ethnic Choices: California's Punjabi Mexican Americans*

Gary Y. Okihiro, *Cane Fires: The Anti-Japanese Movement in Hawaii, 1865–1945*

Sucheng Chan, *Entry Denied: Exclusion and the Chinese Community in America, 1882–1943*